Lecture Notes in Artificial Intelli

Edited by J. G. Carbonell and J. Siekmann

Subseries of Lecture Notes in Computer Science

Stefan Edelkamp   Alessio Lomuscio (Eds.)

Model Checking and Artificial Intelligence

4th Workshop, MoChArt IV
Riva del Garda, Italy, August 29, 2006
Revised Selected and Invited Papers

 Springer

Series Editors

Jaime G. Carbonell, Carnegie Mellon University, Pittsburgh, PA, USA
Jörg Siekmann, University of Saarland, Saarbrücken, Germany

Volume Editors

Stefan Edelkamp
University of Dortmund
Computer Science Department
Otto-Hahn-Straße 14, 44227 Dortmund, Germany
E-mail: stefan.edelkamp@cs.uni-dortmund.de

Alessio Lomuscio
Imperial College London
Department of Computing
180 Queen's Gate, London SW7 2AZ, UK
E-mail: a.lomuscio@cs.ucl.ac.uk

Library of Congress Control Number: 2007932185

CR Subject Classification (1998): I.2.3, I.2, F.4.1, F.3, D.2.4, D.1.6

LNCS Sublibrary: SL 7 – Artificial Intelligence

ISSN   0302-9743
ISBN-10   3-540-74127-5 Springer Berlin Heidelberg New York
ISBN-13   978-3-540-74127-5 Springer Berlin Heidelberg New York

Springer is a part of Springer Science+Business Media

springer.com

© Springer-Verlag Berlin Heidelberg 2007
Printed in Germany

Typesetting: Camera-ready by author, data conversion by Scientific Publishing Services, Chennai, India
Printed on acid-free paper   SPIN: 12103942   06/3180   5 4 3 2 1 0

Preface

Exploration of very large search spaces lies at the heart of many disciplines in computer science and engineering, especially systems verification and artificial intelligence. In particular, the technique of *model checking* is used to automatically verify the properties of a system. In the model checking approach, verifying that a system S satisfies a property P is investigated by automatically checking the satisfiability of the expression $M_S \models \phi_P$, where M_S is a suitable model representing all evolutions of S, and ϕ_P is a logical formula capturing the property P to be checked.

Model checking and artificial intelligence have enjoyed a healthy interchange of ideas over the past few years. On the one hand, model checking techniques have benefited from efficient search algorithms developed in artificial intelligence thereby increasing their efficiency, on the other, model checking techniques have been extended to deal with typical artificial intelligence formalisms, such as epistemic logics, thereby permitting the verification of systems based on artificial intelligence concepts. In addition to this, there remains a keen interest among researchers to use model checking to solve planning problems.

The forth MOCHART workshop aimed at bringing together researchers interested in the interplay of these areas. The workshop was held as a satellite workshop of ECAI 2006, the 17th biennial European conference on Artificial Intelligence. Previous workshops were held in San Francisco in 2005 (as a satellite workshop of CONCUR 2005), Acapulco in 2003 (as a satellite workshop of IJCAI 2003), and Lyon in 2002 (as a satellite workshop of ECAI 2002).

This volume includes extended versions of eight of the nine papers selected for presentation at the workshop after a selective round of reviews, as well as three further papers selected from submissions to the post-proceedings. An article based on an invited presentation to the workshop is also included. The papers are included in the order in which they were presented at the workshop.

The volume begins with the invited contribution by Bertoli et al. on a broad overview of the use of model checking techniques for safety analysis, diagnosability and synthesis in reactive systems. This is followed by an article by Alechina et al. investigating the reasoning capabilities of resource bounded agents. A contribution by Edelkamp on a variety of genetic algorithms operating on pattern databases represented via OBDDs follows.

Hoffman et al. then discuss efficient optmization methods for model checking real-time systems by introducing predicate abstraction to generate efficient heuristic search functions. Analysis for real-time systems also features in the following paper by Edelkamp and Jabber investigating the performance of secondary storage solutions for three search algorithms. Concluding in this line, Lomuscio et al. present and evaluate algorithms for model checking networks of timed-automata with clock differences against epistemic real-time specifications.

Genetic algorithms feature again in the following article where Araragi and Cho suggest a reinforcement learning technique to check liveness in reactive systems. This is followed by a paper by Pecheur and Raimondi on model checking variants of CTL supporting explicit actions via OBDDs. In the next paper, Viganò proposes a methodology based on SPIN to verify the multi-agent frameworks of e-institutions described by an ad-hoc modelling language.

In a change of topic Kurkowski et al. present a SAT-based methodology for the verification of security protocols by modelling principals via networks of communicating automata. Wijs and Lisser conclude the volume by analyzing variations of distributed beam search algorithms to find solutions to scheduling problems via model checking.

All the papers represent solid contributions to the state of the art in the interplay between artificial intelligence and model checking and provide an interesting overview of the current trends of research worldwide.

We very much enjoyed the workshop and wish to thank the authors for their excellent contributions and the program committee for their outstanding service in selecting the papers.

We conclude by thanking Springer for enthusiastically supporting the idea of publishing the post-proceedings of the event. The British Royal Association of Engineering and the Deutsche Forschungsgemeinschaft are also acknowledged for their generous support.

February 2007

Stefan Edelkamp
Alessio Lomuscio

Organization

Program Committee

Massimo Benerecetti, Università di Napoli (Italy)
Armin Biere, University of Linz (Austria)
Rafael H. Bordini, University of Durham (UK)
Edmund Clarke, CMU (USA)
Alessandro Cimatti, ITC-IRST (Italy)
Stefan Edelkamp, University of Dortmund (Germany)
Enrico Giunchiglia, University of Genoa (Italy)
Jörg Hoffmann, Digital Enterprise Research Institute (Austria)
Froduald Kabanza, Université de Sherbrooke (Canada)
Richard Korf, UCLA, California (USA)
Stefan Leue, University of Konstanz (Germany)
Alessio Lomuscio, Imperial College London (UK)
Ron van der Meyden, University of New South Wales / NICTA (Australia)
Charles Pecheur, Université catholique de Louvain (Belgium)
Wojciech Penczek, University of Podlasie (Poland)
Mark Ryan, University of Birmingham (UK)
Brian Williams, MIT (USA)
Michael Wooldridge, University of Liverpool (UK)

Additional Referees

Shahid Jabbar, University of Dortmund (Germany)
Ansgar Fehnker, NICTA (Australia)

Table of Contents

A Symbolic Model Checking Framework for Safety Analysis, Diagnosis, and Synthesis*

Piergiorgio Bertoli, Marco Bozzano, and Alessandro Cimatti

ITC-irst - Via Sommarive 18 - 38050 Povo - Trento - Italy
{bertoli,bozzano,cimatti}@irst.itc.it

Abstract. Modern reactive control system are typically very complex entities, and their design poses substantial challenges. In addition to ensuring functional correctness, other steps may be required: with safety analysis, the behavior is analyzed, and proved compliant to some requirements considering possible faulty behaviors; diagnosis and diagnosability are forms of reasoning on the run-time explanation of faulty behaviors; planning and synthesis allow the automated construction of controllers that implement desired behaviors. Symbolic Model Checking (SMC) is a formal technique for ensuring functional correctness that has achieved a substantial industrial penetration in the last decade. In this paper, we show how SMC can be used as a convenient framework to express safety analysis, diagnosis and diagnosability, and synthesis. We also discuss how model checking tools can be used and extended to solve the resulting computational challenges.

1 Introduction

In recent years, complex applications increasingly rely on implementations based on software and digital systems. Typical examples are transportation domains (e.g. railways, avionics, space), telecommunications, hardware, industrial control. The design of such complex systems is a very hard task. On the one hand, more and more functionalities must be implemented, in order to provide for flexible, user-configurable products. On the other hand, there is a need to achieve higher degrees of assurance, given the criticality of the functions.

For the above reasons, the engineering of complex systems has witnessed the introduction of model-based design techniques and tools. The idea is to write system models, expressed at different levels of abstraction, and to provide support tools to automatically analyze them. Different languages can be used to express such models; in general, they can be encoded and treated in terms of transition systems. Model checking is a verification technique to check whether a system (modeled as a transition system) satisfies certain requirements (modeled as temporal logic).

Goal of this paper is to draw a unifying view between different aspects of engineering, within the framework of model checking. We show how many different stages in model-based design can be cast in the framework of model checking, and can benefit from the advanced symbolic model checking techniques and tools.

---

* This work has been partly supported by the E.U.-sponsored project ISAAC, contract no. AST3-CT-2003-501848.

S. Edelkamp and A. Lomuscio (Eds.): MoChart IV, LNAI 4428, pp. 1–18, 2007.

We proceed in order of increasing complexity. We start by defining the problem of model checking, and providing an overview of the available techniques. Then, we consider the field of *safety analysis*: while in model checking the behavior of the system is analyzed under nominal conditions, in safety analysis the problem is to check the behavior of the design in presence of failures. This phase is carried out at design time. The only increase required in the framework is the specification of a selected set of failure mode variables. The next problem is *diagnosis*, that can be seen as the problem of safety analysis carried out at run-time. On one side, only one trace at the time is considered. On the other side, diagnosis is usually performed on systems which provide limited run-time sensing, making the problem much harder. Another interesting and related problem, known as *diagnosability*, is the analysis, *at design time*, of diagnosis capabilities. We conclude with the problem of planning, which in the general setting used in this paper amounts to the problem of *synthesis*, i.e. automatic generation of controllers from specifications. The problem has been addressed in many variations, and has interesting overlappings with diagnosis. In particular, in the case of planning under partial observability, actions must be planned in order to achieve a given amount of information.

This paper is structured as follows. In Section 2 we describe model checking, and overview the main symbolic implementation techniques. In Section 3 we present the ideas underlying safety analysis. In Section 4 we discuss the role of model checking in diagnosis and diagnosability. In Section 5 we discuss planning based on symbolic model checking, and in Section 6 we draw some conclusions, and outline directions for future work.

2   Symbolic Model Checking

Model checking [21,22,45] is a formal verification technique that is widely used to complement classical techniques such as testing and simulation. In particular, while testing and simulation may only verify a limited portion of the possible behaviors of complex, asynchronous systems, model checking provides a formal guarantee that some given specification is obeyed. In model checking, the verified system is modeled as a state transition system (typically of finite size). The specifications are expressed as temporal logic formulæ, that express constraints over the dynamics of systems. Model checking then consists in exhaustively exploring every possible system behavior, to check automatically that the specifications are satisfied. In the case of finite models, termination is guaranteed. Very relevant for debugging purposes, when a specification is not satisfied, a counterexample is produced, witnessing the offending behavior of the system. Formally, model checking relies on the following definition of a *system*:

Definition 1 (System). *A system is a tuple* $\mathcal{M} = \langle \mathcal{S}, \mathcal{S}_i, \mathcal{I}, \mathcal{R} \rangle$ *where:*

- $\mathcal{S}$ *is a finite set of states,*
- $\mathcal{S}_i \subseteq \mathcal{S}$ *is the set of initial states,*
- $\mathcal{I}$ *is a finite set of inputs,*
- $\mathcal{R} \subseteq \mathcal{S} \times \mathcal{I} \times \mathcal{S}$ *is the transition relation*

The transition relation specifies the possible transitions from state to state, triggered by the applications of inputs to the system. For technical reasons, it is required to be total, i.e. for each state there exists at least a successor state. From such a tuple, abstracting away from inputs, one can immediately extract a *state transition graph*, a Kripke structure that only describes transitions from states to states.

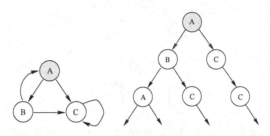

Fig. 1. A State Transition Graph and its unwinding

A path in such a Kripke structure is obtained starting from a state $s \in \mathcal{S}_i$, and then repeatedly appending states reachable through $\mathcal{R}$; since inputs have been abstracted away, a path corresponds to the evolution of the system *for some* sequence of inputs. Given the totality of $\mathcal{R}$, behaviors are infinite. Since a state can have more than one successor, the structure can be thought of as unwinding into an infinite tree, representing all the possible executions of the system starting from the initial states. Figure 1 shows a state transition graph and its unwinding from the initial (colored) state. A Kripke structure is typically associated with a set of propositions $\mathcal{P}$, and with a labeling function that maps each state onto a truth assignment to such propositions. In the following, we assume that one truth assignment to the variables in $\mathcal{P}$ is associated to at most one state, and we write $s \models p$ to indicate that a proposition p holds in a state s.

Traditionally, two temporal logics are most commonly used for model checking, CTL and LTL [31]. Computation Tree Logic (CTL) is interpreted over the computation tree of the Kripke structure, while Linear Temporal Logic (LTL) is interpreted over the set of its paths. These two logics have incomparable expressive power, and differ in how they handle branching in the underlying computation tree: CTL temporal operators quantify over the paths departing from a given state, while LTL operators describe properties of all possible computation paths.

Model checking is the problem of deciding whether a certain temporal formula φ holds in a given Kripke structure $\mathcal{M}$ (see [24] for a detailed overview). In the following we use the notation $\mathcal{M} \models \varphi$. The first model checking algorithms used an explicit representation of the Kripke structure as a labeled, directed graph [21,22,45]. Explicit state model checking is based on the exploration of the Kripke structure based on the expansion and storage of individual states. Over the years, explicit state model checking has reached impressive performance (see for instance the SPIN model checker [38]). The key problem, however, is that explicit state techniques are subject to the so-called state explosion problem, i.e. they need to explore and store the states of the state transition graph. In industrial sized systems, this amounts to an extremely large number of

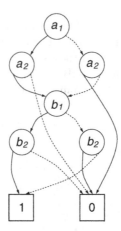

Fig. 2. A BDD for the formula $(a_1 \leftrightarrow a_2) \wedge (b_1 \leftrightarrow b_2)$

states. In fact, the Kripke structure is typically the result of the combination of a number of components (e.g. the communicating processes in a protocol), and the size of the resulting structure may be exponential in the number of components.

A major breakthrough was enabled by the introduction of *symbolic model checking* [40]. In symbolic model checking, rather than individual states and transitions, the idea is to manipulate sets of states and transitions, using a logical formalism to represent the characteristic functions of such sets [26,43,52,15]. Since a small logical formula may admit a large number of models, this results in most cases in a very compact representation which can be effectively manipulated. Each state is presented by an assignment to the propositions (variables) in $\mathcal{P}$ (equivalently, by the corresponding conjunction of literals). A set of states is represented by the disjunction of the formulae representing each of its states. The basic set theoretic operations (intersection, union, projection) are given by logical operations (such as conjunction, disjunction, and quantification). In the following we use x to denote the vector of variables representing the states of a given system; we write $\mathcal{S}_i(x)$ for the formula representing the initial states. A similar construction can be applied to represent inputs (for which we use a vector of variables i). A set of "next" variables x' is used for the state resulting after the transition: a transition from s to s' is then represented as a truth assignment to the current and next variables. We use $\mathcal{R}(x, i, x')$ for the formula representing the transition relation expressed in terms of those variables.

Obviously, the key issue is the use of an efficient logical representation. The first one used for symbolic model checking was provided by Ordered Binary Decision Diagrams [12,13] (BDDs for short). BDDs are a representation for boolean formulas, which is canonical once an order on the variables has been established. This allows equivalence checking in constant time. Figure 2 depicts the BDD for the boolean formula $(a_1 \leftrightarrow a_2) \wedge (b_1 \leftrightarrow b_2)$, using the variable ordering a_1, a_2, b_1, b_2. Solid lines represent "then" arcs (the corresponding variable has to be considered positive), dashed lines represent "else" arcs (the corresponding variable has to be considered negative). Paths from the root to the node labeled with "1" represent the satisfying assignments of the represented boolean formula (e.g., $a_1 \leftarrow 1, a_2 \leftarrow 1, b_1 \leftarrow 0, b_2 \leftarrow 0$).

Such a powerful logical computation machinery provides the ideal basis for the implementation of algorithms manipulating sets of states. In fact, the use of BDDs makes it possible to verify very large systems (larger than 10^{20} states [15,40,14]). Symbolic model checking has been successful in various fields, allowing the discovery of design bugs that were very difficult to highlight with traditional techniques. For instance, in [23] the authors discovered previously undetected and potential errors in the design of the cache coherence protocol described in the IEEE Futurebus+ Standard 896.1.1991, and in [29] the cache coherence protocol of the Scalable Coherent Interface, IEEE Standard 1596-1992 was verified, finding several errors.

A more recent advance in the field originates from the introduction of *bounded model checking* (BMC) [7,6]. The idea is twofold. First, we look for a witness to a property violation that can be presented within a certain bound, say k transitions. Second, we generate a propositional formula that is satisfiable if and only if a witness to the property violation exists. The formula is obtained by unwinding the symbolic description of the transition relation over time. In particular, we use $k + 1$ vectors of state variables $x_0, \ldots, x_k$, whose assignments represent the states at the different steps, and k vectors of input variables $i_1, \ldots, i_k$, that represent the inputs at the different transitions:

$$\mathcal{S}_i(x_0) \wedge \mathcal{R}(x_0, i_1, x_1) \wedge \ldots \wedge \mathcal{R}(x_{k-1}, i_k, x_k)$$

Additional constraints are used to limit such assignments to witness the violation of the property, and to impose a cyclic behaviour when required. The solution technique leverages the power of modern SAT solvers [30], which are able to check the satisfiability of formulae with hundreds of thousands of variables, and millions of clauses.

In comparison to BDD-based algorithms, the advantages of SAT-based techniques are twofold [25]. First, SAT-based algorithms have higher capacity, i.e. they can deal with a larger number of variables. Second, SAT solvers have a high degree of automation, and are less sensitive than BDDs to the specific parameters (e.g. variable ordering). As a result, SAT-based technologies have been introduced in industrial settings to complement and often to replace BDD-based techniques. In addition, SAT has become the core of many other algorithms and approaches, such as inductive reasoning (e.g. [50]), incremental bounded model checking (e.g. [36]), and abstraction (e.g. [35]). A survey of the recent developments can be found in [44].

3   Safety Analysis

The goal of safety analysis is to investigate the behavior of a system in degraded conditions, that is, when some parts of the system are not working properly, due to malfunctions. Safety analysis includes a set of activities, that have the goal of identifying all possible hazards of the system, and that are performed in order to ensure that the system meets the safety requirements that are required for its deployment and use. Safety analysis activities are particularly critical in the case of reactive systems, because hazards can be the result of complex interactions involving the dynamics of the system [51]. Traditionally, safety analysis activities have been performed manually. Recently, there has been a growing interest in model-based safety analysis using formal methods [11,9,1,10] and in particular symbolic model checking.

Model-based safety analysis is carried out on formally specified models which take into account system behavior in the presence of malfunctions, that is, possible *faults* of some components. Symbolically, the occurrence of such faults is modeled with a set of additional propositions, called *failure mode variables*. Intuitively, a failure mode variable is true when the corresponding fault has occurred in the system (different failure mode variables are associated to different faults). In the rest of this section, we assume to have a system $\mathcal{M} = \langle \mathcal{S}, \mathcal{S}_i, \mathcal{I}, \mathcal{R} \rangle$ with a set of failure mode variables $\mathcal{F} \subseteq \mathcal{P}$. Furthermore, for the sake of simplicity, we assume that failure modes are *permanent* (*once failed, always failed*), that is, we assume that the following condition holds:

$$\forall f \in \mathcal{F}, s_1, s_2 \in \mathcal{S}, i \in \mathcal{I} \quad (\langle s_1, i, s_2 \rangle \in \mathcal{R} \wedge s_1 \models f) \Rightarrow s_2 \models f \qquad (1)$$

The theory can be extended to the more general case of *sporadic* or *transient* failure modes, that is, when faults are allowed to occur sporadically (e.g., a sensor showing an invalid reading for a limited period of time), possibly repeatedly over time, or when repairing is possible.

In this section we briefly describe two of the most popular safety analysis activities, that is, *fault tree analysis* (FTA) and *failure mode and effect analysis* (FMEA), and we discuss their relationship with the symbolic model checking techniques illustrated in Section 2. Fault Tree Analysis [53] is an example of deductive analysis, which, given the specification of an undesired state, usually referred to as a *top level event*, systematically builds all possible chains of one of more basic faults that contribute to the occurrence of the event. The result of the analysis is a *fault tree*, that is, a representation of the logical interrelationships of the basic events that lead to the undesired state. In its simpler form (see Fig. 3) a fault tree can be represented with a two-layer logical structure, namely a top level disjunction of the combinations of basic faults causing the top level event. Each combination, which is called *cut set*, is in turn the conjunction of the corresponding basic faults. In general, logical structures with multiple layers can be used. A cut set is formally defined via CTL as follows.

Definition 2 (Cut set). *Let* $\mathcal{M} = \langle \mathcal{S}, \mathcal{S}_i, \mathcal{I}, \mathcal{R} \rangle$ *be a system with a set of failure mode variables* $\mathcal{F} \subseteq \mathcal{P}$, *let* $FC \subseteq \mathcal{F}$ *be a fault configuration, and* $TLE \in \mathcal{P}$ *a top level event. We say that* FC *is a cut set of* TLE, *written* $cs(FC, TLE)$ *if*

$$\mathcal{M} \models EF(\bigwedge_{f \in FC} f \; \wedge \bigwedge_{f \in (\mathcal{F} \setminus FC)} \neg f \; \wedge \; TLE).$$

Intuitively, a fault configuration corresponds to the set of active failure mode variables. Typically, among the possible fault configurations, one is interested in isolating those that are minimal in terms of failure mode variables, that is, those that represent simpler explanations, in terms of system faults, for the occurrence of the top level event. Under the hypothesis of independent faults, these configurations also represent the most probable explanations for the top level event, and therefore they have a higher importance in reliability analysis. Minimal configurations are called *minimal cut sets* and are formally defined as follows.

Definition 3 (Minimal Cut Sets). *Let* $\mathcal{M} = \langle \mathcal{S}, \mathcal{S}_i, \mathcal{I}, \mathcal{R} \rangle$ *be a system with a set of failure mode variables* $\mathcal{F} \subseteq \mathcal{P}$, *let* $F = 2^{\mathcal{F}}$ *be the set of all fault configurations, and*

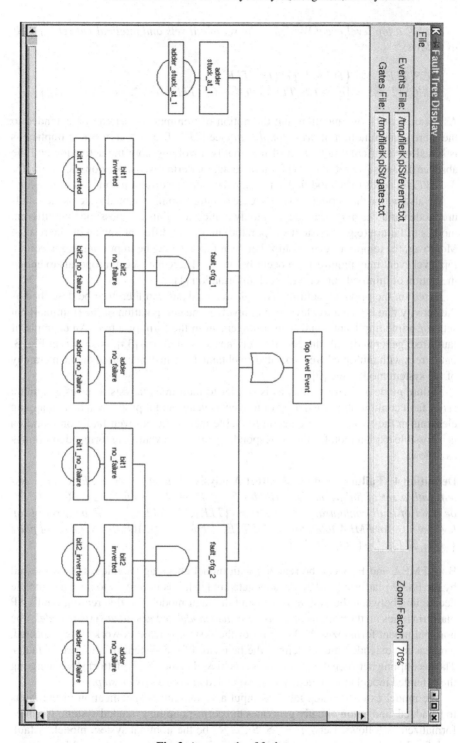

Fig. 3. An example of fault tree

$TLE \in \mathcal{P}$ a top level event. We define the set of cut sets and minimal cut sets of TLE as follows:

$$CS(TLE) \quad = \{FC \in F \mid cs(FC, TLE)\}$$
$$MCS(TLE) = \{cs \in CS(TLE) \mid \forall cs' \in CS(TLE) \ (cs' \subseteq cs \Rightarrow cs' = cs)\}$$

As a side remark, we mention that the notion of minimal cut set can be extended to the more general notion of *prime implicant* (see [27]). The notion of prime implicants is based on a different definition of minimality, involving both the activation and the absence of faults (we refer to [27] for more details). Formally, the previous definition for $MCS(TLE)$ needs to be modified to take into account the different notion of minimality.

We also notice that, compared to the case of purely combinational systems, here failure mode variables may be associated to dynamics, and thus it is possible that different models of failure (e.g. persistent vs sporadic) may have different impact on the results. Moreover, the temporal relationships between failures may be important, e.g. a certain top level event may require f_1 to occur before f_2. There have been proposals to enrich the notion of minimal cut set with such information [1].

Based on the previous definitions, fault tree analysis can therefore be described as the activity that, given a top level event, involves the computation of the (minimal) cut sets (or prime implicants) and their arrangement in the form of a tree. An example of fault tree, generated with the FSAP safety analysis platform [33], is shown in Fig. 3. Fault trees with multiple layers can also be obtained, for instance based on the hierarchy of the system model (see [2]).

Failure mode and effect analysis is similar to fault tree analysis. It takes as input a *set* of fault configurations and a *set* of top level events, and it produces a table mapping elements in the two sets. An entry in the table means that a given fault configuration is a possible explanation for the corresponding top level event. The formal definition is as follows.

Definition 4 (Failure Mode and Effect Analysis). *Let* $\mathcal{M} = \langle \mathcal{S}, \mathcal{S}_i, \mathcal{I}, \mathcal{R} \rangle$ *be a system with a set of failure mode variables* $\mathcal{F} \subseteq \mathcal{P}$, *let* $F = \{FC_1, \ldots, FC_n\} \subseteq 2^{\mathcal{F}}$ *be a set of fault configurations, and* $T = \{TLE_1, \ldots, TLE_m\} \subseteq \mathcal{P}$ *be a set of top level events. An FMEA table for* F *and* TLE, *denoted* $FMEA(F, T)$ *is the set of pairs* $\{\langle FC_i, TLE_j \rangle \mid cs(FC_i, TLE_j)\}$.

Both FMEA and FTA can be realized with model checking techniques, as witnessed by the FSAP platform [33,10]. As advocated in [11], it is important to have a complete decoupling between the system model and the fault model. For this reason, the FSAP platform relies on the notions of *nominal system model* and *extended system model*. The nominal model formalizes the behavior of the system when it is working as expected, whereas the extended model defines the behavior of the system in presence of faults. The decoupling between the two models is achieved in the FSAP platform by generating the extended model automatically via a so-called *model extension step*.

The model extension step takes as input a system and a specification of the faults to be added, and automatically generates the corresponding extended system. It can be formalized as follows. Let $\mathcal{M} = \langle \mathcal{S}, \mathcal{S}_i, \mathcal{I}, \mathcal{R} \rangle$ be the nominal system model. A fault is defined by the proposition $p \in \mathcal{P}$ to which it must be attached to, and by its type, specifying the "faulty behavior" of proposition p in the extended system (e.g., p can non-deterministically assume a random value, or p is stuck at a particular value). Given the proposition p, FSAP introduces a new proposition p^{FM}, the *failure mode variable*, modeling the possible occurrence of the fault, and two further propositions p^{Failed} and p^{Ext}, with the following intuitive meaning. The proposition p^{Failed} models the behavior of p when a fault has occurred. For instance, the following condition (where S' is the set of states of the extended system) defines a so-called *inverted* failure mode (that is, proposition p^{Failed} holds if and only if proposition p does not hold):

$$\forall s \in S' \quad (s \models p^{Failed} \iff s \not\models p) \tag{2}$$

The proposition p^{Ext} models the extended behavior of p, that is, it behaves as the original p when no fault is active, whereas it behaves as p^{Failed} in presence of a fault. Formally, we impose the following conditions:

$$\forall s \in S' \quad s \not\models p^{FM} \Rightarrow (s \models p^{Ext} \iff s \models p) \tag{3}$$

$$\forall s \in S' \quad s \models p^{FM} \Rightarrow (s \models p^{Ext} \iff s \models p^{Failed}) \tag{4}$$

The extended system $M_{Ext} = \langle S', S'_i, \mathcal{I}, \mathcal{R}' \rangle$ can therefore be easily defined in terms of the nominal system by adding the set of propositions $\{p^{FM}, p^{Failed}, p^{Ext}\}$ to the original set $\mathcal{P}$, modifying the definition of the (initial) states and of the transition relation, and imposing the additional conditions (1), (2) (in the hypothesis of an inverted failure mode), (3) and (4). We omit the details for the sake of simplicity. Finally, system extension with respect to a *set* of propositions can be defined in a straightforward manner, by iterating system extension over single propositions.

The extended system model resulting from the extension step is used in FSAP to carry out the safety analysis activities, FMEA and FTA. The corresponding algorithms are implemented as an extension of the NuSMV tool [41,16], a symbolic model-checker developed at ITC-IRST. As far as FTA is concerned, the FSAP platform can be used to compute both the minimal cut sets and the prime implicants of a given top level event. The computation involves two different stages, both of them relying on symbolic techniques. The first stage consists in computing the set of cut sets, that is, the set of fault configurations satisfying the condition of Def. 2. This can be realized, as described in [10], by using model checking symbolic techniques to compute a forward fixpoint of a forward image primitive. The second stage of the computation consists in extracting the set of *minimal* cut sets from the set computed at the previous stage. The extraction is based on classical routines for computing the *prime implicants* of Boolean functions [27,46].

4 Diagnosis and Diagnosability

Rarely physical systems are fully observable: parts of their state are hidden, and sensors are used to expose (partial) information about otherwise unobservable aspects. Diagnosis starts from observed run time behavior of a system, and tries to provide an explanation (in terms of hidden states). In particular, diagnosis is often the problem of identifying the set of possible causes of a specific unexpected or faulty behavior.

The seminal approaches to diagnosis are carried out considering combinational, state-less models. These can be symbolically represented as a propositional formula $\Phi(x, o)$, where x are the hidden variables, and o are the observable variables (e.g. conveyed inputs and observed outputs). Within this framework, it is possible to encompass problems such as fault detection (that is, detecting whether the system is malfunctioning) and fault isolation (i.e. detecting a specific cause of malfunctioning). Let $\mu(o)$ denote an assignment to the observable variables. Then, we say that an assignment $D(x)$ is a diagnosis (alternatively, an explanation) for $\mu(o)$ if $\Phi(x, o)$ is true under the interpretation $\mu(o) \cup D(x)$. Notice that diagnoses need not be total, i.e. some hidden variables may be unassigned (in which case any extension to $D(x)$ is also an explanation).

In general, several possible explanations may exist, and some may be preferable over others, according to some criterion. For example, an explanation may be minimal (i.e. any of its subsets is not an explanation); alternatively, it could be of least cardinality, based on the number of assigned literals, or could be required to have the least number of variables assigned to true. Probabilistic information can be taken into account, in order to require the most likely explanation.

In contrast to model checking and safety analysis, that are typically carried out at design time, diagnosis deals with the run-time of a system. Thus, we reject the assumption (that is used for for verification and safety analysis) that the system is fully observable. When considering the problem of diagnosis for *reactive systems*, failure modes and other hidden variables may have their own dynamics, leading to the following extension of Def. 1:

Definition 5 (Partially Observable System). *A system is a tuple* $\mathcal{M} = \langle \mathcal{S}, \mathcal{S}_i, \mathcal{I}, \mathcal{O}, \mathcal{R}, \mathcal{X} \rangle$ *where:*

- $\mathcal{S}$ *is a finite set of states,*
- $\mathcal{S}_i \subseteq \mathcal{S}$ *is the set of initial states,*
- $\mathcal{I}$ *is a set of inputs to the system,*
- $\mathcal{R} \subseteq \mathcal{S} \times \mathcal{I} \times \mathcal{S}$ *is the transition relation*
- $\mathcal{O}$ *is a set of possible observations;*
- $\mathcal{X} \subseteq \mathcal{S} \times \mathcal{O}$ *is the observation relation;*

We require $\mathcal{X}$ to be total, i.e. for each state s there exists an observation o such that $\mathcal{X}(s, o)$. Two states associated to the same observation may be indistinguishable. Notice that this model of observation is extremely expressive, as it makes it possible for a state to be associated to many different observations.

The symbolic representation used in previous sections can be generalized to deal with the new notions. In particular, the set of observations $\mathcal{O}$ is presented symbolically by introducing a set of *observation variables*; each observation is represented by a valuation to the observation variables. The observation relation is then represented as a formula in the state variables and the observation variables.

Definition 6. *An execution in* $\mathcal{M}$ *is a sequence* $\sigma = s_0, o_0, i_1, s_1, o_1, i_2, \ldots, i_k, s_k, o_k$, *such that* $s_0 \in \mathcal{S}_0$, $\mathcal{R}(s_{i-1}, i_i, s_i)$ *for* $1 \leq i \leq k$, *and* $\mathcal{X}(s_i, o_i)$ *for* $0 \leq i \leq k$. *The observable trace of an execution* σ *is* $w = o_0, i_1, o_1, \ldots, i_k, o_k$, *and we write* $\sigma : s_0 \xrightarrow{w} s_k$. *We also write* $s_0 \xrightarrow{w} s_k$ *if such a* σ *exists.*

The above definition captures the dynamics of a plant and its observable counterpart. If an execution σ has k steps, then it is associated to a trace $w \in \mathcal{O} \times (\mathcal{I} \times \mathcal{O})^k$. The set of traces is in general a subset of $\mathcal{O} \times (\mathcal{I} \times \mathcal{O})^*$. In the following we use σ to denote a feasible execution, and w to denote the corresponding (observable) trace.

The problem of diagnosis in the setting of reactive systems generalizes the combinational case in the following directions. First, an explanation is no longer an assignment to the hidden variables, but rather an assignment to the hidden variables *over time*: in order to explain a sequence of length k, a suitable amount of assignments are in order. Second, the notion of preferable explanation may be generalized according to temporal aspects. As a result, there may be many more definitions of preference between explanations.

Remarkably, given an observable trace w of specific length, it is possible to recast the problem of diagnosis within the framework of bounded model checking. In particular, we start from the formula describing all the executions of length k:

$$\mathcal{S}_i(x_0) \wedge \mathcal{X}(x_0, o_0) \wedge \mathcal{R}(x_0, i_1, x_1) \wedge \mathcal{X}(x_1, o_1) \wedge \ldots \wedge \mathcal{R}(x_{k-1}, i_k, x_k) \wedge \mathcal{X}(x_k, o_k)$$

We then restrict the set of models by conjoining it with the formula that restricts the input and output variables to assume the values required by the observable trace w:

$$w_{[0]}(o_0) \wedge w_{[1]}(i_1) \wedge w_{[2]}(o_1) \wedge \ldots \wedge w_{[2k-1]}(i_k) \wedge w_{[2k]}(o_k)$$

where $w_{[i]}$ stands for the formula encoding the constraint expressed by i-th element of w. With this constraint, the input and output variables are assigned specific truth values: the formula resulting after the simplification only contains state variables, and the set of satisfying assignments to the (temporal instantiations of the) state variables is a description of the sequences of states that may be associated with the observable trace w.

The problem of diagnosis has a design-time counterpart. In fact, it is often an important question whether a diagnoser will be able to carry out its tasks for all possible run-time executions of the observed system. This task, called *diagnosability*, can for instance be used in order to analyze the effectiveness and displacement of sensors in a design.

The task of diagnosability has been tackled with several methods, based on automata theory and similar techniques, see e.g. [39,48,49]. Intuitively, a system is not diagnosable if two executions exist that share the same observable trace, but have different properties (e.g. in one a failure occurs, while the other one models a nominal behavior), and should be distinguishable. In [17], the problem is tackled by means of bounded model checking techniques, by reduction to a so-called *twin model*:

$$\mathcal{S}_i(x_0^l) \wedge \mathcal{X}(x_0^l, o_0) \wedge \mathcal{S}_i(x_0^r) \wedge \mathcal{X}(x_0^r, o_0) \wedge$$
$$\mathcal{R}(x_0^l, i_1, x_1^l) \wedge \mathcal{X}(x_1^l, o_1) \wedge \mathcal{R}(x_0^r, i_1, x_1^r) \wedge \mathcal{X}(x_1^r, o_1) \wedge \ldots \wedge$$
$$\mathcal{R}(x_{k-1}^l, i_k, x_k^l) \wedge \mathcal{X}(x_k^l, o_k) \wedge \mathcal{R}(x_{k-1}^r, i_k, x_k^r) \wedge \mathcal{X}(x_k^r, o_k)$$

Two (left and right, l and r) copies of the system are fed with the same sequence of inputs, and forced to exhibit the same outputs. Additional constraints on the state variables are used to express the required properties of the left and right executions. If the problem is satisfiable, then the system is not diagnosable; in addition, it is possible to provide as diagnostic information the *critical pair*, i.e. the pair of indistinguishable executions. The usage of SMC techniques for this purpose has allowed checking the diagnosability of significantly complex system models developed within Nasa [17].

5   Planning

We now introduce planning, and discuss its relationships with (symbolic) model checking and diagnosis.

Planning is the problem of identifying a plan whose execution controls the system (called in that context *planning domain*) so that, when the system executes under the control of the plan, certain properties (over its states) are obeyed. Several specializations of this general statement are possible and relevant, both theoretically and for practical purposes. For instance, in *classical* planning [32,34] it is assumed that the domain is deterministic, that its state can be observed at runtime, and that the desired execution properties amount to a set of goal states which must be finally reached. The deterministic nature of the controlled system allows restricting to plans structured simply as sequences of inputs that must be provided to the domain. In *strong* planning [20], the assumption that the domain is deterministic is removed. This makes it necessary to consider plans that have a conditional, loop-free structure, and that branch depending on the currently observed system state. Loops are also considered by a relaxation of the problem called *strong cyclic* planning [18]. These same problems can be considered when the hypothesis of full observability of the domain is removed. In *conformant planning* [19], the opposite hypothesis is made: nothing can ever be observed about the status of the domain; therefore, plans may not branch and have a sequential structure like in classical planning. In this case, however, goal achievement has to be guaranteed regardless of nondeterminism - i.e. several different, but equally plausible executions must be considered for the plan. Contingent planning [8,5] deals with the more general case where a domain is partially observable, i.e. it has the same features of the systems considered for diagnosis in Section. 4. On top of having to consider multiple executions, of course, contingent plans have a branching structure, and take choices at runtime depending on the currently perceived observations. Different planning problems have also been tackled where goals are not anymore set of states to be reached, but define constraints over the behavior of the domain during the whole plan execution, using CTL [42] or different logics [28].

In all instantiations of the planning problem, the plan can be interpreted as an automaton, whose execution controls the system (the planning domain) by synchronously reading the system's outputs (the observations) and providing the system's inputs (the planning actions). The specific plan structures considered in the various problems simply correspond to constraints over the structure of the corresponding automata. Thus planning refers to a framework where the system and diagnoser described in the previous sections are complemented by a *controller* (the plan). Here, we provide the most general definition, referring to a partially observable domain - its simplifications for the special cases of full or null observability are trivial.

Definition 7 (controller). *A controller for system* $\mathcal{M} = \langle \mathcal{S}, \mathcal{S}_i, \mathcal{I}, \mathcal{O}, \mathcal{R}, \mathcal{X} \rangle$ *is a tuple* $\Pi = \langle \Sigma, \sigma_0, \alpha, \epsilon \rangle$, *where:*

- Σ *is the set of* contexts.
- $\sigma_0 \in \Sigma$ *is the* initial context.
- $\alpha : \Sigma \times \mathcal{O} \rightharpoonup \mathcal{I}$ *is the* action function; *it associates to a context c and an observation o an input* $a = \alpha(c, o)$ *for the system.*
- $\epsilon : \Sigma \times \mathcal{O} \rightharpoonup \Sigma$ *is the* context evolution function; *it associates to a context c and an observation o a new context* $c' = \epsilon(c, o)$.

Naturally, a symbolic representation in terms of variables is also possible, and indeed used, for the controller as well as for the system. Notice that the controller is a *deterministic* Moore machine; nondeterministic controllers are not useful for our purposes and therefore we will not consider them.

The execution of the system under the control of the plan can be represented by a Kripke structure, called *execution structure*, whose states are configurations that couple system states and plan contexts. In fact, the execution structure is a finite presentation of every possible execution trace, and corresponds to the standard synchronous product of the plan and the system, denoted $\mathcal{M} \times \Pi$.

This makes it possible to define a notion of satisfactory plan, for some property ϕ, in terms of a model checking problem: plan Π satisfies goal ϕ for domain $\mathcal{M}$ if and only if $\mathcal{M} \times \Pi \models \phi$. When the goal ϕ is expressed as a CTL or LTL formula, standard model checking techniques can be used for this purpose.

Therefore, the planning problem can be formulated as follows: *given a system* $\mathcal{M}$ *and a goal* ϕ, *find an executable controller* Π *such that their synchronous execution satisfies the goal* ϕ, *i.e.* $\Pi \times \mathcal{M} \models \phi$.

This statement highlights the main differences and similarities between planning and model checking: they both refer to properties of execution of a system modeled as a finite state automata (eventually constrained by a controller), but the latter is a synthesis problem rather than a verification one. In general, planning is a (theoretically and practically) harder problem than model checking, which intuitively requires searching for a single execution witness, rather than for a complex plan.

The fact that model checking also synthesizes a counterexample for a non-valid property makes it possible to exploit it in a direct way to solve planning problems in the specific 'classical' setting. This is performed by stating, as the property that needs be verified, that the goal ϕ can never be finally achieved. As usual, the application of model checking returns one of two possible answers: either such property holds, or it does not and a counterexample is given. In the former case, this indicates that it is actually impossible to achieve the goal, therefore no plan exists. In the latter, a plan exists, and it corresponds to the sequence of inputs given as a counterexample.

For more complex cases, such a direct usage of model checking to generate solution controllers is not possible, either because controllers have a branching/looping structure or because the goal language must be richer then the CTL/LTL used in model checking.

In these cases, the commonalities between the elements involved in model checking and planning are exploited by making use of model checking's *symbolic* techniques and primitives to manipulate planning domains. For instance, strong planning under full observability can be tackled by a backward fixpoint of a backward image primitive.

Such *strong backward image* must be defined to derive all the strong predecessors of a set of states ϕ, i.e. all those states such that there exists some action whose outcomes, applied to them, all belong to ϕ. This primitive can be defined as a QBF formula and implemented on top of the basic BDD primitives used to compute the semantics of the temporal CTL formula $AX\phi$ in model checking. Similar primitives are adopted for the remaining planning problems: in every case, the ability to manipulate sets of states by means of basic primitives is used to describe (forward/backward) images either on search frontiers, or on sets of observationally equivalent states.

Concerning the relationships between diagnosis and planning, they are evident once partially observable domains are considered. In this case, as stated in [4], CTL is not adequate to express many interesting planning goals. Such inadequacy is related with the fact that in this setting, during plan execution, a monitor has only limited run-time information, which in general is not sufficient to rule out uncertainty about the state of the controlled system. To express that a certain property must not only be achieved, but also detected by the monitor, the knowledge operator **K** must be added to CTL, i.e. the K-CTL logic developed for diagnosis is adopted. For instance, a strong requirement of the form "finally achieve and detect property ϕ", such as those considered in most contingent planning approaches ([5,47,37]), can be written as the K-CTL formula $AF\,K\,\phi$. That is, those approaches solve the problem of identifying a controller Π such that

$$\mathcal{M} \times \Pi \models AF\,K\,\phi$$

Two remarks are in order. First, as discussed in [3], considering CTL goals may nevertheless be interesting in some cases, where goal detection is not possible, and only goal achievement can be pursued. Second, symbolic model checking techniques can also be used when looking for plans that satisfy K-CTL goals. For this purpose one needs to consider the search space called *belief space*, whose nodes are sets of observationally equivalent states called *beliefs*, representing the epistemic knowledge of a universal monitor. Contingent planning on K-CTL goals can be formulated as and/or search in the *belief space* [8], and, as shown in [5,47], it is possible to represent beliefs symbolically, as formulas modeling sets of states, and progress or regress them by appropriate image primitives.

The relationship between diagnosability and (contingent) planning becomes evident when a K-CTL goal formula of the form $AF(K(\phi) \vee K(\neg\phi))$ is used. In this case, the generated plan is one that finally achieves knowing whether ϕ holds or not, i.e. diagnosing ϕ. That is, contingent planning is to diagnosability what classical planning is to model checking: it *generates* a controller that drives the system to achieve a goal that can be otherwise *verified* by a diagnosability check.

This paves the way to the use of K-CTL planning to generate *active diagnosers*, that is controllers that can be used to appropriately drive systems so that faults can be discovered.

Notice the major difference with the passive diagnosing of Section 4: here, we are not given the execution trace for diagnosing, but rather we generate from scratch a controller that - interacting with the system in a non trivial way - drives it so that the observer will obtain a univocal diagnosis. We also remark that the generality of the approach allows conjoining "diagnosis-oriented" goals such as the above with different requirements; e.g a formula of the form $AF\phi$ actually forces the system to finally achieve ϕ, and a formula of the form $AG\psi$ requires that ψ holds throughout the execution of the plan. This way, we obtain a controller that conjoins a diagnosis task with a control task that aims at driving the system according to some desirable behavior. The way in which the different tasks are mixed within a unique controller is responsibility of the specific and/or search algorithm used to visit the belief space, and in particular of search heuristics.

By now, we conducted some preliminary experiments with active diagnosis by enriching the goal language of the MBP system with the modal knowledge operator, and leaving implicit - as usual - the top-level CTL AF operator. We conducted the experiments on a model of the Cassini spacecraft and we were able to synthesize a diagnoser for several goals of the form $AF(K(\phi) \vee K(\neg\phi))$. We implemented a prototype, based on MBP, which is able to synthesize the diagnoser for the given goal and to automatically generate the model corresponding to the synchronous product of the synthesized controller and the original model. The diagnosability properties of the resulting model were further verified using the FSAP platform [33].

6   Conclusions and Future Work

In this paper we have discussed how the framework of symbolic model checking can be used to model several interesting problems for the development of reactive systems: safety analysis, diagnosis, diagnosability, and synthesis. Symbolic model checking also provides effective computational primitives and tools for the implementation of special purpose, highly effective algorithms to tackle the above problems. We believe that one of the most interesting challenges in the field is to provide an effective support toolset, where different design tasks can be cast in a uniform working framework.

References

1. Åkerlund, O., Bieber, P., Böede, E., Bozzano, M., Bretschneider, M., Castel, C., Cavallo, A., Cifaldi, M., Gauthier, J., Griffault, A., Lisagor, O., Lüdtke, A., Metge, S., Papadopoulos, C., Peikenkamp, T., Sagaspe, L., Seguin, C., Trivedi, H., Valacca, L.: ISAAC, a framework for integrated safety analysis of functional, geometrical and human aspects. In: Proc. European Congress on Embedded Real Time Software (ERTS 2006) (2006)
2. Banach, R., Bozzano, M.: Retrenchment, and the Generation of Fault Trees for Static, Dynamic and Cyclic Systems. In: Gorski, J. (ed.) SAFECOMP 2006. LNCS, vol. 4166, pp. 127–141. Springer, Heidelberg (2006)
3. Bertoli, P., Cimatti, A., Pistore, M.: Strong Cyclic Planning under Partial Observability. In: Proc. of 17th European Conference on Artificial Intelligence (ECAI 2006) (2006)
4. Bertoli, P., Cimatti, A., Pistore, M., Traverso, P.: A Framework for Planning with Extended Goals under Partial Observability. In: Proc. International Conference on Automated Planning and Scheduling (ICAPS 2003) (2003)
5. Bertoli, P., Cimatti, A., Roveri, M., Traverso, P.: Strong Planning under Partial Observability. Artificial Intelligence 170, 337–384 (2006)
6. Biere, A., Cimatti, A., Clarke, E., Fujita, M., Zhu, Y.: Symbolic Model Checking Using SAT Procedures instead of BDDs. In: Proceedings of the 36th Design Automation Conference (DAC'99), New Orleans, LA, USA, pp. 317–320. ACM Press, New York (1999)

7. Biere, A., Cimatti, A., Clarke, E., Zhu, Y.: Symbolic model checking without BDDs. In: Cleaveland, W.R. (ed.) ETAPS 1999 and TACAS 1999. LNCS, vol. 1579, pp. 193–207. Springer, Heidelberg (1999)

8. Bonet, B., Geffner, H.: Planning with Incomplete Information as Heuristic Search in Belief Space. In: Proc. 5th International Conference on Artificial Intelligence Planning and Scheduling (AIPS 2000), pp. 52–61 (2000)

9. Bozzano, M., Cavallo, A., Cifaldi, M., Valacca, L., Villafiorita, A.: Improving Safety Assessment of Complex Systems: An industrial case study. In: Araki, K., Gnesi, S., Mandrioli, D. (eds.) FME 2003. LNCS, vol. 2805, pp. 208–222. Springer, Heidelberg (2003)

10. Bozzano, M., Villafiorita, A.: The FSAP/NuSMV-SA Safety Analysis Platform. International Journal on Software Tools for Technology Transfer, 2006. DOI 10.1007/s10009-006-0001-2 (To appear)

11. Bozzano, M., Villafiorita, A., Åkerlund, O., Bieber, P., Bougnol, C., Böde, E., Bretschneider, M., Cavallo, A., Castel, C., Cifaldi, M., Cimatti, A., Griffault, A., Kehren, C., Lawrence, B., Lüdtke, A., Metge, S., Papadopoulos, C., Passarello, R., Peikenkamp, T., Persson, P., Seguin, C., Trotta, L., Valacca, L., Zacco, G.: ESACS: An Integrated Methodology for Design and Safety Analysis of Complex Systems. In: Proc. European Safety and Reliability Conference (ESREL 2003), pp. 237–245. Balkema Publisher, 2003.

12. Bryant, R.E.: Graph-Based Algorithms for Boolean Function Manipulation. IEEE Transactions on Computers C-35(8), 677–691 (1986)

13. Bryant, R.E.: Symbolic Boolean Manipulation with Ordered Binary-Decision Diagrams. ACM Computing Surveys 24(3), 293–318 (1992)

14. Burch, J.R., Clarke, E.M., Long, D.E., McMillan, K.L., Dill, D.L.: Symbolic Model Checking for Sequential Circuit Verification. IEEE Transactions on Computer-Aided Design of Integrated Circuits and Systems 13(4), 401–424 (1994)

15. Burch, J.R., Clarke, E.M., McMillan, K.L., Dill, D.L., Hwang, L.J.: Symbolic Model Checking: 10^{20} States and Beyond. Information and Computation 98(2), 142–170 (1992)

16. Cimatti, A., Clarke, E.M., Giunchiglia, E., Giunchiglia, F., Pistore, M., Roveri, M., Sebastiani, R., Tacchella, A.: NuSMV2: An OpenSource Tool for Symbolic Model Checking. In: Brinksma, E., Larsen, K.G. (eds.) CAV 2002. LNCS, vol. 2404, pp. 359–364. Springer, Heidelberg (2002)

17. Cimatti, A., Pecheur, C., Cavada, R.: Formal Verification of Diagnosability via Symbolic Model Checking. In: Gottlob, G., Walsh, T. (eds.) Proceedings of the International Joint Conference on Artificial Intelligence (IJCAI'03), Acapulco, Mexico, pp. 363–369. Morgan Kaufmann, San Francisco (2003)

18. Cimatti, A., Pistore, M., Roveri, M., Traverso, P.: Weak, Strong, and Strong Cyclic Planning via Symbolic Model Checking. Artificial Intelligence 147(1-2), 35–84 (2003)

19. Cimatti, A., Roveri, M., Bertoli, P.: Conformant Planning via Symbolic Model Checking and Heuristic Search. Artificial Intelligence 159, 127–206 (2004)

20. Cimatti, A., Roveri, M., Traverso, P.: Strong Planning in Non-Deterministic Domains via Model Checking. In: Proc. 4th International Conference on Artificial Intelligence Planning Systems (AIPS-98), Carnegie Mellon University, Pittsburgh, USA, AAAI-Press, Stanford, California, USA (1998)

21. Clarke, E.M., Emerson, E.A.: Synthesis of Synchronization Skeletons for Branching Time Temporal Logic. In: Kozen, D. (ed.) Logics of Programs. LNCS, vol. 131. Springer, Heidelberg (1982)

22. Clarke, E.M., Emerson, E.A., Sistla, A.P.: Automatic Verification of Finite-State Concurrent Systems using Temporal Logic Specifications. ACM Transactions on Programming Languages and Systems 8(2), 244–263 (1986)

23. Clarke, E.M., Grumberg, O., Hiraishi, H., Jha, S., Long, D., McMillan, K.L., Ness, L.: Verification of the FUTUREBUS+ Cache Coherence Protocol. In: Proc. of 11th International Symposium on Computer Hardware Description Languages and their Applications (CHDL-93) (1993)
24. Clarke, E.M., Grumberg, O., Peled, D.: Model Checking. MIT Press, Cambridge, MA (1999)
25. Copty, F., Fix, L., Fraer, R., Giunchiglia, E., Kamhi, G., Tacchella, A., Vardi, M.Y.: Benefits of bounded model checking at an industrial setting. In: Berry, G., Comon, H., Finkel, A. (eds.) CAV 2001. LNCS, vol. 2102, pp. 436–453. Springer, Heidelberg (2001)
26. Coudert, O., Berthet, C., Madre, J.C.: Verification of Synchronous Sequential Machines Using Symbolic Execution. In: Proc. of International Workshop on Automatic Verification Methods for Finite State Systems. LNCS, vol. 407, Springer, Heidelberg (1989)
27. Coudert, O., Madre, J.C.: Fault Tree Analysis: 10^{20} Prime Implicants and Beyond. In: Proc. Annual Reliability and Maintainability Symposium (RAMS 1993) (1993)
28. Dal Lago, U., Pistore, M., Traverso, P.: Planning with a Language for Extended Goals. In: Proc. 18th National Conference on Artificial Intelligence (AAAI'02) (2002)
29. Dill, D.L., Drexler, A J., Hu, A.J., Yang, C.H.: Protocol Verification as a Hardware Design Aid. In: International Conference on Computer Design, VLSI in Computers and Processors, pp. 522–525. IEEE Computer Society Press, Los Alamitos, Ca., USA (October 1992)
30. Eèn, N., Sörensson, N.: An extensible sat solver. In: Proc. of the 6th International Conference on Theory and Applications of Satisfiability Testing, pp. 502–518 (2003)
31. Emerson, E.: Temporal and Modal Logic. In: Handbook of Theoretical Computer Science, vol. B, Formal Models and Semantics, Elsevier, Amsterdam (1990)
32. Fikes, R.E., Nilsson, N.J.: STRIPS: A New Approach to the Application of Theorem Proving to Problem Solving. Artificial Intelligence 2, 187–208 (1971)
33. The FSAP platform. http://sra.itc.it/tools/FSAP
34. Ghallab, M., Nau, D., Traverso, P.: Automated Planning: Theory and Practice. 1, pp. 17–110. Morgan Kaufmann, Washington (2004)
35. Gupta, A., Clarke, E., Strichman, O.: Sat based counterexample-guided abstraction-refinement. IEEE Transactions on Computer Aided Design 23, 1113–1123 (2004)
36. Heljanko, K., Junttila, T.A., Latvala, T.: Incremental and complete bounded model checking for full PLTL. In: Etessami, K., Rajamani, S.K. (eds.) CAV 2005. LNCS, vol. 3576, pp. 98–111. Springer, Heidelberg (2005)
37. Hoffmann, J., Brafman, R.: Contingent Planning via Heuristic Forward Search with Implicit Belief States. In (ICAPS-05). Proc. of 15th International Conference on Automated Planning and Scheduling, Monterey, CA, USA, pp. 71–80. Kaufmann, San Francisco (2005)
38. Holzmann, G.J.: The model checker Spin. IEEE Trans. on Software Engineering, Special issue on Formal Methods in Software Practice. 23(5), 279–295 (1997)
39. Jiang, S., Huang, Z., Chandra, V., Kumar, R.: A polynomial algorithm for testing diagnosability of discrete event systems. IEEE Transactions on Automatic Control 46(8), 1318–1321 (2001)
40. McMillan, K.L.: Symbolic Model Checking. Kluwer Academic Publishers, Dordrecht (1993)
41. The NuSMV model checker, http://nusmv.itc.it
42. Pistore, M., Traverso, P.: Planning as Model Checking for Extended Goals in Nondeterministic Domains. In: Proc. of 17th International Joint Conference on Artificial Intelligence (IJCAI-01) (2001)
43. Pixley, C.: A Computational Theory and Implementation of Sequential Hardware Equivalence. In: DIMACS Workshop on Computer Aided Verification '90, Providence, RI pp. 293–320 (1990)
44. Prasad, M., Biere, A., Gupta, A.: A survey of recent advances in sat-based formal verification. STTT, (7), 156–173 (2005)

45. Queille, J.P., Sifakis, J.: Specification and Verification of Concurrent Systems in CESAR. In: Dezani-Ciancaglini, M., Montanari, U. (eds.) International Symposium on Programming. LNCS, vol. 137, pp. 337–371. Springer, Heidelberg (1982)
46. Rauzy, A.: New Algorithms for Fault Trees Analysis. Reliability Engineering and System Safety 40(3), 203–211 (1993)
47. Rintanen, J.: Backward Plan Construction for Planning as Search in Belief Space. In: Proc. of 6th International Conference on Artificial Intelligence Planning and Scheduling (AIPS'02), pp. 93–102 (2002)
48. Sampath, M., Sengupta, R., Lafortune, S., Sinnamohideen, K., Teneketzis, D.: Diagnosability of discrete-event systems. IEEE Transactions on Automatic Control 40(9), 1555–1575 (1995)
49. Sampath, M., Sengupta, R., Lafortune, S., Sinnamohideen, K., Teneketzis, D.: Failure diagnosis using discrete event models. IEEE Transactions on Control Systems 4(2), 105–124 (1996)
50. Sheeran, M., Singh, S., Stalmarck, G.: Checking safety properties using induction and a sat-solver. In: Johnson, S.D., Hunt Jr., W.A. (eds.) FMCAD 2000. LNCS, vol. 1954, Springer, Heidelberg (2000)
51. Siu, N.O.: Risk Assessment for Dynamic Systems: An Overview. Reliability Engineering and System Safety 43, 43–74 (1994)
52. Touati, H.J., Savoj, H., Lin, B., Brayton, R.K., Sangiovanni-Vincentelli, A.: Implicit State Enumeration of Finite State Machines Using BDDs. In: Proc. of the IEEE International Conference on Computer-Aided Design, pp. 130–133, Santa Clara, CA , IEEE Computer Society Press, Los Alamitos (November 1990)
53. Vesely, W.E., Goldberg, F.F., Roberts, N.H., Haasl, D.F.: Fault Tree Handbook. Technical Report NUREG-0492, Systems and Reliability Research Office of Nuclear Regulatory Research U.S. Nuclear Regulatory Commission (1981)

Verifying Space and Time Requirements for Resource-Bounded Agents

Natasha Alechina[1], Piergiorgio Bertoli[2], Chiara Ghidini[2], Mark Jago[1], Brian Logan[1], and Luciano Serafini[2]

[1] School of Computer Science
University of Nottingham
Nottingham, UK
{nza,mtw,bsl}@cs.nott.ac.uk
[2] ITC-IRST, Trento, Italy
{bertoli,ghidini,luciano.serafini}@itc.it

Abstract. The *effective reasoning capability* of an agent can be defined as its capability to infer, within a given space and time bound, facts that are logical consequences of its knowledge base. In this paper we show how to determine the effective reasoning capability of an agent with limited memory by encoding the agent as a transition system and automatically verifying whether a state where the agent believes a certain conclusion is reachable from the start state. We present experimental results using the Model Based Planner (MBP) which illustrates how the length of the deduction varies for different memory sizes.

1 Introduction

Consider an agent that has a finite knowledge base and some rules of inference which allow it to derive new information from its knowledge base. It is intuitively clear that some derivations require more memory than others (e.g., to store intermediate results), and that two agents with the same knowledge base and the same set of inference rules, but with different amounts of memory, may not be able to derive the same formulas.

The question of how much memory a reasoning agent needs to derive a formula is of considerable theoretical and practical interest. From a theoretical point of view, it is interesting to investigate how the deductive strength of a particular logic changes when only a fixed number of formulas are allowed to be 'active' in a derivation. From a practical point of view, the question of whether an agent will run out of memory or time before achieving its goal(s) is clearly a major concern for the agent developer. As agent tasks become more open ended, the amount of memory required to achieve them becomes harder to predict a priori. For example, the reasoning capabilities of agents assumed by many web service applications is non trivial (e.g., reasoning over complex ontologies or about business processes described by a set of business rules) and the memory requirements correspondingly difficult for the agent developer to determine a priori. At the same time trends towards mobile agents and agents which run on mobile devices such as PDAs and smart phones imply more processor and memory efficient agent designs (e.g., the Micro-FIPA-OS [18] and JADE-LEAP [4] platforms). Such devices typically have a relatively small amount of physical memory (and no virtual memory), which

S. Edelkamp and A. Lomuscio (Eds.): MoChart IV, LNAI 4428, pp. 19–34, 2007.

must be shared between the OS, the agent platform and other applications running on the device. While increased bandwidth and more powerful handheld devices will undoubtedly become available, the rapid growth in, e.g., the number and complexity of ontologies, seems likely to outstrip any increases in hardware capabilities, at least for the foreseeable future.

In this paper, we present a novel procedure for automatically verifying the space and time requirements for resource-bounded reasoning agents. Specifically, we address the question: given an agent and a formula ϕ, does the agent have sufficient memory to derive ϕ, and, if it does, what is the length of the shortest derivation within the specified memory bound? In outline, our approach is as follows. We represent a reasoning agent as a finite state machine in which the states correspond the formulas currently held in the reasoner's memory and the transitions between states correspond to applying the reasoning rules. Our approach is general enough to admit verification of reasoners with any set of inference rules, provided that those rules can be encoded as transitions between FSM states. To illustrate the generality of our approach, we show how to encode two example reasoners: a classical propositional reasoner which can derive all classical consequences of its knowledge base given unlimited memory, and a forward-chaining rule-based agent of the kind found in many applications employing ontological reasoning and business rules. To check whether a reasoner has enough memory to derive a formula ϕ, we specify the FSM as input to the model-based planner MBP [6], and check whether the reasoner has a plan (a choice of memory allocations and inference rule applications), all executions of which lead to states containing ϕ. Using a simple business rules example, we show how MBP can be used to automatically verify the existence of a derivation, and present experimental results which illustrate how the length of the deduction varies for different memory sizes.

The remainder of the paper is organised as follows. In section 2 we introduce our model of the agent's memory and give some examples of the kinds of properties we wish to verify. In section 3, we present our formal model of a resource bounded agent and show how to model two example agents, a simple agent that reasons using rules, and a classical reasoner capable of deriving any classical consequence of its knowledge base. In section 4 we briefly introduce the MBP model-based planner and explain how it is used to verify the memory requirements of a resource-bounded reasoner. In section 5 we present a simple example to illustrate the effects of memory limitations on a rule-based reasoning agent and give results from MBP illustrating how the length of deduction varies for different memory sizes. In section 6 we briefly describe related work before concluding in section 7.

2 Memory Bounds

Consider an agent running on a small device like a mobile phone, a simple PDA, or even a smaller device like a node of a sensor network. The agent has a pool of potentially available information stored in a Knowledge Base (K)[1] and a fixed set of reasoning

---

[1] The information could be stored in a remote database or in a persistent memory like a flash card or obtained in input from a user. In this paper we abstract from these aspects and say only that information is potentially available in a knowledge base K.

rules. Using information from the knowledge base and the inference rules, the agent can infer new formulas. We assume that the knowledge base is too large to fit into the agent's memory, and the agent can store at most n formulas from K in memory at any given time. Loading new information from the KB when the agent's memory is full overwrites some of the information currently in memory. For example, a location-aware device which advises a traveller about local amenities and tourist attractions cannot load an entire database of attractions and ontological definitions in memory when computing a recommendation, and will have to manage the subset of formulas from K which are in memory and available for inference. Given this resource bound, which we call, 'memory of size n', the properties we are interested in verifying are of the form: can a formula ϕ be derived with a memory of size n?; what is the minimum amount of memory required to derive ϕ?; is there a relation between memory size and the number of steps required to derive ϕ? what is the minimum amount of memory required to derive ϕ with the shortest derivation?

To illustrate the impact of memory bounds in the reasoning process, consider an agent with a knowledge base K composed of the following formulas:

$$A, A \rightarrow B, B \rightarrow C, C \rightarrow D. \tag{1}$$

If the only inference rule the agent uses is modus ponens, it will require a memory of at least size 2 to derive D:

1. read A (memory contains $\{A\}$)
2. read $A \rightarrow B$ (memory contains $\{A, \; A \rightarrow B\}$)
3. apply modus ponens and store B, overwrite A (memory contains $\{A \rightarrow B, \; B\}$)
4. read $B \rightarrow C$, overwrite $A \rightarrow B$ (memory contains $\{B, \; B \rightarrow C\}$)
... ...
n. until we apply all the rules and conclude D.

The deduction above requires only two formulas in memory at any given time as we can overwrite the antecedent of an implication with the result of applying modus ponens, load the next implication, apply modus ponens, and store the new result. Notice that after adding new implications, say $E \rightarrow F$, $F \rightarrow G$, we still need only two formulas in memory to derive G. Thus memory requirements do not necessarily depend upon the number of formulas used in the derivation. However, if K contains the following formulas

$$A, A \rightarrow B, A \wedge B \rightarrow C, B \wedge C \rightarrow D \tag{2}$$

and the agent reasons using the inference rules modus ponens (MP) and conjunction introduction ($\wedge_I$), then the derivation requires storing at least 3 formulas in memory at any given time. Notice that the two knowledge bases (1) and (2) are logically equivalent. Thus memory requirements can change for logically equivalent knowledge bases. Also, it can be shown that adding conjunction elimination to the set of rules allows the agent to derive D with only 2 formulas in memory. Thus, memory requirements also depend upon the inference rules available to the agent.

In summary, there is a trade-off between space and time requirements, and the memory required for a derivation will depend on both K and the agent's inference rules. Given a procedure for determining how much memory a given derivation requires (and how much time it takes) for particular inference rules and K, an agent developer can ensure that an agent has sufficient memory for a particular task, or, conversely engineer a K which will allow an agent with particular inference capabilities and memory size to derive a given formula.

3   Formal Model

We model resource-bounded agents as finite state machines (FSM) or transition systems. Let the internal language of the agent be some language L (e.g. propositional language). The definition of a transition system is given relative to the following components:

1. the bound n on the agent's memory size
2. the agent's reasoning rules
3. the agent's knowledge base $K \subseteq L$
4. the agent's goal formula $A_G \in L$

The set of all subformulas of K and A_G will be denoted by Ω. We abstract away from the size of the formulas. However, given K, the maximal size of any formula which the agent's state has information about, will be fixed.

In the remainder of this section, we first define the language and transition systems for 'definite reasoning' agents, which never do reasoning by cases or assumption-based reasoning, and give an example of such an agent (rule-based agent). We then introduce a more complex logic for agents that need to maintain a set of epistemic alternatives, and give an example of such an agent (classical reasoner).

3.1   Definite Reasoners

The language of the logic BML^d (for bounded memory logic, definite case) is defined relative to the agent's internal language L. Well formed formulas (w.f.f.) are defined as follows:

- If A is a formula of L, then B A (the agent believes A) is a w.f.f.
- If ϕ is a w.f.f., then $\neg \phi$, EX ϕ ('in one of the successor states, ϕ') and EF ϕ ('in some future state, ϕ') are w.f.f.
- If ϕ_1 and ϕ_2 are w.f.f., then $\phi_1 \wedge \phi_2$ is a w.f.f.

Other boolean connectives are defined in the usual way. We also define AX ϕ as $\neg$EX $\neg\phi$ and AG ϕ as $\neg$EF $\neg\phi$.

A transition system $M = (S, R, V)$ consists of a set of states S, a serial binary relation R on S (transitions between states) and an assignment $V : S \longrightarrow \mathcal{P}(\Omega)$ (assigning to the state the set of formulas the agent believes in that state). Notice that $V(s)$ is not a classical truth assignment, as it might contain complex formulas, e.g., $A \wedge B$, as well as contradictory formulas, e.g., $A \wedge B, \neg B \in V(s)$. To reflect the fact that the agents have bounded memory, we postulate that V can assign at most n formulas to any given state. The transitions which the agent can make depend on the agent's inference rules. In our model, we assume that one of the agent's possible transitions is 'reading' a K formula into its memory or 'active state'. Reading a formula may correspond to reading from flash memory, asking for user input, or reading data from a server over the network.

The definition of a formula being satisfied in $M, s \in S$ is as follows:

$M, s \models \text{B} A$ iff $A \in V(s)$
$M, s \models \neg\phi$ iff $M, s \not\models \phi$
$M, s \models \phi \wedge \psi$ iff $M, s \models \phi$ and $M, s \models \psi$
$M, s \models \text{EX} \phi$ iff there exists a state t such that $R(s,t)$ and $M, t \models \phi$.
$M, s \models \text{EF} \phi$ iff there exists a sequence of states $t_1, \ldots, t_k$ such that for all $i \in \{1, \ldots, k-1\}$, $R(t_i, t_{i+1})$, $t_1 = s$ and $M, t_k \models \phi$

Let $\mathbf{M}$ be a class of models (for example, all models with the same knowledge base and the same transition rules). A formula is $\mathbf{M}$-satisfiable if it is true in some state in some model in $\mathbf{M}$. A formula is $\mathbf{M}$-valid if it is true in every state in every model in $\mathbf{M}$. The definition of logical consequence is standard.

The bound n on the size of the agent's memory is expressed by the following axiom schema:

B(n) $\text{B} A_1 \wedge \ldots \wedge \text{B} A_n \rightarrow \neg\text{B} A_{n+1}$ where $A_i \neq A_j$ if $i \neq j$.

We can express that the agent can derive its goal A_G from its knowledge base K as $\text{EF} \text{B} A_G$ (there is some future state where the agent believes A_G). The fact that a formula is derivable in k steps can be expressed as $\text{EX}^k \text{B} A_G$ (where EX^k denotes k applications of the operator EX). Similarly, the fact that an agent needs at least $k + 1$ steps to derive a formula A_G can be expressed as $\text{AX}^k \neg\text{B} A_G$.

3.2 Rule-Based Reasoners

In this section we present a simple example of an agent which reasons using rules, e.g., ontology rules, or business rules. We assume that agent's knowledge base consists of ground atomic formulas and rules of the form $A_1 \wedge \ldots \wedge A_n \rightarrow B$, where $A_1, \ldots, A_n, B$ are atomic formulas (see, for example, [13]). An example of such rule would be

$$Parent(x, y) \wedge Brother(y, z) \rightarrow Uncle(x, z)$$

Essentially, such agents can only reason by a single inference rule:

$$\frac{A_1(\bar{a}), \ldots, A_n(\bar{a}) \quad \forall \bar{x}(A_1(\bar{x}) \wedge \ldots \wedge A_n(\bar{x}) \rightarrow B(\bar{x}))}{B(\bar{a})}$$

By generating all possible substitutions of constants occurring in the knowledge base into the rule, we can reduce the knowledge base to a purely propositional set of formulas, consisting of propositional variables and implications of the form $p_1 \wedge \ldots \wedge p_n \rightarrow q$. Then the only rules the agent needs to derive all 'rule-based' consequences are conjunction introduction $\wedge_I$ and modus ponens MP:

$$\frac{A_1, A_2}{A_1 \wedge A_2} \wedge_I \qquad \frac{A_1, A_1 \rightarrow A_2}{A_2} MP$$

We show how to represent this reasoner as an FSM. Let $V'(s)$ be any subset of $V(s)$ which differs from $V(s)$ in at most one formula and has cardinality at most $n - 1$. The rule-based reasoner has the following transitions:

Read $R(s,t)$ if $V(t) = V(s)' \cup \{A\}$ for some $A \in K$
AND $R(s,t)$ if $A_1, A_2 \in V(s)$ and $V(t) = V(s)' \cup \{A_1 \wedge A_2\}$.
MP $R(s,t)$ if $A_1 \in V(s)$, $A_1 \to A_2 \in V(s)$, and $V(t) = V(s)' \cup \{A_2\}$.
Reflexivity $R(s,s)$

For technical convenience (we will discuss a class of models without this assumption later in this section), we also allow (but not require) 'forgetting' transitions of the form $R(s,t)$, where $V(t) = V'(s)$.

Notice that the definition of $V'(s)$ guarantees that after each transition $R(s,t)$, the memory bound is satisfied by $V(t)$, i.e., $|V(t)| \le n$.

A formula A_G is derivable from K using only modus ponens and conjunction introduction with memory of size n if, and only if, $M_{K,A_G}, start \models \text{EF B } A_G$, where M_{K,A_G} is a rule-based transition model where states are assigned only formulas which are subformulas of K and A_G, $V(s)$ for any s contains at most n formulas, and $V(start) = \emptyset$. Indeed, a derivation of A_G from K using only the allowed rules and at most n formulas in memory corresponds to a branch in a state transition system described above from an empty state to a state containing A_G; and conversely, such a branch can be converted into a derivation of A_G from K. Similarly, A_G is derivable from K in k steps iff $M_{K,A_G}, start \models \text{EX}^k \text{B } A_G$.

The logical axioms corresponding to the rule-based reasoner's transition rules are as follows (we assume $n \ge 1$ for **A1**):

A1 $\text{EX B } A$ for $A \in K$
A2 $\text{B } A_1 \wedge \text{B } A_2 \to \text{EX B } (A_1 \wedge A_2)$
A3 $\text{B } A_1 \wedge \text{B } (A_1 \to A_2) \to \text{EX B } A_2$

Finally, we need to express that only transitions which are made according to the rules are possible, and that in each transition at most one new formula is added and at most one formula is overwritten.

A4 $\text{EX } (\text{B } A_1 \wedge \text{B } A_2) \to \text{B } A_1 \vee \text{B } A_2$
A5 $\text{EX } (\neg \text{B } A_1 \wedge \neg \text{B } A_2) \to \neg \text{B } A_1 \vee \neg \text{B } A_2$
A6 $\text{EX B } (A_1 \wedge A_2) \to \text{B } (A_1 \wedge A_2) \vee (\text{B } A_1 \wedge \text{B } A_2)$
A7 $\text{EX B } A_2 \to \text{B } A_2 \vee \bigvee_{A_1 \to A_2 \in K} (\text{B } (A_1 \to A_2) \wedge \text{B } A_1)$ for $A_2 \notin K$ and $A_2 \ne$ $\text{B} \wedge C$

Note that the only axiom schema which depends on K is **A7**. Let $ML(K, n, \text{EX})$ be the logic defined by the set of axiom schemata **A1 - A7, B(n)**, together with the classical and modal axioms for EX:

Cl tautologies of classical logic
K $\text{AX } (\phi \to \psi) \to (\text{AX } \phi \to \text{AX } \psi)$
T $\phi \to \text{EX } \phi$

MP $\vdash \phi, \vdash \phi \rightarrow \psi \Rightarrow \vdash \psi$
N $\vdash \phi \Rightarrow \vdash \text{AX}\,\phi$

Let $\mathbf{M}(K, n)$ stand for the class of models where the knowledge base is K, the memory size is n, and the only possible transitions are defined by the transition rules above. We then have the following completeness result.

Theorem 1. $ML(K, n, \text{EX})$ *is sound and strongly complete with respect to* $\mathbf{M}(K, n)$.

Proof. To prove soundness, we will show validity of axioms **A1 - A7**. Axiom **A1** is valid because by the **Read** condition on R, it is always possible to make a transition to a state which contains a formula from K. Axiom **A2** is valid because by the **AND** condition on R, if $V(s)$ contains A_1 and A_2, it is always possible to make a transition to a state which contains $A_1 \wedge A_2$. Similarly, **A3** is valid because of transition guaranteed by **MP**. **A4** is valid because if in some t reachable from the current state s, $A_1, A_2 \in V(t)$, then (since at most one new formula is added in each transition), either A_1 or A_2 are in $V(s)$. **A5** is valid because if for some t reachable from s, $A_1 \notin V(t)$ and $A_2 \notin V(t)$, then (since at most one formula is dropped), either $A_1 \notin V(s)$, or $A_2 \notin V(s)$. **A6** says that conjunctive formulas can only appear in the next state if both conjuncts are in the current state (note that K only contains literals and implications with a literal in the consequent, so **AND** is indeed the only way to derive a conjunction). Finally, **A7** says that the only way to add a formula A which is not in K and not a conjunction, is to derive it by **MP**.

To prove strong completeness, we show how to construct a satisfying model for any $ML(K, n, \text{EX})$-consistent set of formulas. Take an $ML(K, n, \text{EX})$-consistent set of formulas Γ. Construct the satisfying model $M = (S, R, V)$ for Γ as follows. Let S be the set of all $ML(K, n, \text{EX})$-maximal consistent sets. For any formula A of L, let $A \in V(s)$ iff B $A \in s$. Let $R(s, t)$ hold iff for every $\psi \in t$, EX $\psi \in s$. The definition of R is standard for modal logic completeness proofs, and we immediately get the Truth Lemma: for every ψ and every $s \in S$, $M, s \models \psi$ iff $\psi \in s$. Also, axiom **T** forces R to be reflexive. Since Γ is consistent, it is included in some maximal consistent set s, hence there is a state where Γ is satisfied. All we need to do now is to show that the relation R in M satisfies the conditions defining $\mathbf{M}(K, n)$.

The easiest condition to demonstrate is the memory limit: for any state s, $|V(s)| \leq n$. Indeed, since all maximal consistent sets contain $B(n)$, then none of them can contain more that n distinct formulas of the form B A. Hence, $V(s)$ cannot contain more than n formulas.

Next, we need to show that all **Read, AND** and **MP** transitions required by the conditions on R are possible in M.

Read. Assume s is a state and $A \in K$. We need to show that there is a state t such that $R(s, t)$, $V(t)$ contains A, and lacks at most one formula contained in $V(s)$. Because of axiom **A1**, s has a successor t which contains B A. Hence $V(t)$ contains A. By the axiom **A4**, $V(t)$ has at most one new formula compared with $V(s)$. If A is not in $V(s)$, then this new formula is A. There is also (by **A5**) at most one formula which is in $V(s)$ but not in $V(t)$, so $V(t)$ is of the form $V'(s) \cup \{A\}$. If A is in $V(s)$, then by reflexivity of R, trivially there is a $t = s$ such that $R(s, t)$ and $V(t) = V'(s) \cup \{A\}$.

AND. Assume s is a state and $V(s)$ contains A_1 and A_2. We need to show that there is a state t such that $R(s,t)$, $V(t)$ contains $A_1 \wedge A_2$, and $V(t)$ is of the form $V'(s) \cup \{A_1 \wedge A_2\}$. Because of axiom **A2**, s has a successor t which contains $B(A_1 \wedge A_2)$. Hence $V(t)$ contains $A_1 \wedge A_2$. The rest of the argument is the same as for **Read**.

MP. Similarly, by **A3**, is s contains A_1 and $A_1 \rightarrow A_2$, then it has a successor t such that $A_2 \in V(t)$ and $V(t) = V'(s) \cup \{A_2\}$.

We have shown that all the transitions required by the conditions on $\mathbf{M}(K, n)$ indeed exist. Now we need to show that only allowed transitions exist. We have already seen that if $R(s, t)$ then $V(t)$ has at most one extra formula and at most one missing formula, compared to $V(s)$ (this is forced by axioms **A4** and **A5**). The new formula has to be added by one of the transitions **Read**, **AND** or **MP**: this is guaranteed by **A6** and **A7**. However, we cannot force a condition that a transition always adds a new formula; therefore our technical assumption allowing forgetful transitions.

3.3 More General Reasoners

In this section, we model reasoners which can reason by cases, or in general consider hypothetical states; this means that their transitions do not necessarily follow the logical consequence relation. We also extend the language to express disbelief as well as belief.

Consider a reasoner who believes:

$$A \vee B, A \rightarrow C, B \rightarrow C.$$

To derive C, it has to reason by cases: assume A; derive C. Then, assume B; derive C. Hence, it is safe to believe C. However, if the process of assuming A corresponds to a transition to a state where A is believed, the modelling is not 'safe' — the agent's beliefs are not justified by valid inference steps. In the state where it assumes A, the agent should remember that this is just one of the epistemic alternatives, and that in others A is false and B is true.

To deal with such reasoners, we add an extra set of 'epistemic alternatives' or possible worlds to each state. Intuitively, a formula is now believed in a state if it is true in all of the epistemic alternatives associated with this state. We express this as $\Box B\,A$.

The language of the logic BML (for bounded memory logic) extends the language of BML^d by adding extra clauses:

- If A is a formula of L, then $\bar{B}\,A$ (the agent disbelieves A) is a w.f.f.
- If ϕ is a w.f.f., then $\Diamond\phi$ is a w.f.f.

We also define $\Box\phi$ as $\neg\Diamond\neg\phi$.

For such general reasoners, we can express that the agent can derive A_G from its knowledge base K as $EF\,\Box B\,A_G$ (there is some future state where in all epistemic alternatives the agent believes A_G).

A BML transition system $M = (S, W, R, Y, T, F)$ consists of a set of states S, a set of possible worlds or epistemic alternatives W, a binary relation R on S, a function assigning to each state a set of epistemic alternatives $Y : S \longrightarrow \mathcal{P}(W)$, and two assignments $T : W \longrightarrow \mathcal{P}(\Omega)$ and $F : W \longrightarrow \mathcal{P}(\Omega)$ which say whether the value of an (internal language) formula in a world is true or false (where, as before Ω is the set of subformulas of K and A_G). As before, to reflect the bound on the agent's memory, we require $|T(w)| + |F(w)| \leq n$, for any given state w. Moreover, the truth assignments should be consistent, i.e., $T(w) \cap F(w) = \emptyset$. The following truth definitions have been added or modified compared to BML^d. Note that we talk about truth in a world and truth in a state:

$$M, w \models B \, A \text{ iff } A \in T(w)$$
$$M, w \models \bar{B} \, A \text{ iff } A \in F(w)$$
$$M, s \models \Diamond\phi \text{ iff there exists } w \text{ in } Y(s), \text{ such that } M, w \models \phi.$$

The bound n on the size of the agent's memory is expressed by the following axiom (which replaces **B(n)** defined for BML^d):

B(n)′ $\Box(\tilde{B} \, A_1 \wedge \ldots \wedge \tilde{B} \, A_n \rightarrow \neg \, \tilde{B} \, A_{n+1})$, where $\tilde{B} \, A_i$ stands for either $B \, A_i$ or $\bar{B} \, A_i$ and $A_i \neq A_j$ for all $i, j \in \{1, \ldots, n+1\}$ such that $i \neq j$.

3.4 Classical Reasoners

In this section we present a simple example of a classical reasoner, which, given unlimited memory, is capable of deriving any classical consequence of its knowledge base.

Epistemic alternatives are introduced when the classical reasoner applies non-deterministic rules, such as disjunction elimination. Suppose, for example, that the agent has $A \vee B$ in its knowledge base and starts in a state s_0, which has a single epistemic alternative w_0 with $T(w_0) = F(w_0) = \emptyset$. The agent can read $A \vee B$ and transit to a state s_1 with a single epistemic alternative w_1, such that $A \vee B \in T(w_1)$. Now the agent applies a non-deterministic rule for disjunction; it may assume that both disjuncts are true, or A is true and B is false, or vice versa. Formally, this means that the agent transits to a state s_2 where the epistemic alternatives are:

1. w_{11} with $A, B \in T(w_{11})$,
2. w_{12} with $A \in T(w_{12})$ and $B \in F(w_{12})$,
3. w_{13} with $B \in T(w_{12})$ and $A \in F(w_{12})$.

Note that the classical reasoner cannot derive A from $A \vee B$ in the sense of our criterion of $EF \, \Box B \, A$ being true: A is true in w_{11} and w_{12}, but false in w_{13}, so s_2 does not satisfy $\Box B \, A$.

The transition relation R between states is defined in terms of expansion relation between epistemic alternatives $\preceq$. Expansion corresponds to applying an inference rule to formulas in the epistemic alternative; in the example above, w_1 is expanded (by applying the rule of disjunction elimination) to w_{11}, w_{12}, w_{13}. Formally, $R(s, t)$ holds if $Y(s) = \{w_1, \ldots, w_m\}$, and for some $w_i \in Y(s)$, $Y(t) = (Y(s) \backslash \{w_i\}) \cup \{v : w_i \preceq v\}$.

Before we define the expansion relation, we need a few preliminary definitions and comments. Note that the classical reasoner agent can construct new formulas in addition to decomposing formulas. We only allow the construction of formulas which are in Ω (the set of subformulas of K and A_G). This does not affect the completeness of agent's rules (since these are the only formulas it may possibly need in the derivation of A_G from K), but allows us to represent it as a finite state machine.

Since the agent can both believe and disbelieve formulas (and its language contains negation), an issue of inconsistent possible worlds arises. An agent cannot make a transition to a possible world where the same formula is assigned to true and false. All rules therefore have to have a proviso that if $w \preceq v$ then it impossible, for any formula A, to have $A \in T(w)$ and $A \in F(v)$ or vice versa:

Recall. $w \preceq v$ and $A \in T(v) \Rightarrow A \notin F(w)$, and $w \preceq v$ and $A \in F(v) \Rightarrow A \notin T(w)$

Here is a list of possible types of transitions:

Read. $w \preceq v$ if for some formula $A \in K$, $A \in T(v)$, and otherwise $T(v), F(v)$ contain the same formulas as $T(w), F(w)$, apart from possibly omitting one (overwritten) formula. Observe that w can be expanded by the **Read** transition in as many ways as there are formulas in K, and choices for overwriting a formula in $T(w) \cup F(w)$ (including a choice to overwrite nothing). In the modelling section, these two formulas (a formula added and a formula overwritten) are made explicit parameters in defining the transition.

Split. $w \preceq v_1$ and $w \preceq v_2$ if for some formula $A \in \Omega$ with $A \notin T(w) \cup F(w)$, $A \in T(v_1)$, $A \in F(v_2)$, and otherwise the truth assignment in v_1, v_2 is the same as in w, with at most one formula in each world being overwritten, and **Recall** is satisfied. This transition rule enables the agent to do reasoning by cases, and is equivalent to having $A \vee \neg A$ as an axiom, for every $A \in \Omega$.

ExContradictio. $w \preceq v$ if for some A, $A \in T(w)$ and $\neg A \in T(w)$, or $A \in F(w)$ and $\neg A \in F(w)$, and $T(v)$ contains A_G.

makeNot. $w \preceq v$ if for some $\neg A \in \Omega$, $A \in T(w) \cup F(w)$, and $\neg A \in T(v) \cup F(v)$ with the opposite sign, otherwise the truth assignment in v is the same as in w (with at most one formula possibly overwritten), and **Recall** is satisfied.

elimNot. $w \preceq v$ if for some $\neg A \in \Omega$, $\neg A \in T(w) \cup F(w)$, and $A \in T(v) \cup F(v)$ with the opposite sign, otherwise the truth assignment in v is the same as in w (with at most one formula possibly overwritten), and **Recall** is satisfied.

makeAnd. $w \preceq v$ if for some $A_1 \wedge A_2 \in \Omega$, $A_1, A_2 \in T(w) \cup F(w)$ and $A_1 \wedge A_2 \in T(v) \cup F(v)$, so that the value of $A_1 \wedge A_2$ in v is the logical 'and' of the values of A_1, A_2 in w, otherwise the truth assignment in v is the same as in w (with at most one formula possibly overwritten), and **Recall** is satisfied.

elimAnd. $w \preceq v$ if $A_1 \wedge A_2 \in T(w) \cup F(w)$, $A_1, A_2 \in T(v) \cup F(v)$, so that the logical 'and' of the truth value of A_1 and A_2 in v equals to the value of $A_1 \wedge A_2$ in w, otherwise the truth assignment in v is the same as in w (with at most *two* formulas possibly overwritten), and **Recall** is satisfied. If the conjunction is true in w, there is only one possible truth assignment to the conjuncts in v, but if it is false, then w can be expanded by this rule to worlds where one of the conjuncts is true and another one false, or both false.

Transition rules for other connectives are defined in similar fashion.

Theorem 2. *A classical reasoner with unbounded memory can derive A_G from K whenever A_G is a classical consequence of K.*

Proof. Let A_G be a classical consequence of K. If K is inconsistent, we use **ExContra-dictio** to derive A_G. If K is consistent, the strategy for deriving A_G is as follows. The reasoner does not overwrite any formulas. It reads all formulas from K and decomposes them down to all possible assignments to propositional variables in K. If variables of A_G are a subset of the variables of K, then each branch in the previous execution can be continued with a successful composition of A_G (since every assignment satisfying K satisfies A_G. Else let $Var(A_G)\backslash Var(K) = \{q_1, \ldots, q_m\}$. Then, continue each branch of the previous derivation with m splits on each of q_i. This will generate all possible assignments to $Var(K) \cup \{q_1, \ldots, q_m\}$ which make K true. By assumption, each of them makes A_G true, so again on each branch A_G can be successfully assembled.

4 Verifying Reasoning Capabilities

The problem of identifying the existence (and the minimal length) of a deduction for A_G from a knowledge base K, for an agent with bounded memory modelled as a transition system M can be recast as a *planning problem*: find a control strategy for M (a plan) such that, starting from any state in K, it leads to some state in A_G. The plan is the proof of A_G.

In general, M is a *nondeterministic* transition system, since applying a rule may lead to several epistemic alternatives, as shown e.g. in Sec. 3.4 for the case of disjunction elimination. Thus, we are interested in *strong* plans [6]: tree-structured plans such that their execution leads to the goal, for *every* possible outcome of the actions in the plan.

Among the few planners capable to deal with strong planning for nondeterministic domains, we selected MBP, a system coupling effective algorithms with an input language which allows a concise description of transition systems in logical terms. In this section, we provide a high-level description of the way the proof existence problem is recast as a planning domain in MBP. We take as reference the classical reasoner, leaving the simpler case of rule-based reasoning to the reader. For reasons of space, we will omit the encodings of the rules associated to disjunction and implication, which are analogous to the one for conjunction.

In the following, we partition Ω into the subsets Ω_0, $\Omega_\neg$, $\Omega_\vee$, $\Omega_\wedge$, $\Omega_\rightarrow$ which contain respectively atomic formulae, and formulae whose top-level connective is a negation, disjunction, conjunction or implication. Moreover we define the functions $l(\cdot)$ and $r(\cdot)$ which return the left/right parts of non-atomic formulae. We omit their trivial definition, and we take the convention that $l(\neg\phi) = \phi$.

The core of the encoding consists in representing the state transition system described in Section 3 as a planning domain. Formally, a planning domain is a triple (S, Act, R), where S are the states of the domain, Act is a set of actions, and $R \subseteq S \times Act \times S$ is the transition relation, describing the outcomes of the action execution; an action is executable over a state s iff $\exists(s, \alpha, s') \in R$. Our mapping views actions as deduction rules and domain states as epistemic states of the agent. In a planning domain, the state is represented by means of a set of *state variables*. In our case, the set V will be composed of $|\Omega|$ three-valued state variables. We will denote with $V(\phi)$ the value of the variable associated to ϕ. $V(\phi)$ corresponds to the believed value of ϕ ($\top$ or $\bot$), or indicates that nothing is believed about it (U), representing the T, F

assignments of the transition system for BML. The memory bound condition is enforced by a constraint $\Psi_{\leq n}$ on R, of the form $|\{A : V(A) \neq U\}| \leq n$, directly represented in MBP as a $TRANS\ \Psi_{\leq n}$ construct.

The actions of the domain represent every possible instance of the deduction rules (Read, Split, etc.) over the formulas in Ω. Such instantiation must also explicitly consider, for a given action, every possible choice of the formula(s) to be overwritten by the newly produced formula(s). As such, actions feature one argument in Ω representing the formula to be read, split, or composed, and one or two additional arguments in $\Omega' = \Omega \cup \{A_0\}$, indicating the formula(s) to be overwritten, and the fictitious formula A_0 if no rewriting occurs. This defines the range of the action variable α in the planning domain:

$$\alpha \in \bigcup_{\substack{A \in K \\ B \in \Omega'}} \mathbf{Read}(A,B) \cup \bigcup_{\substack{A \in \Omega \\ B \in \Omega'}} \mathbf{Split}(A,B) \cup \bigcup_{\substack{A \in \Omega \\ B \in \Omega'}} \mathbf{ExC}(A,B) \cup \bigcup_{\substack{A \in \Omega_\neg \\ B \in \Omega'}} \mathbf{makeNot}(A,B) \cup$$

$$\bigcup_{\substack{A \in \Omega_\neg \\ B \in \Omega'}} \mathbf{elimNot}(A,B) \cup \bigcup_{\substack{A \in \Omega_\wedge \\ B \in \Omega'}} \mathbf{makeAnd}(A,B) \cup \bigcup_{\substack{A \in \Omega_\wedge \\ B_1 \neq B_2 \\ B_1, B_2 \in \Omega'}} \mathbf{elimAnd}(A,B_1,B_2)$$

The executability preconditions and the effects of the actions are encoded in MBP as an implicitly conjoined set of constraints over the transition relation, again of the form $TRANS\ \Psi$.

The executability preconditions correspond to the constraints on the current world in the transition rules in Section 3:

$$\alpha = \mathbf{Read}(A,B) \rightarrow A \in K$$
$$\alpha = \mathbf{ExC}(A,B) \rightarrow U \neq V(A) = V(l(A))$$
$$\alpha = \mathbf{makeNot}(A,B) \rightarrow V(l(A)) \neq U$$
$$\alpha = \mathbf{elimNot}(A,B) \rightarrow V(A) \neq U$$
$$\alpha = \mathbf{makeAnd}(A,B) \rightarrow V(l(A)) \neq U \wedge V(r(A)) \neq U$$
$$\alpha = \mathbf{elimAnd}(A,B_1,B_2) \rightarrow V(A) \neq U$$

The (possibly nondeterministic) effects of an action are represented by partitioning the effects over the formula(s) read or built by the rule, and those over the formula(s) that are possibly overwritten by the result(s) of its application. The former are written in terms of the values V must attain for the affected formula(s) after the action execution (i.e. at the next step, denoted with X), constrained by the current values of V, according to the definitions in Section 3.

$$\alpha = \mathbf{Read}(A,B) \rightarrow X(V(A) = \top)$$
$$\alpha = \mathbf{Split}(A,B) \rightarrow X(V(A) \in \{\top, \bot\})$$
$$\alpha = \mathbf{ExC}(A,B) \rightarrow X(V(A_G) = \top)$$
$$\alpha = \mathbf{makeNot}(A,B) \rightarrow X(V(A)) = \neg(V(l(A)))$$
$$\alpha = \mathbf{elimNot}(A,B) \rightarrow X(V(l(A))) = \neg(V(A))$$
$$\alpha = \mathbf{makeAnd}(A,B) \rightarrow X(V(A)) = V(l(A)) \wedge V(r(A))$$
$$\alpha = \mathbf{elimAnd}(A,B_1,B_2) \rightarrow V(A) = X(V(l(A)) \wedge V(r(A)))$$

The following constraints ensure that overwritten formulas become undefined:

$$\alpha = \mathbf{Read}(A, B) \wedge B \notin \{A_0, A\} \rightarrow X(V(B) = U)$$
$$\alpha = \mathbf{Split}(A, B) \wedge B \notin \{A_0, A\} \rightarrow X(V(B) = U)$$
$$\alpha = \mathbf{ExC}(A, B) \wedge B \notin \{A_0, A_G\} \rightarrow X(V(B) = U)$$
$$\alpha = \mathbf{makeNot}(A, B) \wedge B \notin \{A_0, A\} \rightarrow X(V(B) = U)$$
$$\alpha = \mathbf{elimNot}(A, B) \wedge B \notin \{A_0, l(A)\} \rightarrow X(V(B) = U)$$
$$\alpha = \mathbf{makeAnd}(A, B) \wedge B \notin \{A_0, A\} \rightarrow X(V(B) = U)$$
$$\alpha = \mathbf{elimAnd}(A, B_1, B_2) \wedge B_1, B_2 \notin \{A_0, l(A), r(A)\} \rightarrow X(V(B_1) = V(B_2) = U)$$

The constraints above must be conjoined with those representing the **Recall** proviso, and the provisos on the inertiality of the values of non-affected formulas. **Recall** is expressed by adding, for each $A \in \Omega$, two constraints of the form $V(A) = \top \rightarrow X(V(A)) \neq \bot$ and $V(A) = \bot \rightarrow X(V(A)) \neq \top$. Inertiality is expressed by adding constraints stating explicitly that unless a formula is overwritten or produced, it does not change its value, e.g.:

$$\alpha = \mathbf{makeAnd}(A, B) \wedge A' \notin \{A, B\} \rightarrow X(V(A')) = V(A')$$

Given the encoding above, the planning problem is described by an initial state where $\forall A \in \Omega : V(A) = U$, and by a goal state $V(A_G) = \top$.

MBP implements many possible search styles. We chose breadth-first backward search which guarantees that the shortest plan is selected. The computational burden imposed by such a search style is effectively constrained by the use of symbolic representation techniques that allow a very compact encoding, and an efficient handling of extremely large state sets at once; details can be found in [6].

5   Experiments

We present a simple example to illustrate the effect of memory size on the minimum length of a derivation. Consider the set of rules

$A \wedge B \rightarrow H$	$B \wedge I \wedge E \rightarrow L$	$F \wedge G \rightarrow M$
$A \wedge B \rightarrow C$	$D \wedge A \wedge H \rightarrow I$	$I \wedge L \wedge M \rightarrow N$

which may form part of a larger knowledge base. Suppose a designer of a system which uses a knowledge base containing these rules wishes to verify, e.g., that from the following basic facts $\{B, D, E, F, G\}$ an agent running on a PDA with a memory of size n can infer $N \wedge C$. In addition, the designer may be interested in how increases in memory size affect the number steps required for the derivation, e.g., if they wish to trade memory for response time.

Figure 1 shows the length of the shortest deduction of the formula $N \wedge C$ for different memory sizes as determined by the MBP planner. Deriving the target formula requires a memory of at least size 3. For memory size of 1 and 2 the system quickly determines that there are no possible derivations of the target formula. Let us focus on the lower

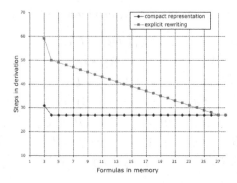

Fig. 1. Running the example

curve. With 3 memory cells the deduction requires 31 steps. With a memory of size 4, the number of steps in the deduction drops to 27. This is because the fourth cell is used to store an intermediate result which is used more than once in the derivation and does not need to be recomputed, thus shortening the inference process. In this example further increases in the amount of memory do not result in further reductions in the length of derivation. These results do not consider explicitly the action of overwriting a memory location, that is, steps in the derivation consist either of the application of an inference rule or reading a formula from K. In computing the length of a deduction we may also want to explicitly consider the action of over-writing a memory location (we can think of this step as choosing which location in memory to over-write). The upper curve in Figure 1 shows the length of the derivations including these extra steps. With a memory of size 3, the number of steps in the derivation is 59 (31 steps + 28 over-write operations). With a memory of size 4 this drops to 50 steps (27 steps + 23 over-write operations). As can be seen, the number of times a cell in over-written continues to drop with increasing memory size, until with a memory of size 27, when we can store all the subformulas used in the derivation in memory, the length of the derivation is the same as in the previous case.

6   Related Work

Our work is related to other work on logics of knowledge and belief, for example [10]. Much of this work assumes that the agent's knowledge is deductively closed, and therefore does not try to model the time and space restrictions on an agent's ability to derive the consequences of its beliefs. There is a growing body of work in which the agent's deduction steps are explicitly modelled in the logic, for example [9,7,2,1]. These approaches make it possible to model the time it takes the agent to arrive at a certain conclusion, but not the space required. A different kind of limitation on the depth of belief reasoning allowed is studied in [12]. Limitations on memory are considered in fewer approaches; for example, in work on the logic of games [19], where an agent with limited memory can base its strategy only on a limited portion of the game's history, and in some of the work on step logic [8], which considers both the time and space limitations on the agent's knowledge. Step logic makes use of the notion of a *step* in reasoning. Given a set of formulas X and a set of inference rules I, an agent performs a step of reasoning by adding the consequents of any applicable inference rule in I to X. If a formula ϕ had been derived in this way at step t, it is said to be a t-theorem. [8] address the issue of the increasing number of t-theorems at each step, which require a larger and larger memory size. However, rather than attempting to verify the space required to solve a given problem, [8] are concerned with restricting the size of short term memory to isolate any possible contradictions, thereby avoiding the problem of *swamping*: deriving all possible consequences from a contradiction. The emphasis on perfect rationality in AI was challenged by Russell in [17] in favour of bounded optimality, (optimality relative to the time and space bounds on the device the agent program is running on).

The problem of formal verification of multi agent systems has lead to a growing body of work, especially in the area of multi agent model checking [3,15]. The existing work, however, is mainly focused on logically omniscient agents, that is, agents who instantaneously believe all the logical consequences of their basic beliefs, and no time and space limitations are taken into account.

The connection between deduction and planning has long been established for a variety of logics, e.g. temporal, linear and propositional logics, see [14,5,16,11]. The existing work, however, focused on using effective theorem provers to build plans, rather than exploiting a planner to build a deduction. To the best of our knowledge, ours is the first experiment in this direction.

7   Conclusions and Future Work

In this paper, we have attempted to take seriously the idea that reasoning is a process which requires memory, and developed a framework for representing and verifying memory-bounded reasoners. While the temporal aspect of reasoning has been studied before, we believe that our treatment of the memory aspect is novel. We have proposed a new kind of epistemic logic where memory is explicitly modelled. The logic is interpreted on state transition systems, where the reasoner's state can contain only a fixed finite number of formulas (beliefs), and transitions correspond to application of inference rules by the agent. By specifying the state transition system as an input to the MBP planner, we can automatically verify the lower bounds on memory required by the agent to derive a certain formula.

In future work, we plan to remove some idealisations made in the present work, such as constant size of formulas, and paying no penalty in terms of memory for backtracking.

Acknowledgements. This work was supported by the Royal Society UK-Italy Joint Project grant 'Model-checking resource-bounded agents'.

References

1. Ågotnes, T., Walicki, M.: Complete axiomatizations of finite syntactic epistemic states. In: Baldoni, M., Endriss, U., Omicini, A., Torroni, P. (eds.) DALT 2005. LNCS (LNAI), vol. 3904, pp. 33–50. Springer, Heidelberg (2006)
2. Alechina, N., Logan, B., Whitsey, M.: A complete and decidable logic for resource-bounded agents. In: Proceedings of the Third International Joint Conference on Autonomous Agents and Multi-Agent Systems (AAMAS 2004), pp. 606–613. ACM Press, New York (July 2004)
3. Benerecetti, M., Giunchiglia, F., Serafini, L.: Model Checking Multiagent Systems. Journal of Logic and Computation, Special Issue on Computational & Logical Aspects of Multi-Agent Systems 8(3), 401–423 (1998)
4. Berger, M., Bauer, B., Watzke, M.: A scalable agent infrastructure. In: Proceedings of the Second Workshop on Infrastructure for Agents, MAS and Scalable MAS (held in conjuction with Autonomous Agents'01), Montreal (2001)
5. Bibel, W.: A deductive solution for plan generation. New Generation Computing 4, 115–132 (1986)
6. Cimatti, A., Pistore, M., Roveri, M., Traverso, P.: Weak, Strong, and Strong Cyclic Planning via Symbolic Model Checking. Artificial Intelligence 147(1,2), 35–84 (2003)
7. Duc, H.N.: Reasoning about rational, but not logically omniscient, agents. Journal of Logic and Computation 7(5), 633–648 (1997)
8. Elgot-Drapkin, J., Miller, M., Perlis, D.: Memory, reason and time: the Step-Logic approach. In: Philosophy and AI: Essays at the Interface, pp. 79–103. MIT Press, Cambridge, Massachusetts (1991)
9. Elgot-Drapkin, J.J., Perlis, D.: Reasoning situated in time I: Basic concepts. Journal of Experimental and Theoretical Artificial Intelligence 2, 75–98 (1990)
10. Fagin, R., Halpern, J.Y., Moses, Y., Vardi, M.Y.: Reasoning about Knowledge. MIT Press, Cambridge, Massachusetts (1995)
11. Fikes, R.E., Nilsson, N.J.: STRIPS: A new approach to the application of theorem proving to problem solving. Artificial Intelligence 2, 187–208 (1971)
12. Fisher, M., Ghidini, C.: Programming Resource-Bounded Deliberative Agents. In: Proceedings of the Sixteenth International Joint Conference on Artificial Intelligence (IJCAI'99), pp. 200–206. Morgan Kaufmann, San Francisco (1999)
13. Horrocks, I., Patel-Schneider, P.F.: A proposal for an OWL rules language. In: Proceedings of the 13th international conference on World Wide Web, WWW 2004, pp. 723–731. ACM, New York (2004)
14. Jacopin, E.: Classical AI planning as theorem proving: The case of a fragment of linear logic. In: AAAI Fall Symposium on Automated Deduction in Nonstandard Logics, pp. 62–66. AAAI Press, Palo Alto, California (1993)
15. Kacprzak, M., Lomuscio, A., Penczek, W.: Verification of multiagent systems via unbounded model checking. In: Kudenko, D., Kazakov, D., Alonso, E. (eds.) Adaptive Agents and Multi-Agent Systems II(AAMAS). LNCS (LNAI), vol. 3394, Springer, Heidelberg (2005)
16. Kautz, H., Selman, B.: Pushing the envelope: Planning, propositional logic, and stochastic search. In: Proceedings of the Thirteenth National Conference on Artificial Intelligence, pp. 1194–1201. AAAI Press, Stanford, California, USA (1996)
17. Russell, S.J.: Rationality and intelligence. Artificial Intelligence 94(1-2), 57–77 (1997)
18. Tarkoma, S., Laukkanen, M.: Supporting software agents on small devices. In: Proceedings of the First International Joint Conference on Autonomous Agents and Multiagent Systems (AAMAS'02), pp. 565–566. ACM Press, New York, NY, USA (2002)
19. van Benthem, J., Liu, F.: Diversity of agents in games. Philosophia Scientiae, vol. 8(2) (2004)

Automated Creation of Pattern Database Search Heuristics

Stefan Edelkamp

Computer Science Department
University of Dortmund
stefan.edelkamp@cs.uni-dortmund.de

Abstract. Pattern databases are dictionaries for heuristic estimates storing state-to-goal distances in state space abstractions. Their effectiveness is sensitive to the selection of the underlying patterns. Especially for multiple and additive pattern databases, the manual selection of patterns that leads to good exploration results is involved.

For automating the selection process, greedy bin-packing has been suggested. This paper proposes genetic algorithms to optimize its output. Patterns are encoded as binary strings and optimized using an objective function that predicts the heuristic search tree size based on the distribution of heuristic values in abstract space.

To reduce the memory requirements we construct the pattern databases symbolically. Experiments in heuristic search planning indicate that the total search efforts can be reduced significantly.

1 Introduction

The ultimate goal for an efficient exploration is the automated creation of (admissible) search heuristics. By applying state space abstractions, heuristic estimates correspond to solutions in simplified problem spaces. The underlying problem graph is *abstracted*, e.g., in a form that nodes are contracted or new edges are inserted. Such abstractions are *homomorphisms*, i.e., for each path in the concrete state space there is a corresponding path in the abstract one. This notion of abstraction matches the one used in verification for abstraction refinement [4] and predicate abstraction [1,45].

Gaschnig [17] proposed that the cost of solutions can be computed by exact solution in abstract space. He observed that search with abstract information can be more time-consuming than with breadth-first search. Voltorta [49] has proven this conjecture, showing that heuristic search algorithms that explore state space abstractions for each encountered state from scratch (and that do not memorize abstract states) cannot possibly be better than blind search [20]. Absolver [40] was the first system to break the barrier imposed by his theorems. In order to reduce the number of revisits in abstract state one either has to memorize abstract state information on-the-fly or precompute it for the entire search space. Pattern databases [5] correspond to complete scans of the (inverted) abstract space *before* applying the search algorithm in the concrete space. A

S. Edelkamp and A. Lomuscio (Eds.): MoChart IV, LNAI 4428, pp. 35–50, 2007.
© Springer-Verlag Berlin Heidelberg 2007

mixed strategy (between memorizing and precomputing) is considered in [30] and revisited in [27].

The success story of searching with pattern databases is long, starting with first optimal solutions in Rubik's Cube [35] and large savings in sliding-tile puzzles [5,36]. Applied for the multiple sequence alignment problem, pattern databases correspond to lookup tables for alignments of a smaller number of sequences [38,52]. In finding the best parse of a sentence [33], a pattern database entry correlates to the cost of completing a partial parse; the abstraction is derived by simplifying the grammar. TSP with asymmetric costs and precedence constraints has been analyzed by [24] using pattern database techniques. Pattern database heuristics have been applied for co-operative planning in computer games [47], where many agents search for individual paths but are allowed to help each other to succeed. First successful applications of pattern databases for verification are due to [11] (explicit-state model checking), [44] (symbolic model checking), and [39] (real-time model checking). In all approaches, even though the construction is automated, patterns were provided manually, such that, in essence, pattern selection remains a domain-dependent feature.

As they operate at the limit of main memory, a compact and space-efficient representation of pattern databases is essential. This paper exploits a space-efficient representation of pattern databases based on BDDs [3], which – by sharing binary state vectors – can lead to large memory savings. Instead of transforming an already constructed database, we apply a construction process that is throughout symbolic. Nonetheless, the main objective of this paper is to address the problem of automated pattern selection for an improved search. We embed our approach in domain-independent action planning, where automated pattern selection is mandatory. In this research area, the use of multiple [29] (often disjoint [36]) databases is frequent. So far, only greedy bin packing algorithms have been applied that terminates with the first established pattern set [7,21].

The number of possible patterns for selection is large. In case of state space abstractions that include don't cares in the state vector, the complexity is exponential in the number of remaining vector entries. In case of general relaxations of the state vector (e.g. by data abstraction, mapping variable domains to smaller sets) the number of possible choices almost becomes intractable. So even for the choice of a single pattern, we are facing a hard combinatorial optimization problem. If multiple abstractions are used, the number of choices is even worse.

In order to predict their pruning[1] effect, pattern databases have to be constructed. Unfortunately, the efforts for constructing pattern databases are high, as their sizes (measured in the number of abstract states) are large.

Especially in combinatorial problems with large state spaces and unknown structures, optimization algorithms adapted from nature – such as evolutionary

---

[1] Pattern database heuristics do not *prune* the exploration in the strong sense in that they eliminate transitions from the state space. If no error/goal is present, then there is no search reduction. On the other hand, if there is, then the enforced order of expansion can save many states to be looked at.

strategies or swarm optimization techniques [6] – are recommended. Given the discrete structure of the pattern selection problem, we have chosen genetic algorithms [26], which are widely used and adapt nicely: the proposed encoding of patterns into chromosomes is accessible for a human, and we can expect to obtain insights to important *schemas* for pattern selection. There are already some reports on attempts to unify planning and evolutionary computing [2,18,51,41,48], but all are concerned about plan finding (or plan refinement) and none of them addresses the problem of the automated creation of search heuristics.

The paper is structured as follows. First we review pattern databases as applied in optimal heuristic search planning. Then we turn to genetic algorithms for the automated inference of the patterns. Starting with the encoding of patterns into chromosomes, we present the design of genetic operators for the pattern selection problem. Experiments report on improving the mean heuristic value and on reducing the resulting search efforts for a selection of challenging planning domains. Finally, we draw conclusions and indicate further research avenues.

2   Pattern Databases in Planning

Action planning refers to a world description in logic[2]. A number of atomic propositions, *atoms* for short, describe what can be true or false in each state of the world. By applying operations in a world, we arrive at another world where different atoms might be true or false. Usually, only few atoms are affected by an operator, and most of them remain the same.

Let AP be the set of atoms. A planning problem (in STRIPS notation) [16] is a finite state space problem $\mathcal{P} = < \mathcal{S}, \mathcal{O}, \mathcal{I}, \mathcal{G} >$, where $\mathcal{S} \subseteq 2^{AP}$ is the set of states, $\mathcal{I} \in \mathcal{S}$ is the initial state, $\mathcal{G} \subseteq \mathcal{S}$ is the set of goal states, and $\mathcal{O}$ is the set of operators that transform states into their successors. We often have that $\mathcal{G}$ is described by a simple list of atoms. Operators $O \in \mathcal{O}$ have preconditions $pre(O)$, and effects $(add(O), del(O))$, where $pre(O) \subseteq AP$ is the *precondition list* of O, $add(O) \subseteq AP$ is its *add list* and $del(O) \subseteq AP$ is its *delete list*. Given a state S with $pre(O) \subseteq S$, its successor $S' = O(S)$ is defined as $S' = (S \setminus del(O)) \cup add(O)$.

2.1   Admissible Heuristics in Planning

Admissible heuristics for planning underestimate the shortest path distance of the current state to the goal. They are important to guarantee optimality in heuristic search algorithms like A* and IDA*. The *max-atom* heuristic [22] is an approximation of the optimal cost for solving a relaxed problem in which the delete lists are ignored. Its extension *max-pair* improves the information without loosing admissibility, approximating the cost of atom pairs. The heuristic h^+ [25] is another extension to *max-atom* defined as the length of the shortest plan that

---

[2] For the sake of brevity, the presentation of the paper restricts to propositional planning. However, the design of planning pattern databases is applicable to complex planning formalisms too.

solves the relaxed problem with ignored delete lists. The heuristic is admissible, but solving relaxed plans is computationally hard.[3]

2.2 Explicit-State Planning Pattern Databases

Explicit-state planning pattern databases as proposed by [7,21] refer to state space abstraction, where some atoms are omitted from the problem description.

The basic idea for computing a heuristic with pattern databases is to analyze the abstraction of the concrete state space prior to the search [5]. In this abstract state space, a (complete) backward exploration (starting with the abstract goal) computes accurate goal distances and stores them in a lookup table[4]. This then information guides the concrete search process. More formally, the *abstraction* [34] of a planning problem $\mathcal{P} = <\mathcal{S}, \mathcal{O}, \mathcal{I}, \mathcal{G}>$ wrt. a set of atoms R is defined as $\mathcal{P}|_R = <\mathcal{S}|_R, \mathcal{O}|_R, \mathcal{I}|_R, \mathcal{G}|_R>$ with $\mathcal{S}|_R = \{S \cap R \mid S \in \mathcal{S}\}$, $\mathcal{G}|_R = \{G \cap R \mid G \in \mathcal{G}\}$, and $\mathcal{O}|_R = \{O|_R \mid O \in \mathcal{O}\}$, where $O|_R$ for $O \in \mathcal{O}$ is given as $(pre(O) \cap R, add(O) \cap R, del(O) \cap R)$. As the goal distance in abstract state space drop by not more than 1, pattern databases are consistent, leading to monotone cost functions in A* [42]. The principle of abstracting atoms has been extended to (automatically inferred and mutually exclusive) *atom groups* [7]. The approach reflects a multi-variate (finite domain) variable encoding of a state [23]. As an example, in Blocksworld the variable $on(X, a)$ (where X represents any available block a, b, c, or d), encodes the atoms $on(d, a)$, $on(c, a)$, $on(b, a)$ and $on(a, a)$. As only one block can lay on top of a, all atoms in a state variable (group) are mutually exclusive. Variables are distributed into *patterns*, where each pattern corresponds to an abstraction of the state space: abstract states are assignments of atoms to state variables of the chosen pattern. Using this approach each concrete state is mapped to an abstract state. As seen above the projection extends to operators, intersecting the precondition, add and delete list with the pattern. The selection of patterns that lead to the best search reduction is computationally hard and critically influences the quality of the estimate [21].

For multiple pattern databases [29], in each abstraction i, $i \in \{1, \ldots, k\}$, and for each state S we compute estimated costs $h_i(S)$. The maximum $h_m(S) = \max_{i=1}^k h_i(S)$ is a consistent estimate, the cumulation $h_a(S) = \sum_{i=1}^k h_i(S)$, however, is not necessarily admissible, since in general we cannot expect that each operator contributes to only one pattern database abstraction. In case an admissible heuristic is obtained by adding the values, we call the databases *disjoint* [36]. In order to resolve the admissibility problem in general, we have to grant that each operator has zero costs for all but one pattern databases. This induces that the backward in abstract space operates on a weighted problem graph. For this particular single-source shortest-paths problem, we adapt BFS. In each BFS level, each zero-cost operator is fired until a fixpoint is reached.

---

[3] The heuristic h^+ can, however, efficiently be approximated by the number of operators in a parallel plan that solves the relaxed problem. The applied approximation sacrifices the admissibility of the estimate making it inadequate for optimal planning.

[4] As inverse operator application is not always immediate, it is possible to apply backward search to the inverse of the state space graph generated in forward search [11].

2.3   Symbolic Planning Pattern Databases

The main limitation for applying pattern databases in practice is the restricted amount of (main) memory. Many strategies for leveraging the problem have been proposed. *Symmetries* allow reusing pattern databases [5], while lookups in *dual* pattern databases additionally apply to permutation problems [15]. Compressed pattern databases [14] approximate abstract states-to-goal distances. Given an upper bound on the optimal goal distance in the concrete state space, pattern database construction can be pruned [52]. *On-demand* pattern databases [13] suspend and resume a backward A* exploration of the abstract space.

A space-saving alternative for pattern databases that allow sharing of the state vector is the *trie* data structure. In a trie, each path from the root to a leaf corresponds to a scan of the state vector. Tries are commonly used in pattern databases for the multiple sequence alignment problem [46]. States with same prefixes share their representations. Tries can be *multi-variate* (each branch corresponds to a state vector entry of finite domain) or *binary* (each path corresponds to the binary representation of the state vector). Tries can be contracted by merging edges.

The main advantage of using BDDs [3] is an efficient and unique representation for sets of states. Intuitively, BDDs are binary tries in which further reduction rules have been applied to obtain a directed and acyclic graph structure. More precisely, a BDD represents the *characteristic function* of a set of states, which evaluates to 1 if and only if the binary state vector is a member of that set. The characteristic function is identified with the set itself.

Transitions are also formalized as relations, i.e., as sets of tuples of predecessor and successor states, or, more precisely, as the characteristic function of such sets. This allows to compute the image in form of a relational product. It conjoins the state set (formula) with the transition relation (formula) and quantifies the predecessor variable. This way, all states are determined, that can be reached by applying one action to a state in the input set. Iterating the process starting with the characteristic function of the initial state yields a symbolic implementation of BFS. The application of A* with BDDs has been initially proposed by [12], extensions are found in [31] (branching partitioning), [43] (weak heuristics), and [19] (ADDs). All implementations rely on small edge weights.

Symbolic pattern databases [8] are pattern databases that have been constructed symbolically for a latter lookup in either symbolic or explicit-state heuristic search. The bi-directional definition of the transition relation allows to change the search direction by quantifying the posterior variables set in the relational product. Each state set (in a breadth-first/shortest paths layer) is efficiently represented by a corresponding characteristic function. Different to the compression of the state set by *compiling* the outcome of an explicit-state pattern database, the symbolic construction operates on the compressed representation of the state and the action sets. External symbolic planning pattern databases [53] are symbolic planning databases that additionally exploit secondary storage devices such as hard disks to lessen the RAM load during construction and search.

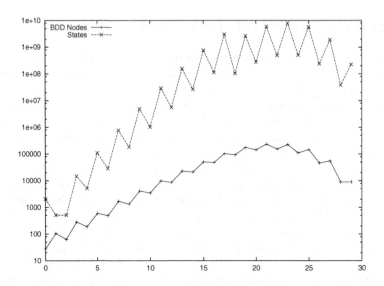

Fig. 1. Effect of symbolic pattern database construction

A better memory performance often favors symbolic to explicit-state pattern database construction: Fig. 1 displays an example of a typical Blocksworld problem instance. The number of BDD nodes is by far smaller than the number of represented states. Moreover, BDD nodes are small,[5] while the explicit-state sizes grow with size the problem instance. The mean heuristic value (for both cases) is 22.16. Besides memory savings the key performance of symbolic pattern databases for the purpose of this paper are time savings. For example, the above pattern database contains 27.22 billion entries generated in 109 seconds. Compared to explicit-state search, this corresponds to about 250 million expanded states per second.

3   Automated Pattern Selection

We have indicated that finding good patterns is involved, as there are many possible choices, especially if multiple pattern databases have to be considered. Manual pattern selection is tedious and implies that the planning process inevitably becomes problem-dependent. So far, automated pattern selection is a rather unresolved challenge, even if some recent progress has been made.

For explicit-state construction of multiple pattern databases, one has simplified the problem of finding a suitable partition to the *bin-packing* problem [7,21]. The general idea is to distribute state variables into bins in such a way that a minimal number of patterns is used; a state variable is added to an already existing bin, until the (expected) abstract state space size exceeds main memory.

---

[5] BDD nodes frequently consume a small number of bytes for encoding the level, the 0- and 1-successor and some auxiliary information like a hash value and markings.

Procedure GA
   $t \leftarrow 0$
   $P^{(t)} \leftarrow Initialize$
   $Evaluate(P^{(t)})$
   while $(\kappa(P^{(t)}))$
          $P'^{(t)} \leftarrow Recombination(P^{(t)})$
          $P''^{(t)} \leftarrow Mutation(P'^{(t)})$
          $Evaluate(P''^{(t)})$
          $P^{(t+1)} \leftarrow Selection(P''^{(t)})$
          $t \leftarrow t + 1$

Fig. 2. Standard genetic algorithm

Adding a variable to the pattern corresponds to a multiplication of its domain size to the (already computed) abstract state size (if possible). As a result, the bin-packing variant needed for automated pattern selection is based on multiplying variable domain sizes (rather than adding). Bin-packing is NP-complete, but efficient approximations like the first- or best-fit have been used.

For the implementation of automated pattern selection we adapt a genetic algorithm (GA) [26]. A generic implementation using the evolutionary operations for evaluation, recombination, mutation, and selection is shown in Fig. 2, where κ is the termination criterion, and t is the current iteration.

Representation. Patterns are represented as binary chromosomes of size $p \times n$, where n is the number of atoms (groups) and $p \leq n$ is the number of active patterns. In the columns, state variables are indexed, while in the rows patterns are selected. Therefore, a chromosome represents the distribution of state variables into multiple pattern databases. Fig. 3 illustrates an example: in the first pattern the groups 1, 5, 6, 8 and n are included, whereas in the second pattern the groups 3, 5 and 7 are present.

Chromosomes are *valid*[6] if all patterns respect the memory threshold M (the bin size). Formally speaking, if v_i denotes the set of atoms in state variable i, $i \in \{1, \ldots, n\}$, and $c_{i,j}$ is a bit indicating whether or not variable v_i is selected in pattern p_j, $j \in \{1, \ldots, p\}$, then for all j we have $\prod_{1 \leq i \leq n} c_{i,j} \cdot |v_i| \leq M$. (We assume that at least one variable is selected in each pattern, i.e., for all j we have $\sum_{i=1}^{n} c_{i,j} > 0$). For generating disjoint pattern databases, we additionally impose the condition that in each column there is exactly one 1, i.e., for all i we have $\sum_{j=1}^{p} c_{i,j} = 1$. Since the columns > 3 have more than one bit set, the chromosome in Fig. 3 is not disjoint.[7]

---

[6] Invalid chromosomes are assigned to a bad fitness value and discarded by Darwin's evolutionary rule for the *survival of the fittest*.

[7] As planning operators can modify more than one state variable at a time, in difference to the set of well-studied $(n^2 - 1)$-puzzle pattern databases [36] this condition is only a necessary but not a sufficient condition for disjointness. As checking disjointness based on the pattern selection may be involved, for each operator we assign cost 1 to only one abstraction.

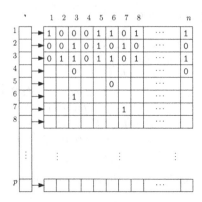

Fig. 3. Bitvector representation of a chromosome

Initialization. For the initialization phase we could generate random chromosomes, but we found that the amount of work to find an acceptable partitioning by performing a randomized assignment of the chromosomes is by far larger as with prior bin packing with no significant advantage within the overall search process. Therefore, we initialize the chromosomes with bin packing. To avoid all chromosomes of the initial population to be identical, we choose a random permutation to the atom groups prior to their automated partitioning into patterns. This leads to comparably good but different distributions of groups into patterns and a feasible initial population for the genetic algorithm.

Recombination. The motivation of *recombination* of two parent chromosomes is the hope, that the good properties of the one parent combines well with the good properties of the other. One of the simplest techniques that we looked at is *crossover*: the parent chromosomes exchange parts of their patterns. If the two parents have a different number of patterns, so do the two children.

Mutation. For *mutation* chromosome bits are flipped with a small probability. This corresponds to extending or reducing the corresponding abstract space. For our case, we had to allow the addition or deletion of entire patterns. In the bin packing analogy of multiple pattern partition, adding a pattern corresponds to opening a bin, and deleting a pattern corresponds to closing a bin.

Selection. During *selection* an enlarged population (as produced by either recombination or mutation) is truncated to its original size based on the fitness value(s). The normalized fitness evaluation for the population is interpreted as a distribution function, which governs the selection process for the next population. Chromosomes with a better fitness are chosen with higher probability.

Objective Functions. The objective function plays a central role in a genetic algorithm. It defines a fitness to determine the evolutionary strength of chromosomes. The construction of a meaningful objective function is often difficult, like in our case, where the conditions for *good* patterns are hardly accessible.

A fundamental question concerns the relationship between the contents of a pattern database, and the number of nodes expanded when the heuristic is used to guide the search. Korf [35] gives first insights in such performance predictions of pattern databases: he characterizes the effectiveness of a heuristic h by its expected value $\overline{h}$ (the mean) over the problem space. The main line of reasoning is the following: if the heuristic value of every state was equal to its expected value $\overline{h}$, then a search to depth d would be equivalent to searching to depth $d - \overline{h}$ without a heuristic, since the priority for every state would be its depth plus $\overline{h}$. This means that in most search spaces, a linear gain in $\overline{h}$ corresponds to an exponential gain in the search.

For the pattern selection problem we conclude that the higher the average heuristic value, the better the corresponding pattern database. As a consequence, we compute the mean heuristic value for each database. For one pattern database PDB we compute

$$\overline{h} = \sum_{h=0}^{\max} \frac{h \cdot |\{u \in PDB \mid h^*(u) = h\}|}{|PDB|},$$

where $h^*(u)$ is the accurate abstract goal distance stored for the abstract state u, and where the size of a pattern database (layer) is determined by counting the number of accepting paths in the BDD.[8] For multiple pattern databases, we have k distributions. As an example, the distributions of the heuristic estimates for three pattern databases are shown in Fig. 4 in the form of histograms. For computing the evolutionary strength for an entire chromosome we compute the mean heuristic value for each of the databases individually and cumulate (or maximize) the outcome. More formally, if PDB_i is the i-th pattern database, $i \in \{1, \ldots, k\}$, then the additive *fitness* of a chromosome is computed as

$$fitness(c) = \sum_{i=1}^{k} \sum_{h_i=0}^{\max_i} \frac{h_i \cdot |\{u \in PDB_i \mid h_i^*(u) = h_i\}|}{|PDB_i|}.$$

Using the mean heuristic estimate is not the only choice. We have also experimented with a derivate not based on the number of states that share the same heuristic value, but on the number of BDD nodes to represent them. Unfortunately, the results were consistently weaker.

A Note on Search Tree Prediction. Applying the mean heuristic value for the fitness extends to the formula for search tree prediction [37]. It approximates $E(N, c, P)$, the expected number of nodes expanded by IDA* up to depth c, given a problem-space tree with N_i nodes of cost i, and a heuristic characterized by the equilibrium distribution P. The formula denotes that in the limit of large c, we expect $E(N, c, P) = \sum_{i=0}^{c} N_i P(c - i)$ nodes to be generated. It has already been used for the analysis of pattern database performance [28] and to explain anomalies that many small pattern databases are often more effective than few

---

[8] There are linear time algorithms for performing model counting [3].

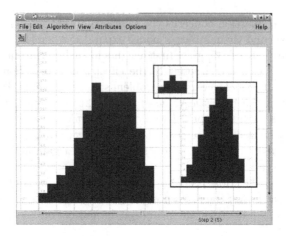

Fig. 4. Histograms of heuristic values

big ones of same total size [29]. However, the growth of search trees for general problems as addressed in action planning is not immediate [32]. Hence, we prefer $\bar{h}$ for the fitness evaluation.

4   Experiments

For implementing genetic algorithms we adapt the library GAlib[9] [50] to our hybrid (explicit-state and symbolic) planner MIPS [9]. One advantage is that it is portable to different operating systems. Another gain is that there is already a 2D chromosome data structure that satisfies our requirement. It was sufficient to provide an objective function. A fitness function could be derived automatically, using the fitness scaling approach. As a consequence, only the genetic operations for recombination mutation and selection are to be configured. These configurations have been implemented without modifying the existing source code for the standard genetic algorithm.

After some initial testing[10] we turned off recombination completely. This actually simplifies the genetic algorithm to a randomized local search strategy. As indicated above, the mutation operator adds and deletes groups to an existing pattern and allows to extend patterns in a disjoint partition. For the automated construction of both explicit-state or symbolic pattern databases, the maximum size of the abstract state spaces is taken as an additional parameter – actually the only information that has to be provided manually.

4.1   Explicit-State Pattern Databases

In a first test suite, we studied explicit-state pattern databases constructed with greedy bin packing and optimized genetic algorithms (with different parameters).

---

[9] http://lancet.mit.edu/galib-2.4/

[10] We conducted all experiments on a 3 GHz Linux PC. Time in CPU seconds was limited to 1,800; space was limited to 1 GB.

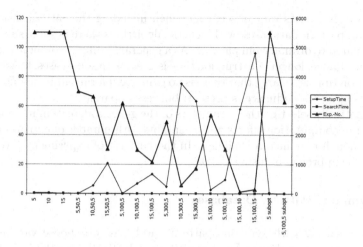

Fig. 5. Explicit pattern databases in Logistics

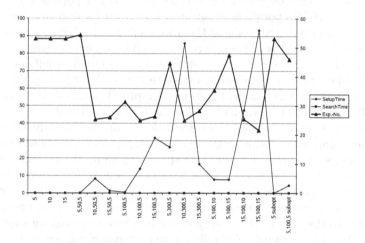

Fig. 6. Explicit pattern databases in DriverLog

The aim was to learn about the parameter setting of genetic algorithms in planning domains, as they are known to be sensitive to parameter selection.

We use several runs applying the mean of the heuristic value as a comparison guideline. As the iterated tests were involved, we depict the change in the exploration efficiencies for some interesting domains only. The horizontal axes denote the choice of parameters as follows.

Label	Meaning
5	Bin Packing with a memory threshold of 2^5 abstract states
5,50,5	GA with a memory threshold of 2^5 abstract states, 50 epocs, 5 genes

In Fig. 5 the setup time, the search time (in seconds, left label) and the number of expansions (right label) for different genetic parameters settings in the *Logistics* domain are shown. As we can see, even when including the entire construction time for all pattern databases, with genetic algoirthms there is some substantial gain compared to ordinary bin packing. As a general finding we observe that for a better guidedance, longer construction time is needed. In some cases, however, the construction time is so large that there is no gain in exploration. In the *DriverLog* domain (Fig. 6) the influence is present, but less apparent.

Automatically selecting the parameters of the genetic algorithm in such a way that the pre-computation efforts are acceptable with number of expansions that is small enough remained a challenge. In the next set of experiments, we try to scale-up the approach by using BDDs.

4.2 Symbolic Pattern Databases

For experimenting with symbolic pattern databases, we choose various problems from international planning competition (IPC-2, IPC-3, IPC-5).[11] For the construction of symbolic pattern databases we choose a population size of 5, and a number of 20 epocs (resulting in at most 100 pattern databases to be constructed and evaluated; some of them were eliminated due to size and state variable constraints). The random seed was fixed for all experiments.

The initial population the genetic algorithm is computed as follows. We first randomize the order of variables in the state vector. Next, we apply the bin-packing strategy.[12] The search algorithm we applied is symbolic A* search with full duplicate elimination. We have added the heuristic estimates.

In Table 1 symbolic exploration results for comparing greedy bin-packing with genetic pattern selection in the benchmark problems are shown. Headings read as follows: 2^l is the abstract state space size limit; the searching time t_s is compared to the total running time [13] In other words, the setup time $t - t_s$ for the genetic construction covers the time for computing *all* pattern databases during the optimization process. The additional time for pattern optimization contributes to the gain in the quality of the heuristic estimate, measured in $\overline{h}$, the mean heuristic estimate of the first (greedy bin-packing) or best surviving (genetic algorithm) pattern.

As the Logistics and DriverLog domains were less complex in the explicit than in the symbolic case, we have recognize that the application of symbolic pattern databases pays off (cf. Fig. 1). We also observe that pattern optimization generally leads to much better mean heuristic values and to smaller search times. When scaling the problems the savings in search dominate the additional workload during construction and take over to the total search time.

---

[11] For domains from IPC-4 good exploration results of symbolic pattern databases are already known [10].

[12] As there is no unshuffled bin packing result, invoking search without optimization can produce better results than with optimization.

[13] Total time includes the parsing efforts of the planning problem and pattern database construction. Time for grounding the domain is not counted as we apply an individual but same program to both strategies.

Table 1. Symbolic A* search with and without genetic optimized pattern databases

problem	2^l	Greedy Bin Packing					GA-Optimization				
		length	images	$\bar{h}$	t_s	t	length	images	$\bar{h}$	t_s	t
logistics-4-1	10	19	63	9.28	0.39	0.77	19	63	8.57	0.37	0.79
logistics-6-1	20	14	42	21.9	0.39	0.77	14	39	20.34	0.30	1.01
logistics-8-1	20	44	166	26.32	11.98	19.92	44	44	29.51	5.7	1.42
logistics-10-1	30	-	-	-	-	-	42	351	38.82	33.78	85.69
logistics-12-1	30	-	-	-	-	-	69	826	51.49	138.02	498.76
blocks-9-0	30	30	79	8.86	0.47	52.51	30	358	20.03	8.89	19.4
blocks-10-0	40	-	-	-	-	-	34	692	25.15	8.53	34.94
blocks-11-0	40	-	-	-	-	-	32	1,219	24.20	49.30	58.44
blocks-12-0	40	-	-	-	-	-	34	942	25.36	101.95	104.55
zeno-2	10	6	6	6.37	0.17	0.55	6	14	3.83	0.19	0.57
zeno-4	10	8	19	5.74	0.27	0.73	8	14	3.83	0.19	0.57
zeno-6	20	11	24	6.6	0.64	1.21	11	14	8.58	0.58	1.51
zeno-10	25	-	-	-	-	-	22	23	15.7	43.12	190.56
zeno-11	25	-	-	-	-	-	14	37	15.06	15.11	833.16
driverlog-9	25	22	109	12.9	86.76	87.59	22	107	15.3	52.46	72.25
driverlog-11	25	-	-	-	-	-	19	110	10.67	34.48	44.60
driverlog-13	35	-	-	-	-	-	26	143	13.7	553.01	778.03
openstack-1	20	23	96	3.71	0.51	1.29	23	116	5.06	0.60	3.04
openstack-3	20	23	96	3.71	0.51	1.29	23	110	5.40	0.60	3.02
openstack-6	30	20	65	4.99	70.38	96.17	20	39	5.44	52.42	216.19
openstack-7	30	-	-	-	-	-	20	38	6.88	31.05	484.19
pipesworld-2	20	12	91	6.53	0.77	2.82	12	82	7.01	0.23	4.72
pipesworld-4	20	11	34	4.75	4.37	6.44	11	50	6.63	1.55	4.62
pipesworld-6	20	10	23	5.44	3.31	5.44	10	29	7.33	0.95	4.82
pipesworld-8	20	11	25	6.12	55.08	60.07	11	29	7.57	6.79	12.58
pipesworld-10	53	-	-	-	-	-	19	203	10.97	45.30	97.27

5 Conclusion

We have seen a flexible attempt to optimize pattern database exploration prior
to the overall search process using genetic algorithms[14]. The approach optimizes
the partition of multi-variate variables into disjoint patterns. We showed that
pattern optimization is essential and optimization with genetic algorithms can
increase not only the search time, but also the total run time. While the greedy
bin packing strategy often runs out of memory, improved pattern selection with
genetic algorithm scales better and can find solutions where bin packing fails.

Given the time and space efficiency of symbolic search, we could construct
and evaluate many large pattern databases in a limited amount of time. Driven

---

[14] To the author's knowledge, optimization of patterns has not been considered before.
We are aware some (unpublished) work on the automated generation of pattern
databases by Holte and Hernádvölgyi. Their approach enumerates *all* possible (un-
subsumed) pattern partitions that are not subsumed by already considered ones.

by the theory of search tree prediction, we have chosen the mean heuristic value as a fitness function. For the evaluation of each chromosome we have computed an entire set of pattern databases. Faster construction of larger databases favors a symbolic construction, and the exploration gains obtained in the experiments are promising. The encoding of pattern partition in a 2D gene allows experts to reason on the structure of good patterns and to perform pattern fine-tuning.

Constructing the pattern databases for each fitness evaluation consumes a considerable amount of time, especially if pattern databases become large. Future work will address *learning* of the fitness functions in smaller instances for bootstrapping in a genetic algorithm for larger instances. We also plan to consider alternative optimization methods as the search efficiency varies a lot in different runs. This suggests to apply *randomized local search* with *random restarts* [32].

Acknowledgements. Stefan Edelkamp is supported by DFG in the projects *Heuristic Search* (Ed 74/3) and *Directed Model Checking* (Ed 74/2).

References

1. Ball, T., Majumdar, R., Millstein, T.D., Rajamani, S.K.: Automatic predicate abstraction of c programs. In: SIGPLAN Conference on Programming Language Design and Implementation, pp. 203–213 (2001)
2. Brie, A.H., Morignot, P.: Genetic planning using variable length chromosomes. In: ICAPS, pp. 320–329 (2005)
3. Bryant, R.E.: Symbolic manipulation of boolean functions using a graphical representation. In: ACM/IEEE Design Automation Conference, pp. 688–694 (1985)
4. Clarke, E.M., Grumberg, O., Long, D.: Model checking and abstraction. ACM Transactions on Programming Languages and Systems 16(5), 1512–1542 (1994)
5. Culberson, J.C., Schaeffer, J.: Pattern databases. Computational Intelligence 14(4), 318–334 (1998)
6. Dorigo, M., Stützle, T.: Ant Colony Optimization. MIT Press, Cambridge (2005)
7. Edelkamp, S.: Planning with pattern databases. In: ECP, pp. 13–24 (2001)
8. Edelkamp, S.: Symbolic pattern databases in heuristic search planning. In: AIPS, pp. 274–293 (2002)
9. Edelkamp, S.: Taming numbers and durations in the model checking integrated planning system. Journal of Artificial Intelligence Research 20, 195–238 (2003)
10. Edelkamp, S.: External symbolic heuristic search with pattern databases. In: ICAPS, pp. 51–60 (2005)
11. Edelkamp, S., Lluch-Lafuente, A.: Abstraction in directed model checking. In: ICAPS-Workshop on Connecting Planning Theory with Practice (2004)
12. Edelkamp, S., Reffel, F.: OBDDs in heuristic search. In: KI, pp. 81–92 (1998)
13. Felner, A., Alder, A.: Solving the 24 puzzle with instance dependent pattern databases. In: Zucker, J.-D., Saitta, L. (eds.) SARA 2005. LNCS (LNAI), vol. 3607, pp. 248–260. Springer, Heidelberg (2005)
14. Felner, A., Meshulam, R., Holte, R.C., Korf, R.E.: Compressing pattern databases. In: AAAI, pp. 638–643 (2004)
15. Felner, A., Zahavi, U., Schaeffer, J., Holte, R.: Dual lookups in pattern databases. In: IJCAI, pp. 103–108 (2005)

16. Fikes, R., Nilsson, N.: STRIPS: A new approach to the application of theorem proving to problem solving. Artificial Intelligence 2, 189–208 (1971)
17. Gaschnig, J.: A problem similarity approach to devising heuristics: First results. In: IJCAI, pp. 434–441 (1979)
18. Godefroid, P., Khurshid, S.: Exploring very large state spaces using genetic algorithms. STTT 6(2), 117–127 (2004)
19. Hansen, E.A., Zhou, R., Feng, Z.: Symbolic heuristic search using decision diagrams. In: Koenig, S., Holte, R.C. (eds.) SARA 2002. LNCS (LNAI), vol. 2371, Springer, Heidelberg (2002)
20. Hansson, O., Mayer, A., Valtora, M.: A new result on the complexity of heuristic estimates for the A* algorithm (research note). Artificial Intelligence 55, 129–143 (1992)
21. Haslum, P., Bonet, B., Geffner, H.: New admissible heuristics for domain-independent planning. In: AAAI, pp. 1163–1168 (2005)
22. Haslum, P., Geffner, H.: Admissible heuristics for optimal planning. pp. 140–149 (2000)
23. Helmert, M.: A planning heuristic based on causal graph analysis. In: ICAPS, pp. 161–170 (2004)
24. Hernádvölgyi, I.T.: Automatically Generated Lower Bounds for Search. PhD thesis, University of Ottawa (2003)
25. Hoffmann, J., Nebel, B.: Fast plan generation through heuristic search. Journal of Artificial Intelligence Research 14, 253–302 (2001)
26. Holland, J.: Adaption in Natural and Artificial Systems. PhD thesis, University of Michigan (1975)
27. Holte, R.C., Grajkowski, J., Tanner, B.: Hierarchical heuristic search revisited. In: Zucker, J.-D., Saitta, L. (eds.) SARA 2005. LNCS (LNAI), vol. 3607, pp. 121–133. Springer, Heidelberg (2005)
28. Holte, R.C., Hernádvögyi, I.T.: A space-time tradeoff for memory-based heuristics. In: AAAI (1999)
29. Holte, R.C., Newton, J., Felner, A., Meshulam, R., Furcy, D.: Multiple pattern databases. In: ICAPS, pp. 122–131 (2004)
30. Holte, R.C., Perez, M.B., Zimmer, R.M., Donald, A.J.: Hierarchical A*: Searching abstraction hierarchies. In: AAAI, pp. 530–535 (1996)
31. Jensen, R.M., Bryant, R.E., Veloso, M.M.: SetA*: An efficient BDD-based heuristic search algorithm. In: AAAI, pp. 668–673 (2002)
32. Junghanns, A.: Pushing the Limits: New Developments in Single-Agent Search. PhD thesis, University of Alberta (1999)
33. Klein, D., Manning, C.: A* parsing: Fast exact Viterbi parse selection. In: Human Language Technology Conference of North American Chapter of the Association for Computational Linguistics (2003)
34. Knoblock, C.A.: Automatically generating abstractions for planning. Artificial Intelligence 68(2), 243–302 (1994)
35. Korf, R.E.: Finding optimal solutions to Rubik's Cube using pattern databases. In: AAAI, pp. 700–705 (1997)
36. Korf, R.E., Felner, A.: Chips Challenging Champions: Games, Computers and Artificial Intelligence. In: chapter Disjoint Pattern Database Heuristics, pp. 13–26. Elsevier, Amsterdam (2002)
37. Korf, R.E., Reid, M., Edelkamp, S.: Time Complexity of Iterative-Deepening-A*. Artificial Intelligence 129(1–2), 199–218 (2001)
38. Korf, R.E., Zhang, W., Thayer, I., Hohwald, H.: Frontier search. Journal of the ACM 52(5), 715–748 (2005)

39. Kupferschmid, S., Hoffmann, J., Dierks, H., Behrmann, G.: Adapting an ai planning heuristic for directed model checking. In: Valmari, A. (ed.) Model Checking Software. LNCS, vol. 3925, Springer, Heidelberg (2006)

40. Mostow, J., Prieditis, A.E.: Discovering admissible heuristics by abstracting and optimizing. In: IJCAI, pp. 701 – 707 (1989)

41. Muslea, I.: A general-propose AI planning system based on genetic programming. In: Genetic Programming Conference (Late Breaking Papers), pp. 157–164 (1997)

42. Pearl, J.: Heuristics. Addison-Wesley, London (1985)

43. Qian, K., Nymeyer, A.: Heuristic search algorithms based on symbolic data structures. In: ACAI, pp. 966–979 (2003)

44. Qian, K., Nymeyer, A.: Guided invariant model checking based on abstraction and symbolic pattern databases. In: Jensen, K., Podelski, A. (eds.) TACAS 2004. LNCS, vol. 2988, pp. 497–511. Springer, Heidelberg (2004)

45. Graf, S., Saidi, H.: Construction of abstract state graphs with PVS. In: Grumberg, O. (ed.) CAV 1997. LNCS, vol. 1254, pp. 72–83. Springer, Heidelberg (1997)

46. Schroedl, S.: An improved search algorithm for optimal multiple sequence alignment. Journal of Artificial Intelligence Research 23, 587–623 (2005)

47. Silver, D.: Cooperative pathfinding. In: Conference on Artificial Intelligence and Interactive Digital Entertainment, pp. 117–122 (2005)

48. Spector, L.: Genetic programming and AI planning systems. In: AAAI, pp. 1329–1334 (1994)

49. Valtorta, M.: A result on the computational complexity of heuristic estimates for the A* algorithm. Information Sciences 34, 48–59 (1984)

50. Wall, M.: GAlib – A C++ Library of Genetic Algorithm Components. Massachusetts Institute of Technology (2005)

51. Westerberg, H., Levine, J.: Optimising plans using genetic programming. In: ECP, page Poster (2001)

52. Zhou, R., Hansen, E.: Space-efficient memory-based heuristics. In: AAAI, pp. 677–682 (2004)

53. Zhou, R., Hansen, E.: External-memory pattern databases using structured duplicate detection. In: AAAI (2005)

Using Predicate Abstraction to Generate Heuristic Functions in UPPAAL

Jörg Hoffmann[1,*], Jan-Georg Smaus[2], Andrey Rybalchenko[3,4],
Sebastian Kupferschmid[2], and Andreas Podelski[2]

[1] Digital Enterprise Research Institute (DERI), Innsbruck, Austria
[2] University of Freiburg, Germany
[3] Max Planck Institute for Computer Science, Saarbrücken, Germany
[4] Ecole Polytechnique Fédérale de Lausanne, Switzerland
joerg.hoffmann@deri.org

Abstract. We focus on checking safety properties in networks of extended timed automata, with the well-known UPPAAL system. We show how to use predicate abstraction, in the sense used in model checking, to generate search guidance, in the sense used in Artificial Intelligence (AI). This contributes another family of heuristic functions to the growing body of work on *directed model checking*. The overall methodology follows the *pattern database* approach from AI: the abstract state space is exhaustively built in a pre-process, and used as a lookup table during search. While typically pattern databases use rather primitive abstractions ignoring some of the relevant symbols, we use *predicate abstraction*, dividing the state space into equivalence classes with respect to a list of logical expressions (predicates). We empirically explore the behavior of the resulting family of heuristics, in a meaningful set of benchmarks. In particular, while several challenges remain open, we show that one can easily obtain heuristic functions that are competitive with the state-of-the-art in directed model checking.

1 Introduction

When model checking safety properties, the ultimate goal is to prove the absence of error states. This can be done by exploring the entire reachable state space. UPPAAL is a tool doing this, for networks of extended timed automata.[1] UPPAAL has a highly optimized implementation, but still the reachable state space often is prohibitively large in realistic applications. A potentially much easier task is to try to *falsify* the safety property, by identifying an error path: for this, we can use a *heuristic* that determines in what order the states are explored. If the heuristic is perfect, then only the states on a shortest error path will have to be explored.

More formally, a heuristic, or *heuristic function*, is a function that maps states to integers, estimating the state's distance to the nearest error state. The heuristic is called

---

* Corresponding author.
[1] Such (networks of) automata feature synchronization, integer variables, and real-valued clock variables. We assume the reader is (vaguely) familiar with these concepts; a brief explanation will be given. The ideas and results of the paper should be easily accessible without detailed background knowledge.

S. Edelkamp and A. Lomuscio (Eds.): MoChart IV, LNAI 4428, pp. 51–66, 2007.

admissible if it provides a lower bound on the real error state distance. The search gives a preference to states with lower h value. There are many different ways of doing the latter. The A^* method, where the search queue is a priority queue over start state distance plus the value of h, guarantees to find an optimal (shortest possible) solution (error) path if the heuristic is admissible. Herein, we instead use *greedy best-first search*. There, the search queue is a priority queue over the value of h. This does not give any guarantee on the solution length, but tends to be much faster than A^* in practice.

The application of heuristic search to model checking was pioneered a few years ago by Edelkamp et al [6,7], christening this research direction *directed model checking*, and inspiring various other approaches of this sort, e.g. [5,9,13,15]. The main difference between all the approaches is how they define and compute the heuristic function: *How does one estimate the distance to an error state?*

A brief overview of the heuristic functions defined so far is this. Edelkamp et al [6] base their heuristics on the "graph distance" within each automaton – the number of edge traversals needed, disregarding synchronization and all state variables. This yields a rather simplistic estimation, but can be computed very quickly. Groce and Visser [9] define heuristics inspired from the area of testing, with the idea to prefer covering yet unexplored branches in the program. Qian and Nymeyer [15] ignore some of the state variables to define heuristics which are then used in a pattern database approach (see below). Kupferschmid et al [13] adapt a heuristic method from the area of AI Planning, based on a notion of "monotonicity" where it is assumed that a state variable accumulates, rather than changes, its values. Dräger et al [5] iteratively "merge" a pair of automata, i.e., compute their product and then merge locations until there are at most N locations left, where N is an input parameter. The heuristic function is read off the overall merged automaton.

We add another family of heuristic functions into the above arsenal, based on an abstraction method already established quite broadly in model checking – *predicate abstraction* [8]. A predicate abstraction of a system is defined by a set of logical expressions – the predicates. In general, one could use arbitrary expressions; herein, we consider expressions of the form $lfn(X) \bowtie c$ where $lfn(X)$ is a linear function in variable set X, $\bowtie \in \{<, \leq, =, \geq, >\}$, and c is a constant (a number). The idea is to divide the state space into equivalence classes with respect to the truth values of the predicates: the abstraction of a system state s is a tuple $\bar{b}$ of truth values, stating which of the predicates are true or false in s; we have an abstract transition $\bar{b} \to \bar{b}'$ for every transition $s \to s'$ of the original system. The abstract system thus over-approximates the real system, which enables us to analyze the abstract system in order to draw (certain kinds of) conclusions about the real system. If an error state (condition) is not reachable in the abstract system, then it is neither reachable in the real system. Such methods have been extremely successful in the verification of temporal safety properties, e.g. [1,2,10].

Herein, predicate abstraction is, for the first time as far as we are aware, used to define heuristic functions instead. In a manner reminiscent of the *pattern database* approach [3], we build the (entire) abstract state space before search starts; during search, the abstract state space is used as a lookup table, i.e., states are mapped onto their abstract counterparts, and the error distance of the counterpart is taken as the heuristic estimate.

In difference to our approach, pattern databases traditionally use simple abstractions, mostly (like [15] above) based on ignoring some of the relevant symbols.

An important characteristic of our method (which it shares with traditional pattern databases) is that it yields a very large family of heuristics, rather than just a single one. Every different set of predicates yields a different abstract state space, which gives a different heuristic function. The main question is: *How should we choose the predicates?* This is the same "main" question as in the standard use of predicate abstraction. However, in our approach the abstraction does not have to be precise enough to verify the property of interest, in order to be useful. So we got much more freedom of design. Herein, we explore two approaches. The first one simply collects the predicates from the syntax (e.g. transition guards) of the automata network, which is not likely to be property-preserving. The second one uses the standard *error path guided abstraction refinement* life cycle: (1) start with an empty set of predicates; (2) find an error path; (3) check if the error is real or spurious; (3a) if it is real, stop; (3b) if it is spurious, *analyze the error path* to create new predicates that exclude this path, and goto (2). For our purposes, we can stop the process at any time – we do not have to wait until a real error path is found. In our experiments, we simply fix a number of refinement iterations (which becomes an input parameter).[2] Generating the predicates using abstraction refinement is, we think, particularly promising: this technique has the power to adapt the heuristic function quite flexibly and intelligently to the individual problem instance at hand. Surprisingly, we weren't yet able to obtain entirely convincing results with the technique; we believe there is hope for the future. This will be discussed in detail later.

Apart from the parameterization given by the choice of predicates, we explore another parameter defining how the automata network is *split* into several parts. It turns out that predicate abstraction is much too time-consuming when done on the entire network. So we apply another abstraction method beforehand. We define a partitioning of the set of automata (we "split" the network), and hand each part to the predicate abstraction engine *in separate*. The splits are made so that few potential "interactions" are violated. The transition guards responsible for the violated interactions are removed. During search, a heuristic value is looked up in each part (in the corresponding abstract state space). These values are aggregated by taking their sum as the overall heuristic value. Since we removed the guards responsible for violated interactions, this aggregated heuristic value is still admissible. There are many possible strategies for making the split. We use a simple greedy strategy parameterized by the *split bound b* – the maximal number of automata in a single part of the partitioning (the maximal number of automata considered within a single predicate abstraction).

For testing, we use a set of benchmarks that is meaningful in that it includes examples from two industrial case studies [4,12]. Table 1 gives a summary of our results. Examples "FAn" and "FBn" are variants of the Fischer protocol for mutual exclusion, examples "Mi", "Ni", and "Ci" come from the industrial case studies (some more details are given later). In Table 1, "RDF" is standard UPPAAL's fastest search strategy, a randomized depth-first search. "[13]-best" gives, for each example, the better result of

---

[2] We will see that, by using abstraction refinement for a heuristic – combining abstraction refinement and state space search – we can solve examples that cannot be solved by either method (abstraction refinement or blind state space search) alone.

Table 1. Summary of results. Number of explored states/runtime (sec.) for RDF, [13]-best, and [5]-b50. Overhead/number of explored states/runtime (sec.) for Syntax-b2 and ARMC-b3-r4. Explanation see text.

Exp.	RDF	[13]-best	[5]-N50	Syntax-b2	ARMC-b3-r4
FA5	526/0.0	27/0.0	80/0.1	0.0/80/0.1	0.3/29/0.3
FA10	6371/0.4	42/0.0	130/0.2	0.0/130/0.1	0.4/44/0.4
FA15	20010/1.3	57/0.0	180/0.5	0.1/180/0.1	0.6/59/0.6
FB5	356/0.0	74/0.0	21/0.0	0.1/21/0.1	0.5/23/0.5
FB10	7885/0.5	274/0.0	36/0.1	0.3/36/0.3	0.5/38/0.5
FB15	58793/3.8	599/0.1	51/0.4	0.5/51/0.5	0.5/53/0.5
M1	29607/0.7	5656/0.7	19063/0.9	1.1/23257/1.8	3.9/12121/4.1
M2	118341/3.3	30743/2.8	46545/1.5	1.2/84475/3.9	4.0/50599/5.1
M3	102883/4.6	18431/2.0	64522/2.0	1.1/92548/4.4	4.0/28022/4.4
M4	543238/6.1	88537/9.9	168692/3.3	1.3/311049/11.4	4.5/116570/5.8
N1	41218/2.0	16335/2.4	27275/2.0	1.0/36030/3.8	7.3/12439/8.1
N2	199631/10.1	132711/9.9	102097/5.2	1.4/178333/14.0	7.8/97219/11.3
N3	195886/9.7	28889/3.3	135783/6.8	1.3/196535/15.4	7.5/43159/9.6
N4	878706/43.5	226698/23.1	483623/23.1	1.2/983344/75.1	8.2/469363/24.4
C1	25219/0.9	2368/0.8	871/0.5	2.8/1588/2.8	10.8/1172/10.8
C2	65388/1.0	5195/1.5	1600/0.6	3.0/3786/3.1	12.2/3256/12.2
C3	85940/1.7	6685/1.7	2481/0.8	2.6/3846/2.7	12.5/4278/12.5
C4	892327/9.7	55480/6.5	22223/1.4	4.6/30741/5.0	14.3/46837/14.8
C5	8.0e+6/81.9	465796/41.9	160951/3.2	5.0/185730/8.0	15.4/473470/20.0
C6	–	4.5e+6/353.0	1.7e+6/15.5	5.2/1.9e+6/33.9	16.5/2.6e+6/42.5

the two heuristic functions defined in [13]. "[5]-N50" gives the result for the heuristic from [5] with $N = 50$.[3] "Syntax-b2" is predicate abstraction based on automata syntax, with split bound 2. "ARMC-b3-r4" is predicate abstraction based on abstraction refinement, with split bound 3 and 4 refinement iterations. The implementation interfaces to ARMC [14,16], which does the abstraction refinement. The "overhead" given for "Syntax-b2" and "ARMC-b3-r4" is the total time taken to build abstract state spaces.

"Syntax-b2" and "ARMC-b3-r4" are, overall, the most successful configurations, of the many possible configurations of our code, that we found in our experiments. The experiments, in particular the effects of the different parameters on performance, are described in detail later (Sections 4 and 5). From a quick glance at Table 1, one sees that our new heuristics are indeed competitive with the heuristics defined by [13] and [5] (which, in turn, have been shown to outperform [6] and some other simple heuristics in these examples). "[13]-best" explores very few states in the "Mi" and "Ni" examples, "[5]-N50" and "Syntax-b2" are best in the "Ci" examples. Note that the blind search "RDF" cannot solve C6 (consumes more than 1GB memory). It is also notable that "[13]-best" takes more time to compute than the other heuristics – e.g., this can be seen in C5 where "[13]-best" takes 41.9 seconds to explore 465796 states, but "ARMC-b3-r4" takes only 4.6 seconds (20.0-15.4) to explore a slightly larger number of states.[4]

---

[3] This is the sweet-spot; when increasing N, the number of explored states does not decrease much, but the overhead for merging the automata increases a lot.

[4] "[13]-best" is the only one of the tested heuristics that is *not* organized as a lookup table (the abstract problem has to be solved in every search state). Note that the results reported in [13] are better than those in Table 1; this is due to the additional "bitstate hashing" technique used there. Here, we focus exclusively on the heuristic functions.

The main surprise in the data, for us, was the good performance of syntax-based predicate abstractions, like "Syntax-b2": we didn't expect that one can do so good with such a simple form of abstraction predicates. In particular, we expected abstraction refinement to yield much better heuristics. The reason why this is not (yet) the case appears to lie in the following oddity. One would expect that a more refined heuristic yields a smaller search space.[5] However, in disquietingly many cases, refining the abstraction yielded a *larger* search space in our experiments. We believe there is hope to overcome this with modified refinement strategies; see Section 5.

The paper is organized as follows. The next section provides a brief background of, and some notations for, predicate abstraction. Section 3 summarizes the technical details of our approach: the formal definition of the predicate abstraction heuristic, a method to implement the needed "lookup tables" efficiently, and the technicalities of our network split operation. Section 4 gives detailed empirical observations for syntax-based predicate abstractions, Section 5 gives detailed empirical observations for predicate abstractions based on abstraction refinement. Section 6 concludes.

2 Predicate Abstraction

In principle, the idea behind this sort of abstraction is very simple. Say we have a transition system, specified declaratively via a set of transition rules, and a set X of variables. The state space of the system is the directed graph S where the nodes are all states (variable valuations) s, and the edges are the possible state transitions, as induced by the transition rules; we will use S also to denote the set of states. A predicate abstraction is defined by a finite set $\mathcal{P}$ of predicates over X. In our context, as said earlier, each $p \in \mathcal{P}$ has the form $lfn(X) \bowtie c$. Denote by a *bitvector* for $\mathcal{P}$ any conjunction that contains (exactly) each $p \in \mathcal{P}$, possibly negated. For a bitvector $\bar{b}$, denote by $[\bar{b}]$ the *extension* of $\bar{b}$, $[\bar{b}] := \{s \mid s \in S, s \models \bar{b}\}$. The $[\bar{b}]$ are equivalence classes in S; for $s \in [\bar{b}]$, we denote $[s] := [\bar{b}]$. The *abstract state space* for $\mathcal{P}$, denoted $[S]^{\mathcal{P}}$, is the directed graph where the nodes are all bitvectors for $\mathcal{P}$, and there is an edge from $\bar{b}_1$ to $\bar{b}_2$ iff there exist $s_1 \in [\bar{b}_1]$ and $s_2 \in [\bar{b}_2]$ so that there is an edge from s_1 to s_2 in S. Obviously, $[S]^{\mathcal{P}}$ is an over-approximation of S: if s_2 is reachable from s_1 in S, then $[s_2]$ is reachable from $[s_1]$ in $[S]^{\mathcal{P}}$.

Matters get a little more complicated once one starts to think about how to actually handle this sort of abstraction. When building the abstract state space, one has to frequently decide if there is an edge from a bitvector $\bar{b}_1$ to a bitvector $\bar{b}_2$. Enumerating $[\bar{b}_1]$ and $[\bar{b}_2]$ is, of course, nonsense. Instead, one formulates the transition rules of the real system as (conjunctions of) constraints on variable values (before and after the transition), so that the needed test comes down to the satisfiability of a conjunction of constraints. Both our own implementation and ARMC use this method, regressing from the error condition in a breadth-first manner to build the fraction of the abstract state space that is reachable from that condition. Concretely, both methods repeatedly consider a formula ϕ that formulates the properties of the state(s) that should be inserted next into the state space: ϕ is initially the error condition, and later the conjunction

---

[5] It is easy to see that a more refined heuristic *dominates* a less refined heuristic; see Section 3.

of the constraints given by the regressed abstract state, and the transition. The precise method to find the corresponding abstract states would be to enumerate all bitvectors and check if they are satisfiable in conjunction with ϕ. Instead, both our own implementation and ARMC additionally use a "cartesian" abstraction, and set the resulting state to $\bigwedge\{p \mid p \in \mathcal{P}, \phi \models p\} \wedge \bigwedge\{\neg p \mid p \in \mathcal{P}, \phi \models \neg p\}$. That is, one just checks which "bits" are definitely implied, and leaves the others unspecified. We denote such partial bitvectors with $\bar{c}$, keeping the notation $[\bar{c}] := \{s \mid s \in \mathcal{S}, s \models \bar{c}\}$. By $[c\mathcal{S}]^{\mathcal{P}}$ we denote the abstract state space – the graph of partial bitvectors – built in this way.

3   Technicalities

Before we start explaining the technical details of our approach, we fill in some details on the framework. As said, we consider networks of extended timed automata, which are finite automata (whose "states" are called "locations" in here) annotated with: 1. Effects and guards (constraints on edge executability) on integer variables; 2. Effects and guards on real-valued clock variables. The latter are a restricted form of real-valued variables: they always increase with the same speed as a linear function over time; their only allowed guards take the form $x \bowtie c$ or $x - y \bowtie c$; their only allowed effects take the form $x := c$ (where c denotes a constant). Networks of extended timed automata feature a set of such automata, that can share global integer and clock variables, and that can synchronize via synchronization actions. The latter actions generally take the form "send signal a" or "receive signal b". If (and only if) "a" and "b" match, the two edges can (and must) be taken simultaneously, as a single transition of the system. Arbitrarily many edges may be involved in such a transition if, e.g., the "send" action is a broadcast. In our implementation, so far we allow binary synchronization only, involving exactly two automata (one sender, one receiver).

Our safety properties take the form of formulas ϕ. In our implementation, so far we restrict to reachability, i.e., the question of whether a state fulfilling ϕ is reachable, where ϕ specifies a set of *target locations* and/or conditions on the clocks and integer variables.

UPPAAL tests safety properties in networks of extended timed automata by enumerating the space of reachable states. The search states correspond not to single system states, but to sets of such states. Namely, instead of concrete clock valuations, of which there are infinitely many, UPPAAL considers clock regions, whose (relevant) number is finite. A clock region is given in the form of a (normalized) set of unary or binary constraints on the clock values, called *difference bound matrix*.

3.1   Predicate Abstraction Heuristics

To turn a predicate abstraction into a heuristic function, we simply map the state into the abstract state space, and read the error distance from there. Precisely, if ϕ is the error condition, $\mathcal{P}$ is the predicate set, and s is a system state, we get:

$$h^{\mathcal{P}}(s) := min\{dist^{\mathcal{P}}(\bar{c}_1, \bar{c}_2) \mid \bar{c}_1, \bar{c}_2 \in [c\mathcal{S}]^{\mathcal{P}}, s \in [\bar{c}_1], \exists s' \in [\bar{c}_2] : s' \models \phi\}.$$

Here, $dist^{\mathcal{P}}(.,.)$ is graph distance in $[c\mathcal{S}]^{\mathcal{P}}$, which is ∞ if there is no path from the first to the second argument. Note here that, since the bitvectors $\bar{c}$ in $[c\mathcal{S}]^{\mathcal{P}}$ are partial, there may be several $\bar{c}_1$ so that $s \in [\bar{c}_1]$. $h^{\mathcal{P}}(s) = \infty$ if no error state is reachable in $[c\mathcal{S}]^{\mathcal{P}}$ from any such $\bar{c}_1$, which implies that no error state is reachable in $\mathcal{S}$ from s. Since we minimize over all $\bar{c}_1$ (and $\bar{c}_2$), $h^{\mathcal{P}}$ is admissible:

Proposition 1. *For any non-temporal formula ϕ, predicate set $\mathcal{P}$, and $s \in S$, we have $h^{\mathcal{P}}(s) \leq min\{dist(s, s') \mid s' \in \mathcal{S}, s' \models \phi\}$, where $dist(.,.)$ is graph distance in $\mathcal{S}$.*

Another interesting property of this kind of heuristics is that they are monotone in the predicate set, in the following sense:

Proposition 2. *For any non-temporal formula ϕ, predicate sets $\mathcal{P}_1$ and $\mathcal{P}_2$ such that $\mathcal{P}_1 \subseteq \mathcal{P}_2$, and $s \in S$, we have $h^{\mathcal{P}_1}(s) \leq h^{\mathcal{P}_2}(s)$.*

This is simply because, in particular, $[\mathcal{S}]^{\mathcal{P}_2}$ makes all distinctions that $[\mathcal{S}]^{\mathcal{P}_1}$ makes. What it tells us is that, if we refine a predicate set $\mathcal{P}$ by inserting new predicates into it, we obtain a heuristic function that *dominates* the previous one, in that it provides a (potentially) better lower bound.

For use in UPPAAL, we have to modify the definition of $h^{\mathcal{P}}$ to work on UPPAAL *search* states – which correspond to *sets* of system states. Let s be a UPPAAL search state, and $[s]$ be the corresponding set of system states. We define:

$$h^{\mathcal{P}}(s) := min\{dist^{\mathcal{P}}(\bar{c}_1, \bar{c}_2) \mid \bar{c}_1, \bar{c}_2 \in [c\mathcal{S}]^{\mathcal{P}}, [s] \cap [\bar{c}_1] \neq \emptyset, \exists s' \in [\bar{c}_2] : s' \models \phi\}.$$

Obviously, again this leads to an admissible heuristic function, and the monotonicity in the predicate set is preserved. While the definition looks fairly complicated, we will see in the next section that, once the abstract state space $[c\mathcal{S}]^{\mathcal{P}}$ is built, the function can be implemented quite efficiently.

3.2 Predicate Abstraction Pattern Databases

For every search state UPPAAL encounters, the heuristic function must be computed. This makes it time-critical to implement that function efficiently. Our two main tricks are: 1. We formulate the mapping of search states into $[c\mathcal{S}]^{\mathcal{P}}$ as a "bitset" inclusion problem; 2. We use a tree data structure to address that inclusion problem efficiently.

Remember that the abstract states in $[c\mathcal{S}]^{\mathcal{P}}$ are partial bitvectors $\bar{c}$: sets of possibly negated predicates from $\mathcal{P}$ – sets of bits. Given a UPPAAL search state s, by $\phi(s)$ we denote the constraint conjunction corresponding to s: location and integer valuations plus difference bound matrix. We define the following bitset:

$$\bar{c}(s) := \{p \mid \phi(s) \models p\} \cup \{\neg p \mid \phi(s) \models \neg p\} \cup \{p, \neg p \mid \phi(s) \not\models p, \phi(s) \not\models \neg p\}.$$

In words, $\bar{c}(s)$ contains all bits that may possibly be true in s (that are satisfied by at least one system state in $[s]$). While the definition of $\bar{c}(s)$ involves entailment checks, due to our particular circumstances $\bar{c}(s)$ can be computed efficiently. First, the UPPAAL search state contains precise valuations for all locations and integer variables; the uncertainty is exclusively about the clocks. So predicates not involving clocks can simply be evaluated in s. Second, since UPPAAL itself allows only clock constraints of the form $x \bowtie c$ or $x - y \bowtie c$, it is reasonable to also restrict to such constraints in the predicate sets. Whether such a predicate is implied by s or not can be read off from a single pass over the difference bound matrix of s. We observe:

$$[s] \cap [\bar{c}_1] \neq \emptyset \Leftrightarrow \bar{c}(s) \supseteq \bar{c}_1.$$

This is because $[s] \cap [\bar{c}_1] \neq \emptyset$ iff $\bar{c}_1$ contains no bit that is known to be false in s – in other words, if all bits contained in $\bar{c}_1$ may be true in s. We obtain:

$$h^{\mathcal{P}}(s) = min\{dist^{\mathcal{P}}(\bar{c}_1, \bar{c}_2) \mid \bar{c}_1, \bar{c}_2 \in [c\mathcal{S}]^{\mathcal{P}}, \bar{c}(s) \supseteq \bar{c}_1, \exists s' \in [\bar{c}_2] : s' \models \phi\}.$$

This is a syntactic characterization except for $\exists s' \in [\bar{c}_2] : s' \models \phi$; but that we have dealt with already when building $[c\mathcal{S}]^{\mathcal{P}}$: we simply mark, during that pre-process, the respective $\bar{c}_2$ (namely, the start state in our backward search) as error states. Of course, we also annotate each state $\bar{c}$ with its distance to the nearest error state (building $[c\mathcal{S}]^{\mathcal{P}}$ backward breadth-first, we get that distance for free).

We are left with the problems to: 1. In the pre-process, store $[c\mathcal{S}]^{\mathcal{P}}$ as a set of bitsets annotated with their error distance; 2. During search, quickly find all bitsets that are contained in $\bar{c}(s)$. Both can be accomplished using a data structure called *Unlimited Branching Tree* [11]. In a nutshell, this is a tree structure that stores sets of sets, exploiting shared elements between the sets to optimize space usage and access time for answering subset queries of the precise kind we need here. The details are not essential for the paper at hand, so we omit them. (A node in the tree may have as many branches as there are distinct elements in the sets, hence the name.)

3.3   Network Splitting

A very simple abstraction method is to partition the set of automata contained in a network. As said, we use this abstraction prior to predicate abstraction, in order to make the latter feasible. One simply considers each part of the partitioning – a subset of the automata – in separate. The only problem with this approach is that, of course, the automata typically interact with each other in various ways, and cannot be split without violating such interactions. We identify a possible definition of what "interaction" means. We approximate that definition to obtain an admissible splitting strategy.

Let e be an edge of automaton a, and e' be an edge of automaton $a' \neq a$. Let ψ be an effect of e (an assignment to a variable, or a synchronization action), and let ϕ be a guard of e' (a constraint over variables, or a synchronization action). We say that ψ *affects* ϕ if there is an execution trace P (a path in $\mathcal{S}$) so that: e occurs before e' on P; when removing ψ from e and simulating the execution of P by ignoring the guards between e and e', ϕ is no longer satisfied at the point where e' should be executed. Similarly, this definition is made also for location invariants ϕ. We say that an automaton a affects an automaton a' if there is an effect of an edge in a that affects a guard of an edge, or a location invariant, in a'. We say that a and a' *interact* if a affects a', or vice versa.

Proposition 3. *Say we have a network with automata A, a set of target locations ϕ, and a set $A_1 \subseteq A$ such that no automaton in $A \setminus A_1$ affects any automaton in A_1. Then,* *for any $s \in S$, we have $min\{dist_{|1}(s_{|1}, s') \mid s' \in S_{|1}, s' \models \phi_{|1}\} \leq min\{dist(s, s') \mid s' \in S, s' \models \phi\}$, where $s_{|1}$ is s restricted to the locations and variables mentioned in A_1, $S_{|1}$ is the state space of A_1, $\phi_{|1}$ is the subset of ϕ mentioned in A_1, and $dist(., .)$ ($dist_{|1}(., .)$) is graph distance in S ($S_{|1}$).*

In words, the isolated automata A_1 provide an admissible distance estimate. The reason for this is, simply, that we can take any solution path for A, and restrict it onto the edges present in A_1, to obtain a solution for A_1 in isolation – otherwise, if that restricted path wasn't a solution for A_1, a constraint in A_1 would be unsatisfied, and we could construct a contradiction since an edge on the sub-path for $A \setminus A_1$ would have to affect that constraint. Note that, in particular, Proposition 3 says that, if A is solvable, then A_1 in isolation is also solvable. We further have:

Proposition 4. *Say we have a network with automata A, a set of target locations ϕ, and a partitioning $A_1, \ldots, A_m$ of A so that no pair of automata $a \in A_i$, $a' \in A_j$, $i \neq j$, interacts. Then, for any $s \in S$, we have $\sum_{i=1}^{m} min\{dist_{|i}(s_{|i}, s') \mid s' \in S_{|i}, s' \models \phi_{|i}\} \leq min\{dist(s, s') \mid s' \in S, s' \models \phi\}$, where the notations are as in Proposition 3.*

This tells us that we can safely add the individual heuristic values. The reason is that we can partition any solution path for A into (independent) solution paths for each of $A_1, \ldots, A_m$.

What we have just seen is not yet practical since there normally is no split that doesn't violate *any* interaction (otherwise there would be no point in posing both parts of the network within the same problem). We become practical by finding *potential* interactions, and simply removing guards that constitute violated potential interactions. Concretely, we use the simplistic notion saying that effect ψ can not affect condition ϕ if the variable x affected by ψ, and any variable that can, transitively, be affected by the value of x, does not appear in ϕ. For example, $x := 1$ can affect $x + y > 2$. On the other hand, $x := 1$ can affect $y > 2$ if there also is an effect $y := x$ somewhere, but not if there is no chain of variables from x to y. In our pre-process, we simply consider all pairs of occuring ψ and ϕ, and see if they satisfy this criterion; if not, we say that they have a potential interaction. We then greedily put automata together (into one part of the partitioning) so that few potential interactions to automata in other parts remain. For those interactions that do remain, we remove the responsible ϕ. Note that the latter will, in particular, remove synchronization actions that also occur in other parts.

With Proposition 4, our resulting heuristic function is still admissible, *except* for the effects of synchronization. In a solution path to A, a set of synchronized edges will be counted as a single transition, while in the partitioned network every edge will be counted separately.[6] We feel that this potential non-admissibility is benign. For example, if only binary synchronization is allowed, then the real error state distance is overestimated by at most a factor 2 – in the *worst case*, which one can realistically expect to be far away from the typical case. We ran a number of tests using our heuristics with A^*, and never obtained a sub-optimal solution.

---

[6] Note that the automata network "A" we have here, in the application of Proposition 4, is no longer the original network, but one where several synchronization actions have been removed.

Table 2. Results for syntax-based abstractions. Notation as in Table 1; empty entries are identical to their left neighbour; "–/" means time-out during pre-processing.

Exp.	Syntax-b1	Syntax-b2	Syntax-b3	Syntax-b4	Syntax-all
FA5	0.1/80/0.1	0.0/80/0.1	0.3/80/0.3	0.2/80/0.2	1.5/27/1.5
FA10	0.1/130/0.1	0.2/130/0.2	0.4/130/0.4	0.6/130/0.6	7.4/42/7.4
FA15	0.1/180/0.1	0.3/180/0.3	0.7/180/0.7	1.2/180/1.2	28.8/57/28.8
FB5	0.1/21/0.1	0.1/21/0.1	0.2/21/0.2	0.3/21/0.3	0.7/21/0.7
FB10	0.1/36/0.1	0.3/36/0.3	0.4/36/0.4	0.5/36/0.5	2.1/36/2.1
FB15	0.1/51/0.1	0.5/51/0.5	0.8/51/0.8	0.9/51/0.9	3.4/51/3.4
M1	0.3/16446/0.8	1.1/23257/1.8	6.3/12780/6.8	6.6/12780/7.0	
M2	0.3/68956/3.5	1.2/84475/3.9	9.6/37780/10.3	37.1/34947/37.8	
M3	0.3/62731/2.6	1.1/92548/4.4	9.1/55726/11.5	36.5/55098/37.8	
M4	0.4/275433/7.0	1.3/311049/11.4	13.5/198407/20.5	57.3/139875/62.6	–/
N1	0.5/22304/2.7	1.0/36030/3.8	8.8/17357/9.9	8.5/17357/10.2	
N2	0.5/122398/8.1	1.4/178333/14.0	11.7/87471/19.8	47.8/63596/53.3	
N3	0.5/140201/8.7	1.3/196535/15.4	11.2/115074/21.7	46.8/96202/56.7	
N4	0.6/738680/37.9	1.2/983344/75.1	16.3/720350/78.8	70.1/445359/120.3	–/
C1	0.9/1455/1.1	2.8/1588/2.8	9.5/4698/9.6	–/	–/
C2	1.4/3273/1.4	3.0/3786/3.1	9.5/10843/9.6	35.7/10507/35.9	–/
C3	1.4/5879/1.5	2.6/3846/2.7	9.7/10375/9.8	35.7/10195/35.9	–/
C4	1.6/44837/2.3	4.6/30741/5.0	21.2/66336/22.7	104.3/66761/105.7	–/
C5	1.8/301065/6.4	5.0/185730/8.0	21.7/436678/34.0	109.4/435309/121.5	–/
C6	1.6/2.8e+6/39.8	5.2/1.9e+6/33.9	26.7/4.1e+6/137.2	103.2/3.8e+6/230.0	–/

4   Syntax-Based Abstractions

In our syntax-based abstractions, as indicated before, the abstraction predicates are simply read off the description of the automata network. Given a set A of automata, the created set of predicates consists of all expressions e that appear as a transition guard, or as a location invariant, of some automaton in A. Further, the abstraction distinguishes between the locations (which is equivalent to including the predicate $loc(a) = l$ for each $a \in A$ and location l of a).

Simply collecting all mentioned constraints, there is no parameterization to this sort of abstraction – except the need to split the automata network before the abstraction is applied. Table 2 shows our results. The data, and all other data reported herein, were obtained on a PC running at 1.2GHz with 1GB main memory and 1024KB cache running Linux. We set a time-out of 300 seconds for pre-processing. Search always ran out of memory before we ran out of patience (within a few minutes, that is).

Before considering the data, let us describe the examples in some more detail. Recall that our aim is *falsification* of safety properties, i.e., the systems we consider are unsafe in that an error state is reachable. Since the examples we considered were originally safe, we *injected* an error into them.

Examples "FAn" and "FBn" are variants of the Fischer protocol for mutual exclusion, which asks if at least two of n similar automata can be in a certain location simultaneously. We made the error possible by weakening one of the temporal conditions in the automata (from ">" to "≥"). The variants differ in the way they encode the error condition. Variant A adds additional automata with synchronisation. Variant B selects and specifies two of the automata for the error condition. Examples "Mi" and "Ni", $i = 1, \ldots, 4$, come from a study called "Mutual Exclusion". This study models a real-time protocol to ensure mutual exclusion of states in a distributed system via asynchronous communication. The protocol is described in full detail in [4]. By increasing an upper time bound in the model we got a flawed specification that we transformed into its timed automata semantics by applying various abstractions techniques. Examples "Ci", $i = 1, \ldots, 6$, come from a case study called "Single-tracked Line Segment". This study stems from an industrial project partner of the UniForM-project [12] and the problem is to design a distributed real-time controller for a segment of tracks where trams share a piece of track. A distributed controller was modeled in terms of PLC-Automata [4,12], and translated into timed automata. We injected an error by manipulating a delay such that the asynchronous communication between some automata is faulty. The given set of PLC-Automata had eight input variables and we constructed six models with decreasing size by abstracting more and more of these inputs.

In Table 2, the split bound increases from left to right as obvious; in "Syntax-all" there is no split bound, meaning that the entire network is handed to the abstraction engine in one piece. The foremost observation is that the latter is *bad* – except in the Fischer toy examples and the smaller "M" and "N" cases, the abstract state space could never be built within the alloted time (300 sec). ("M1" .. "M3" and "N1" .. "N3" have ≤ 4 automata so there is no change from "Syntax-b4" to "Syntax-all".) Consider the "M" and "N" examples, and what happens as b increases from 1 to 4. The overhead increases sharply, quickly becoming larger than the time spent in search. Strangely, the number of explored states also grows, from $b = 1$ to $b = 2$, before decreasing again from $b = 2$ to $b = 4$. It is unclear to us what causes this behavior. The smallest search spaces are obtained with $b = 4$, the smallest overall runtimes are obtained with $b = 1$. Note that the "M" and "N" examples can all be solved quite quickly even with a blind search, c.f. Table 1. The "C" examples are more interesting in that respect (blind search scales badly). They exhibit very similar behavior in terms of the overhead.[7] The number of explored states now decreases sharply from $b = 1$ to $b = 2$, and increases sharply from $b = 2$ to $b = 3$. Again, the reason for this behavior is unclear. C6 is the first example (in the scaling pattern here) where the larger overhead pays off in runtime – "Syntax-b2" is faster than "Syntax-b1" due to the reduced search space. Note here that C6 is the most relevant example.

All in all, the syntax-based abstractions give surprisingly good performance – e.g. "Syntax-b2" is very competitive in the "C" examples – but they don't seem to have much potential for further improvements. One could try to allow more freedom in the selection of the predicates, but such an approach is likely to be wild guesswork, at least without a deeper analysis of the system. An idea worth trying is to integrate syntax-based predicate selection into abstraction refinement: as a start, one could select (amongst others) the guards that are not satisfied by the spurious error path.

5   Abstraction Refinement

We implemented this sort of abstraction via an interface to the ARMC tool [14,16]. This is a recent model checker based on error path guided abstraction refinement.

---

[7] C1 is exceptionally hard for the pre-process since there are only 4 automata, which have a large abstract state space together; in C2 ... C6, one of these automata is split away.

Predicates are generated from spurious error paths by an analysis using a constraint based interpolation [17] to find a concise reason for the failure (the spuriousness) of the path. We modified ARMC to feature a maximal number of iterations as an input parameter. If ARMC finds a correct abstraction (no error paths), it stops with no output, causing our overall program to terminate – if there is no abstract error path, then there is no real one. (In our examples, of course this did not happen.) If ARMC finds a feasible (real) error path, it stops and outputs the abstract state space.[8] The same happens otherwise, i.e. if the maximum iteration is reached. The abstract state space is read in, and stored in a UBTree structure for lookup.

The configuration of our heuristic function now has two parameters: the split bound, and the number of refinement iterations. This makes our data field 3-dimensional. Table 3 restricts to the "C" examples – which are the most relevant anyway – to save space. The data are arranged in a slightly unusual way, grouped by example rather than by configuration parameters, to ease observing how the behavior for an example changes as a function of the configuration parameters.

Let us start with some of the simpler observations to be made in Table 3. First, we see that, like for the syntax-based abstractions, without network splitting we don't get far. The overhead needed with "-b all" is huge with 0 or 1 refinement iterations ("-r 0" or "-r 1") already, exhausting the available runtime for C6 respectively C5.[9] With 4 or more refinement iterations, runtime is exhausted in even the smallest example C1. Second, for "-b 1" and "-b 2", the table entry with "-r 7" is always identical to that with "-r 4". This is because ARMC finds feasible error paths. Precisely, with "-b 1" ARMC finds feasible error paths, in all examples and in all parts of the partitionings (meaning, in each single automaton), in 4 refinement iterations. So increasing the maximum number of refinement iterations beyond 4 does not have any effect. With $b = 2$, ARMC finds feasible error paths in 3 refinement iterations already.

Now, consider what happens as we let the configuration parameters vary. Consider first the split bound "-b": compare the data when moving up or down in the table. Like for the syntax-based abstractions in Table 2, the overhead consistently grows over growing split bound, particularly much when the number of refinement iterations is high.[10] The number of explored search states, on the other hand, behaves more stably, and a little more expectedly, than for the syntax-based abstractions in Table 2. In most cases, the number stays the same, or decreases, over increasing split bound. Particularly with many refinement iterations, there is a relatively sharp monotonic decrease over increasing split bound. Notable exceptions to this rule are a few configurations for C1, and the increase from 2.6e+6 states to 3.8e+6 states when moving from "-b 3" to "-b 4" in C6. We observe that the decreased search space size never pays off in runtime: when moving downwards in a column within one part of the table (within one example), the runtime (almost) always increases monotonically.

---

[8] Since ARMC gets only parts of the network, i.e. due to our splitting operation, a feasible error path here is *not* a solution to the overall problem.

[9] The observations for C6 here show that combining ARMC and UPPAAL enables us to solve examples that neither tool can solve on its own. ARMC, *if* it can solve C6, would definitely run for a *very* long time. UPPAAL, as said before, runs out of memory on this example.

[10] Regarding the huge overhead for C1 with split bound 4, see Footnote 7.

Table 3. Results for abstraction refinement based abstractions. Notation as in Table 1; "-r": number of refinement iterations in ARMC; "-b": split bound; empty entries are identical to their left neighbour; "–/" means time-out during pre-processing; "/–" means out of memory during search.

-b \ -r	0	1	4	7
	C1			
1	0.8/19778/1.0	0.8/17330/1.0	1.6/2806/1.6	
2	1.9/8769/2.0	2.6/8861/3.1	6.0/1508/6.0	
3	1.7/8769/1.8	3.0/8861/3.1	10.8/1172/10.8	36.2/6362/36.2
4	10.0/16291/10.3	32.9/12044/33.0	176.0/3630/174.3	–/
all	30.2/8769/30.2	120.2/9627/120.2	–/	–/
	C2			
1	1.0/62046/1.4	1.2/59031/1.7	1.5/8143/1.6	
2	1.7/39710/2.0	3.1/35245/3.4	6.3/4898/6.3	
3	1.7/39710/2.0	4.1/35245/4.4	12.2/3256/12.2	38.2/25601/38.4
4	2.1/39710/2.6	5.2/35245/5.5	17.2/3256/17.2	63.8/25601/63.9
all	43.0/39710/43.1	189.1/40122/189.8	–/	–/
	C3			
1	0.9/88015/1.6	0.9/89194/1.6	1.6/10191/1.7	
2	1.6/67166/2.2	3.1/53616/3.4	6.4/5583/6.4	
3	1.6/67166/2.2	3.8/53616/4.2	12.5/4278/12.6	40.2/30407/40.4
4	2.0/67166/2.5	5.2/53616/5.6	18.0/4278/18.0	67.6/30407/67.8
all	44.6/67166/45.0	198.2/52042/198.9	–/	–/
	C4			
1	1.2/897900/6.8	1.5/872580/7.2	2.0/79069/2.7	
2	2.1/516282/5.8	3.0/511180/6.8	6.8/41831/7.1	
3	2.1/516282/5.8	4.8/511180/8.6	14.3/46837/14.8	45.6/279374/47.4
4	2.1/516282/5.8	6.0/511180/9.9	20.6/46837/21.0	73.3/279374/74.9
all	67.6/516282/71.2	288.9/540013/291.7	–/	–/
	C5			
1	1.1/9.0e+6/64.1	1.3/8.4e+6/61.0	2.4/1.1e+6/11.8	
2	2.2/4.9e+6/38.8	3.2/6.8e+6/57.0	7.6/425264/11.6	
3	2.2/4.9e+6/38.8	5.2/6.8e+6/59.1	15.4/473470/20.0	48.7/2.3e+6/66.2
4	2.2/4.9e+6/38.8	7.0/6.8e+6/62.2	24.1/288614/26.7	79.9/1.9e+6/94.3
all	94.1/4.9e+6/132.2	–/	–/	–/
	C6			
1	/–	/–	2.4/4.4e+6/40.5	
2	/–	/–	7.9/2.8e+6/34.1	
3	/–	/–	16.5/2.6e+6/42.5	/–
4	/–	/–	30.5/3.8e+6/63.4	/–
all	/–	–/	–/	–/

In terms of runtime, the number of refinement iterations definitely is a better parameter to invest overhead in: most notably, C6 is not solved with less than 4 refinement iterations. Then again, refining "too much" apparently isn't a good idea, either. We get back to this below. First, observe that, when moving from left to right in the table (when increasing the number of refinement iterations), as expected we get a consistent increase of overhead. The number of explored search states consistently (with few exceptions) decreases a little when stepping from "-r 0" to "-r 1", decreases sharply when stepping from "-r 1" to "-r 4", and increases sharply when stepping from "-r 4" to "-r 7". In terms of runtime, the decrease in search space size does not pay off (due to the larger overhead) in C1 .. C4, but does pay off in C5 and C6, when the search spaces explode.

The most curious observation in this data is definitely the *increase* in search space size that we often get when we make the abstraction more refined. Particularly, this is a surprise since, c.f. Section 3.1, every time we refine the abstraction we obtain a heuristic that dominates the previous one. At first sight, we were irritated this is even possible – a heuristic that dominates another one, but yields a larger search space. Looking more closely, however, this is possible quite naturally. Imagine a state has two successors s and s', of which s leads to an error state on a narrow path (not much branching) of length 10, while s' is the start of a huge part of the state space containing no error state at all. Let's say $h(s) = 5$ and $h(s') = 8$. Let's further say $h'(s) = 9$ and $h'(s') = 8$. Obviously, h' is a more precise heuristic than h – it refined h in its judgement of s – but will yield a much larger search space. The "mistake" made in the refinement step here is that the focus of the refinement is exclusively on s, not on s'. This sort of thing may be precisely what happens (sometimes) when we do a refinement step with ARMC. In fact, the defining characteristic of the refinement step is that it *excludes the detected spurious error path* – which means, one shortest spurious error path (ARMC does a breadth-first search) is removed. But other spurious error paths of the same length may remain. The heuristic values "along" the removed spurious error path will increase (that region of the state space is refined), but the heuristic values "along" the other spurious error paths will remain the same. If the removed spurious error path happens to be the (only) one that actually corresponds to a real solution, then the refinement will increase our search space in pretty much the way as illustrated with s and s' in the example above.

Our intuition was confirmed quite clearly when we ran the following test on example C4 with split bound 3 (middle row of C4 part of Table 3). We incrementally increased the number of refinement iterations, and measured the search space size as well as the length of the shortest error path found in the abstractions at the maximum level. The partitioning for this example in this setting has two parts, giving us two abstractions. The data we obtained are as follows. "-r 0": 516282 nodes, error path lengths 6 and 5. "-r 1": 511180, lengths 9 and 7. "-r 2": 49384, lengths 13 and 10. "-r 3": 56081, lengths 13 and 12. At this point, we first notice the hypothesized effect. In difference to before, the error path length of the first abstraction didn't increase, and promptly the search space size went (slightly) up. The error path in the second abstraction became feasible at this level, so it stays fixed and we don't report it from now on. "-r 4": 46837, length 13. "-r 5": 63606, length 13. "-r 6": 279374, length 13 – this step seems to correspond most closely to the example above. "-r 7": 279374, length 13. "-r 8": 279374, length 13. "-r 9": 361555, length 13. "-r 10": 50060, length 16. In this step, the error path length finally increases again, and promptly the search space size goes sharply down. The error path found in refinement step 10 is feasible, so here our experiment stops.

One can try to overcome this phenomenon by making the refinement mechanism less focussed on a single error path, trying to exclude the spurious error paths more "broadly". The straightforward idea is to introduce predicates so that *all* shortest spurious error paths are removed (not just a single one). This may require too much overhead. It remains to be seen if one can define successful selection heuristics and greedy strategies that remove the most "relevant" error paths, and/or that introduce only the most "relevant" predicates (an idea for the latter may be to define relevance of a predicate based on how many error paths it serves to remove). Another idea might be to use a sort of perimeter search within the abstraction, where the error condition would be "broadened" to the final layer of a depth-bounded backwards breadth-first search. Alternatively, of course, one can use our above observations simply to design an automatic selection of the number of refinement steps: refine until, in an iteration k, the length of the shortest spurious error path does, for the first time, not increase; take the heuristic function defined by the abstract state space from iteration $k - 1$.

6 Conclusion

There clearly is promise in defining heuristic functions for model checking based on predicate abstraction. It is straightforward to spell this idea out formally. Apart from the idea, we have contributed a method to efficiently store and query the heuristic information, a method to split an automata network without losing admissibility, and a first empirical exploration. Our (empirical) results are not yet at a level that would be thoroughly satisfying, but we are competitive with the other techniques that have been tried so far. It remains to be seen if, how, and in what sort of applications this kind of heuristic can be made more efficient. We are optimistic that a refinement-based approach will eventually turn out to be quite useful.

References

1. Ball, T., Majumdar, R., Millstein, T., Rajamani, S.: Automatic predicate abstraction of C programs. In: PLDI'2001: Programming Language Design and Implementation, pp. 203–213 (2001)
2. Chaki, S., Clarke, E., Groce, A., Jha, S., Veith, H.: Modular verification of software components in C. In: ICSE'2003: Int. Conf. on Software Engineering, pp. 385–395 (2003)
3. Culberson, J., Schaeffer, J.: Pattern databases. Computational Intelligence 14(3), 318–334 (1998)
4. Dierks, H.: Comparing model-checking and logical reasoning for real-time systems. Formal Aspects of Computing 16(2), 104–120 (2004)
5. Dräger, K., Finkbeiner, B., Podelski, A.: Directed model checking with distance-preserving abstractions. In: Valmari, A. (ed.) Model Checking Software. LNCS, vol. 3925, Springer, Heidelberg (2006)
6. Edelkamp, S., Lluch-Lafuente, A., Leue, S.: Directed explicit model checking with HSF-SPIN. In: Dwyer, M.B. (ed.) Model Checking Software. LNCS, vol. 2057, pp. 57–79. Springer, Heidelberg (2001)
7. Edelkamp, S., Lluch-Lafuente, A., Leue, S.: Directed explicit-state model checking in the validation of communication protocols. International Journal on Software Tools for Technology Transfer (2004)
8. Graf, S., Saïdi, H.: Construction of abstract state graphs with PVS. In: Grumberg, O. (ed.) CAV 1997. LNCS, vol. 1254, pp. 72–83. Springer, Heidelberg (1997)
9. Groce, A., Visser, W.: Model checking Java programs using structural heuristics. In: International Symposium on Software Testing and Analysis, pp. 12–21 (2002)
10. Henzinger, T., Jhala, R., Majumdar, R., McMillan, K.: Abstractions from proofs. In: POPL'2004: Principles of Programming Languages, pp. 232–244 (2004)
11. Hoffmann, J., Koehler, J.: A new method to query and index sets. In: 16th International Joint Conference on Artificial Intelligence (IJCAI-99), pp. 462–467 (1999)
12. Krieg-Brückner, B., Peleska, J., Olderog, E., Baer, A.: The UniForM Workbench, a universal development environment for formal methods. In: Wing, J.M., Woodcock, J.C.P., Davies, J. (eds.) FM 1999. LNCS, vol. 1708, pp. 1186–1205. Springer, Heidelberg (1999)

13. Kupferschmid, S., Hoffmann, J., Dierks, H., Behrmann, G.: Adapting an AI planning heuristic for directed model checking. In: Valmari, A. (ed.) Model Checking Software. LNCS, vol. 3925, Springer, Heidelberg (2006)
14. Podelski, A., Rybalchenko, A.: ARMC: the logical choice for software model checking with abstraction refinement. In: Hanus, M. (ed.) PADL 2007. LNCS, vol. 4354, pp. 245–259. Springer, Heidelberg (2007)
15. Qian, K., Nymeyer, A.: Guided invariant model checking based on abstraction and symbolic pattern databases. In: Jensen, K., Podelski, A. (eds.) TACAS 2004. LNCS, vol. 2988, pp. 497–511. Springer, Heidelberg (2004)
16. Rybalchenko, A.: A model checker based on abstraction refinement. Master's thesis, Universität des Saarlandes (2002)
17. Rybalchenko, A., Sofronie-Stokkermans, V.: Constraint solving for interpolation. In: Cook, B., Podelski, A. (eds.) VMCAI 2007. LNCS, vol. 4349, Springer, Heidelberg (2007)

Real-Time Model Checking on Secondary Storage

Stefan Edelkamp and Shahid Jabbar

University of Dortmund
Otto-Hahn Straße 14
Germany
{stefan.edelkamp,shahid.jabbar}@cs.uni-dortmund.de *

Abstract. In this paper, we consider disk based exploration in priced timed automata for resource-optimal scheduling. State spaces for large problems can easily go beyond the main memory capacity. We propose the use of hard disk to store the generated state space induced by priced timed automata. We contribute three algorithms: External Breadth First Search for reachability analysis in ordinary timed automata, External Breadth First Branch-and-Bound for cost-optimal reachability analysis in priced timed automata, and Iterative Broadening External Breadth First Branch-and-Bound for a partial exploration in priced timed automata. The third algorithm achieves its completeness by trying to find an upper bound on the optimal solution in an incomplete search tree. Iteratively, the upper bound is made tighter and the coverage of the search space is widened. We present correctness and completeness proofs for the suggested algorithms along with experimental results on different instances of aircraft landing scheduling to validate the practicality of our approach.

1   Introduction

Real-time model checking with timed automata [2] is an important decidable subfield of the analysis of hybrid automata [11] with a number of industrial applications. UP-PAAL [21] is one very successful verification tool based on timed automata. It can be used for modeling, simulation and validation of real-time systems. It deals with non-deterministic processes with finite control structure, channel or shared variable communication, and real-valued clocks. UPPAAL CORA [20] is the extension of UPPAAL designed for efficient cost-optimal reachability analysis in priced timed automata. UP-PAAL CORA is also competitive in resource-optimal scheduling [23].

The main limitation to the exploration of real-time systems are bounded main memory resources. Relying on virtual memory slows down the exploration due to excessive page faults. External algorithms [24] exploit harddisk space and organize the access to secondary memory. Originally designed for explicit graphs, external search algorithms have shown considerable performances in the large-scale breadth-first and guided exploration of single-agent games [16,9] and in the analysis of model checking problems [13,14,18]. While [14] provides a distributed implementation of [13] for model checking safety properties, a recent extension [8] extends the approach to general LTL

---

* The authors are supported by DFG under projects *Directed Model Checking* and *Heuristic Search*.

S. Edelkamp and A. Lomuscio (Eds.): MoChart IV, LNAI 4428, pp. 67–83, 2007.

properties. The approaches in [8,13,14] have been implemented on top of Spin model checker and have succeeded in exploring state spaces as large as 3 Terabytes. In [25] the model checker Murφ has been extended to use hard disk to store intermediate states.

In this paper, we extend external search algorithms for exploration in unweighted and weighted real-time models. The challenge is to I/O efficiently deal with the external representation and elimination of redundant states. We propose three algorithms: External Breadth First Search for reachability analysis in ordinary timed automata, External Breadth First Branch-and-Bound for cost-optimal reachability analysis in priced timed automata, and Iterative Broadening External Breadth First Branch-and-Bound for a partial exploration in priced timed automata. The proposed algorithms provide a controlled and guided exploration of the state space.

The paper is structured as follows. First, we review real-time model checking with priced timed automata. Then, we consider external exploration and introduce delayed duplication detection in breadth-first search. Next, we present external search in real-time domains. An introduction to priced timed automata is presented next. Since in the priced timed automata, we are interested in a cost optimal solution, we combine external search with branch-and-bound. Later, we present an iterative broadening variant of the algorithm that tries to find a good upper bound by searching in only a fragment of the state space. We have implemented our approach in UPPAAL CORA. Results for various problems of aircraft landing scheduling are presented.

In this text we consider real-time model checking with timed automata, for which the reachability problem is decidable but PSPACE-hard [2]. We furthermore restrict overselves to the cost optimization variant of reachability analysis for linearly priced timed automata. For extending these explorations to real-time model checking with respect to temporal properties we refer the reader to [6]. Moreover,

2   Timed Automata

Timed Automata can be viewed as an extension of classical finite automata with clocks and constraints defined on these clocks. These constraints, when corresponding to states are called *invariants*, and restrict the time allowed to stay at the state. When corresponding to transitions these constraints are called *guards*, and restrict the use of the transition. The clocks C are real-valued variables and are used to measure durations. The values of all the clocks in the system are denoted as a vector, also called as clock valuation function $v : C \rightarrow I\!R^+$. The constraints are defined over clocks and can be generated by the following grammar: for $x, y \in C$, a constraint α is defined as,

$$\alpha ::= x \prec d \mid x - y \prec d \mid \neg\alpha \mid (\alpha \wedge \alpha),$$

where $d \in Z\!\!\!Z$ and $\prec \in \{<, \leq\}$. These constraints yield two different kinds of transitions. The first one (*delay* transition) is to wait for some duration in the current state s - provided the *invariant*(s) holds. This lets only the clock variables increase. The other operation (*edge* transition) resets some clock variables while taking the transition t. The operation is possible given that the *guard*(t) holds. We allow an edge transition to be taken without an increase in the clock variables, i.e., in time 0. *Trajectories* are alternating sequences of states and transitions and define a path within the automata. The reachability task is to determine, if the goal in form of partial assignment to the ordinary and clock variables can be reached or not. The optimal reachability problem is to find a trajectory that minimizes the overall path length.

For a reachability analysis on timed automata, one faces the problem of an infinite-state space. This infiniteness is due to the fact that the clocks are real-valued and, hence, an exhaustive state space exploration can yield to infinite branches. This problem was solved with the introduction of a partitioning scheme based on regions [2]. A region automata creates finitely many partitions of the infinite state space based on the equivalent classes of the clock valuations. In model checking tools like Uppaal, though, a coarser representation called as *zone* [2] is used. Formally, a *zone* Z over a set of clocks C is a finite conjunction of simple difference constraints of the form $x - y \leq d$ or $x - y < d$, with $x, y \in C$ and integer d^1. The semantics for delay and edge transitions in a timed automata are based on some basic operations. We restrict to changes in clock variables. For a clock vector u and a zone Z we write $u \in Z$ if u satisfies the constraints in Z. The two main operations on (clock) zones are clock *reset* $\{x\}Z = \{u[0/x] \mid u \in Z\}$ that resets all the clocks x, *delay* or *future* (d time units) $Z^\uparrow = \{u + d \mid u \in Z\}$. The reachability problem in timed automata can then be reduced to the reachability analysis in *zone automata*. In a zone automata, each state is basically a *symbolic state* corresponding to one or many states in the original Timed Automata. The new state is represented as a tuple (l, Z), with l being the discrete part containing the local state of the automata, and Z is the convex $|C|$-dimensional hypersurface in Euclidean space. Semantically, (l, Z) now represents the set of all states (l, u) with $u \in Z$. Let $\mathcal{B}(C)$ denotes the set of constraints defined on clocks C and $\mathcal{P}(C)$ the power set of C. Formally, a Timed automata can be defined as follows:

Definition 1 (Timed Automata). *A timed automata is a tuple $A = (\mathcal{S}, l_0, \mathcal{R}, \text{Inv}, \mathcal{T})$, where $\mathcal{S}$ is the set of states, (l_0, Z_0) is the initial state with an empty zone, $\mathcal{R} \subseteq \mathcal{S} \times \mathcal{B}(C) \times \mathcal{P}(C) \times \mathcal{S}$ is the transition relation making states to their successors, given the constraints on the edge are satisfied, $\text{Inv} : \mathcal{S} \to \mathcal{B}(C)$ assigns invariants to the states, and $\mathcal{T}$ is the set of final states.*

3   External Breadth First Search

Most modern operating systems hide secondary memory accesses from the programmer, but offer one consistent address space of *virtual memory* that can be larger than the internal memory. When the program is executed, virtual addresses are translated into physical addresses. Only those portions of the program currently needed for the execution are copied into main memory. Caching and pre-fetching heuristics have been developed in order to reduce the number of page faults (the referenced page does not reside in the cache and has to be loaded from the hard disk). However, these methods are general-purpose and can not always take full advantage of the locality inherent in algorithms. Algorithms that explicitly manage the memory hierarchy can lead to substantial speedups, since they are more informed to predict and adjust future memory access.

---

[1] Unary constraints $x \leq d$ or $x < d$ are rewritten as $x - x_0 \leq d$ and $x - x_0 < d$ for some start time clock variable x_0, $x - y \geq d$ as $y - x \leq -d$ and $x = y$ as $x - y \leq 0$ and $y - x \leq 0$.

The standard model for comparing the performance of external algorithms consists of a single processor, a small internal memory that can hold up to M data items, and an unlimited secondary memory. The size of the input problem (in terms of the number of records) is abbreviated by N. Moreover, the *block size* B governs the bandwidth of memory transfers[2]. Typically $M = \sqrt{B}$. It is usually assumed that at the beginning of the algorithm, the input data is stored in contiguous block on external memory, and the same must hold for the output. Only the number of block reads and writes are counted, computations in internal memory do not incur any cost. The single disk model for external algorithms has been invented by [1]. It is convenient to express the complexity of external-memory algorithms using a number of frequently occurring primitive operations:

1. $scan(N)$ with an I/O complexity of $\Theta(\frac{N}{B})$ that can be achieved through trivial sequential access.
2. $sort(N)$ with an I/O complexity of $\Theta(\frac{N}{B} \log_{M/B} \frac{N}{B})$ that can be achieved through *External Merge* or *Distribution Sort*

Finite State Systems. One of the first efforts towards a search algorithm that works on external memory is due to Munagala and Ranade [22]. The authors presented an external memory Breadth First Search(BFS) algorithm for explicit graphs, i.e., the graphs that are completely available beforehand in the form of adjacency lists. For example, a road network. Later the algorithm has been adapted for the implicit graphs that are generated on-the-fly from an initial state and a set of rules/transitions, and has been called *delayed duplicate detection* for *frontier search*. Both of the these algorithms assume an unweighted and undirected graph and work on a similar principle. Let *Succ* be the successor generation function. The algorithms maintain BFS layers on disk[3]. Let $Open(j)$ represent the set of states at layer j. Layer $Open(j-1)$ is scanned and the set of successors is put into a buffer of size close to the main memory capacity. If the buffer becomes full, internal sorting followed by a scanning generates a sorted duplicate-free state sequence in the buffer that is flushed to disk. This results in a file with states belonging to depth j stored in the form of sorted buffers. To remove the duplicates, *external sorting* is applied to unify the buffers into one sorted file. Due to sorting, all duplicates will come close to each other and a simple scan is enough to generate a duplicate free file. One also has to eliminate/subtract previous layers from $Open(j)$ to avoid re-expansions. In [22], the authors argue that for undirected graphs, subtracting two previous layers is enough to guarantee that no state is expanded twice.

The process is repeated until $Open(j-1)$ becomes empty, or the goal has been found. Delayed duplicate detection applies $O(sort(|Succ(Open(j-1))|) + scan(|Open(j-1)| +$

---

[2] On the hardware level the block size B is fixed by the computer architecture. From the application program point of view it is possible to vary B according to the given resources. If only a constant number c of internal buffers are required, the block size can be scaled to $M = cB$.

[3] As BFS traverses the graph in layers, only two active files are needed, one for reading the expanded states and one for writing the generated states. To I/O optimally cope with sparse graphs, the BFS layers can be maintained in one large file together with file pointers locating their offsets and with two internal buffers for reading and writing. With respect to the previous footnote this implies that $M = 2B$.

$|Open(j-2)|))$ I/Os. Since each edge contributes to one state, $\sum_j |Succ(Open(j))| = O(|\mathcal{R}|)$ and $\sum_j |Open(j)| = O(|\mathcal{S}|)$. This gives a total I/O complexity of $O(sort(|\mathcal{R}|) + scan(|\mathcal{S}|))$ I/Os, which – assuming delayed duplicate detection on general state vectors is needed – proves to be optimal [3].

The algorithm shares similarities with internal *Frontier Search* [15,17] that was used for solving multiple sequence alignment problems, an idea that goes back to Hirschberg [12]. The sorting complexity can be improved in practice by using a hash-based delayed duplicate detection scheme. Frontier search has been used to fully explore the 15-Puzzle with 1.4 Terabytes of harddisk in about three weeks [16]. Since harddisk operations are several times slower than the internal operations, interleaving expansion and merging through threads also accelerated the performance. It has also been used to generate very large abstract state spaces that exceed main memory capacity [27].

4 External Search in Real-Time Systems

One of the involved differences between real-time reachability and ordinary reachability analysis is the *inclusion-check*. While in (delayed) duplicate elimination we omit all identical states from further consideration, in real-time model checking we have to check inclusions of the form $Z \subseteq Z'$ to detect duplicate states. Once Z is *closed under entailment*, in the sense that no constraint of Z can be strengthened without reducing the solution set, the time-complexity for inclusion checking is linear to the number of constraints in Z.

Subsequently, while porting real-time model checking algorithms to an external setting, we have to provide an option for the elimination of zones. Since we cannot define a *total* order on zones, trivial external sorting schemes are useless in our case. In our proposal of External Breadth First Search we exploit the fact that two states (l, Z) and (l', Z') are comparable only when $l = l'$. This motivates the definition of *zone union* $\mathcal{U}$ where all zones correspond to the states sharing a common discrete part l, and for all $Z, Z' \in \mathcal{U}$, we have $Z \not\subseteq Z'$.

Duplicate states can now be removed by first sorting with respect to the discrete part l, which will bring all states sharing the same l close together, and then doing a one-to-one comparison among all such states. The result of this phase is a file where states are sorted according to the discrete parts l forming duplicate free zone unions.

However, the one-to-one comparison of all the zones for a particular l can only be performed I/O-efficiently when all the states sharing the same l can be read into the main memory. Throughout this presentation, we assume that this requirement holds. The same approach of internalizing zone unions is available during set refinement with respect to predecessor files. We load both the zone union from the predecessor file and the one in the unrefined file and check for the entailment condition.

State spaces that appear in model checking are usually directed and hence just removing duplicates with respect to the last previous two layers is not sufficient. The crucial complexity parameter is the locality or duplicate elimination scope as defined in [26], which defines the number of previous levels to be considered. In the text, this notion of locality for an automaton A is referred to as *locality(A)*. Let Z_0 denotes the

Procedure External Breadth First Search
Input: A timed automata $A = (S, l_0, R, Inv, T)$; a symbolic initial state (l_0, Z_0).
begin
  $Open(0) \leftarrow \{(l_0, Z_0)\}$;; START WITH THE INITIAL STATE
  $j \leftarrow 1$
  while $(Open(j - 1) \neq \emptyset)$
    $A(j) \leftarrow Succ(Open(j - 1))$
    forall $(l, Z) \in A(j)$;; ITERATE ON ALL SUCCESSORS
      if $(l \cap T \neq \emptyset)$;; GOAL FOUND
        return $ConstructSolution()$;; RETURN SOLUTION
    $A'(j) \leftarrow$ *remove redundant zones within* $A(j)$;; DUPLICATES WITHIN THE LAYER
    for $loc \leftarrow 1$ **to** $locality(A)$;; DUPLICATES SEEN IN PREVIOUS LAYERS
      $A''(j) \leftarrow A'(j) \backslash$
        $\{(l, Z') \in Open(j - loc) \mid (l, Z) \in A'(j), Z \subseteq Z'\}$
    $Open(j) \leftarrow A''(j)$
    $j \leftarrow j + 1$
end

Fig. 1. External Breadth First Search: (l_0, Z_0) is the initial state of the timed automaton A and T are the desired goal states

empty zone. The locality of a directed search graph with (l_0, Z_0) being the start state is defined as

$$\max\{\delta((l_0, Z_0), (l, Z)) - \delta((l_0, Z_0), (l', Z'))\} + 1$$

for all states (l, Z), (l', Z'), with (l', Z') being a successor of (l, Z) and δ being the shortest-path distance between two states. For undirected graphs the above equation evaluates to 2 – validating the proof of Munagala and Ranade.

In Figure 1, we depict the pseudo-code of the algorithm that performs an External Breadth First Search on real-time systems with *symbolic states* representation. There is no hash-table involve in the algorithm but we rely on alternative duplicates removal techniques. Starting with the initial state, the algorithm performs generates all the nodes of layer $j - 1$ generating the successors in layer $j - 1$. Duplicates are removed in two steps: removing all the redundant zones from within a layer, and wrt. *locality*(A) many previous layers. The sets A, A', and A'' act as temporary sets. Each set is mapped to a file and a corresponding internal memory buffer. New states are first inserted into the buffer and flushed to the file once the buffer is full.

For a timed automaton A with S as the set of states and R the set of transitions in a real-time system A, we obtain the following worst-case I/O complexity of External Breadth First Search.

Theorem 1. *For the problem of symbolic reachability in timed automata, if all zone unions individually fit into the main memory External Breadth First Search for can be executed in $O(\text{sort}(|R|) + \text{locality}(A) \cdot \text{scan}(|S|))$ I/Os.*

Proof. The proof extends the I/O complexity of external Breadth-First search for undirected graphs. For directed graphs, the duplicate elimination scope is equal to

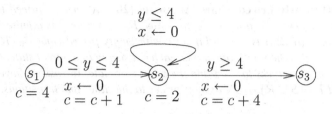

Fig. 2. Example of a priced timed automaton.

locality(A), which, in turn, effects the number of layers that we have to scan in order to remove all the duplicates.   □

The memory assumption is almost always fulfilled in practice, as current amounts of main memory can maintain several millions of zones. If some zone unions still fail to fit into main memory, we have to rescan the zone unions in one file again and again. If the size of the largest zone union is $\mathcal{U}_{max}$, this will accumulate to $O(locality(A) \cdot \frac{|E|}{\mathcal{U}_{max}} \cdot scan(\mathcal{U}_{max})^2)$ I/Os in the worst case for checking the duplicates in the previous layer and for compacting a sorted file.

4.1 Linearly Priced Timed Automata

Linearly Priced Timed Automata (LPTA) are timed automata with (linear) cost variables. For the sake of brevity, we restrict their introduction to one cost variable c. Cost increases at states with respect to a predefined rate and in transitions with respect to an update operation. The cost-optimal reachability problem is to find a trajectory that minimizes the overall path costs. Figure 2 shows a timed automata with 3 states s_1 (*init*), s_2 (*intermediate*), s_3 (*goal*) with two clock variables x and y and the clock constraints defined on the transitions. The rate of cost variable c is 4 at s_1 and 2 at state s_2. The minimum cost of reaching location s_3 with cost 13 correspond to the trajectory $(d(0), t_1, d(4), t_2)$ of waiting 0 steps in s_1 and then taking the transition to s_2, where four time steps are spent until the transition to the goal in s_3.

Similar to the timed automata, for LPTAs we use the notion of priced zone to represent the symbolic states. Let Δ_Z be the unique clock valuation of Z such that for all $u \in Z$ and $\forall x \in C$, we have, $\Delta_Z \leq u(x)$, i.e., it represents the lowest corner of the $|C|$-dimensional hypersurface representing a zone. In the following, we Δ_Z is referred as the zone offset.

For the internal state representation, we exploit the fact that prices are linear cost hyperplanes of zones. A *priced zone* $\mathcal{Z}$ is a triple (Z, c, r), where Z is a zone, integer c describes the cost of Δ_Z and $r : C \to \mathbb{Z}$ gives the rate for a given clock. In other words, prices of zones are defined by the respective slopes that the cost function hyperplane has in the direction of the clock variable axes. Furthermore, with $f : \mathcal{Z} \to \mathbb{Z}$, we denote the cost evaluation function based on priced zones $\mathcal{Z}$. The cost value f for a given clock $x \in C$ in the priced zone $\mathcal{Z} = (Z, c, r)$ can then be computed as $c + \sum_{x \in C} r(x)(v(x) - \Delta_z(x))$. Formally, a priced timed automata can be described as follows:

Definition 2 (Linearly Priced Timed Automata [20]). *A linearly priced timed automaton* $\mathcal{A}$ *over clocks* C *is a tuple* $(S, l_0, \mathcal{R}, \text{Inv}, P, \mathcal{T})$, *where* S *is a finite set of automata locations,* $(l_0, \mathcal{Z}_0)$ *is the initial state with empty priced zone* $\mathcal{Z}_0$, $\mathcal{R} \subseteq S \times \mathcal{B}(C) \times \mathcal{P}(C) \times S$ *is the set of transitions, each consisting of a parent state, the guard on the transition, the clocks to reset and the successor state,* Inv *assigns invariants to locations, and* $P : (S \cup \mathcal{R}) \rightarrow I\!N$ *assigns prices to the states and transitions.*

5   External Breadth First Branch-and-Boundin Priced Real-Time Systems

Until now, we have been mainly discussing external search in directed and unweighted state spaces. But, as we move towards priced real-time systems where timed automata are extended with a cost variable, we find ourselves dealing with a weighted state space. Moreover, we are no longer interested in just some path to a particular goal state, but in an optimal path with respect to our new cost variable.

In priced real-time systems, cost f is a monotonically increasing function implying that for all $(u, v) \in \mathcal{R}$, we have $f(u) \leq f(v)$. If f^* is the optimal solution cost, the following definition captures the notion of cost-optimality for a set of goals T and a start state $(l_0, \mathcal{Z}_0)$.

Definition 3. *(Cost-Optimality) An algorithm is* Cost-Optimal, *if and only if, it terminates with a state* $t \in T$ *and* $f(t) = f^*$.

In such directed and weighted graphs, BFS does not guarantee an optimal solution. A natural extension of BFS is to continue the search when a goal is found and keep on searching until a *better* goal is found or the state space is exhausted. A Branch-and-Bound (BnB) search algorithm is an extension to an uninformed search algorithm that does not stop when it finds the first goal, but instead *prunes* all the states that do not improve on the last solution cost. Given that the cost function is monotone, which is the case with f, BnB always terminates with an optimal solution.

The main traversal policy of a Branch-and-Bound algorithm can be borrowed from either breadth-first search, depth-first search, or best-first search. A Best-First BnB algorithm, though very well suited for small-sized problems can create a bottleneck for larger problems. Best-first search picks a state u such that for all $v \in Open$, we have $f(u) \leq f(v)$, for the next expansion. This selection criteria calls for a much larger horizon to be saved in the memory as compared to the Breadth First Search or a Depth First Search. Moreover, both depth-first and best-first traversal policies show no locality in the way they expand states - unlike Breadth First Search , where every state in a layer j is expanded before any state of the layer $j + 1$. This property makes Breadth First Search a good candidate for branch-and-bound.

Because of being in a weighted state space, we have to pay an overhead by reopening already seen states. Consider the following example as illustrated in Fig. 3. A Breadth-First search visits state v for the first time (top right copy) and stores it. Goal state g is also visited and its cost is saved. When the search reaches state v for the second time along a longer path (bottom left copy), but this time with a better cost, v will be pruned away while subtracting previous layers and g will never be reached. If the

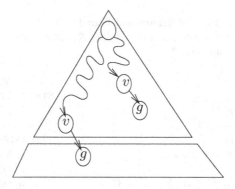

Fig. 3. Anomaly in the Breadth-First Branch-and-Bound. g is a goal state

new path to g has a better cost, we lose our claim for optimality. Due to this anomaly, the duplicate detection policy has to be adapted to make it compatible with weighted state spaces. Now we are not allowed to remove a duplicate state if its cost is better than what we have seen earlier.

Definition 4. **Duplicate state in priced domains** $(l, \mathcal{Z})$ *is a duplicate state of* $(l', \mathcal{Z}')$ *if and only if* $l = l'$, $\mathcal{Z} \subseteq \mathcal{Z}'$ *and* $f(\mathcal{Z}) \geq f(\mathcal{Z}')$.

In Figure 4, we formulate our discussion on External Breadth First Branch-and-Bound in pseudo-code. The set *Open* represents the BFS layer and the sets A, A' and A'' are temporary variables to construct the search frontier for the next iteration. Initially the goal cost *Cost* is initialized with ∞ and a goal state with a better value is searched in the successor set $A(j)$. States with a higher value than the best goal cost are pruned and saved in $A'(j)$. In the next step, we remove redundant states based on our definition of duplicate states.

The working of the algorithm is depicted in Figure 5. On x-axis we denote the layers of Breadth First exploration. Each layer is sorted with increasing cost value. Upon arriving at the first goal t_1, the next layer is pruned to only consider the nodes that have a better cost value. The exploration terminates when the last goal t_4 with the minimal cost value is expanded and no successor of t_4 improves the cost.

The I/O complexity of External Breadth First Branch-and-Bound algorithm depends on the number of times a state is re-expanded. The worst-case scenario is when the whole state space fits into one layer and the next layer has the same states but with better cost values. The following theorem states the cost-optimality and I/O complexity of the algorithm.

Theorem 2. *For the problem of cost-optimal symbolic reachability in priced timed automata with monotonic costs, if all zone unions individually fit into the main memory, External Breadth First Branch-and-Bound is* Cost-Optimal *and can be executed in* $O(D \cdot (sort(|\mathcal{R}|) + \text{locality}(\mathcal{A}) \cdot scan(|\mathcal{S}|)))$ *I/Os, where D is the maximal depth explored.*

Proof. Since External Breadth First Branch-and-Bound expands at least all states $(l, \mathcal{Z})$ with $f(l, \mathcal{Z}) < f^*$, the algorithm terminates with the optimal solution. The *I/O*

Procedure External Breadth First Branch-and-Bound
Input: A linearly priced timed automaton $\mathcal{A} = (\mathcal{S}, l_0, \mathcal{R}, Inv, P, \mathcal{T})$;
        A symbolic initial state $(l_0, \mathcal{Z}_0)$.
begin
    $Cost \leftarrow \infty; j \leftarrow 1$;; BEST GOAL COST IS ∞
    $Open(0) \leftarrow \{(l_0, \mathcal{Z}_0)\}$;; START WITH THE INITIAL STATE
    while $(Open(j - 1) \neq \emptyset)$
      $A(j) \leftarrow Succ(Open(j - 1))$
      forall $(l, \mathcal{Z}) \in A(j)$;; ITERATE ON ALL SUCCESSORS
        if $(l \cap \mathcal{T} \neq \emptyset \wedge f(\mathcal{Z}) < Cost)$;; ANOTHER GOAL FOUND
          $Cost \leftarrow f(\mathcal{Z})$;; COST OF THE NEW GOAL
      $A'(j) \leftarrow A(j) \setminus \{(l, \mathcal{Z}) \in A(j) \mid f(\mathcal{Z}) \geq Cost\}$;; PRUNE THE EXPENSIVE STATES
      $A''(j) \leftarrow$ remove redundant zones within $A'(j)$;; DUPLICATES WITHIN THE LAYER
      for $loc \leftarrow 1$ **to** $locality(\mathcal{A})$;; DUPLICATES SEEN IN PREVIOUS LAYERS
        $A''(j) \leftarrow A''(j) \setminus$
          $\{(l, \mathcal{Z}') \in Open(j - loc) \mid (l, \mathcal{Z}) \in A''(j), \mathcal{Z} \subseteq \mathcal{Z}' \wedge f(\mathcal{Z}) \geq f(\mathcal{Z}')\}$
      $Open(j) \leftarrow A''(j)$
      $j \leftarrow j + 1$
    if $(Cost \neq \infty)$
      return $ConstructSolution()$;; CONSTRUCT SOLUTION IF FOUND
end

Fig. 4. External Breadth First Branch-and-Bound: $(l_0, \mathcal{Z}_0)$ is the symbolic initial state of the graph $\mathcal{A}$ and $\mathcal{T}$ are the desired goal states

complexity of the algorithm is inherited from the External Breadth First Search search (cf. Theorem 1). The factor D is introduced due to re-openings.   □

Furthermore, we can say that if there are several goal states in the state space with different solution costs, then an External Breadth First Branch-and-Bound run will explore at most as many states as a complete External Breadth First Search run.

Lemma 1. *If m is the number of states expanded by External Breadth First Branch-and-Bound and n is the number of states expanded by a complete exploration of External Breadth First Search, then $m \leq n$.*

Proof. External Breadth First Branch-and-Bound does not change the order in which states are looked at during a complete External Breadth First Search exploration. There can be two cases:

1. $|\mathcal{T}| = 1$: There exist just one goal state t which is also the last state in a breadth-first search tree. For this case clearly $n = m$.
2. $|\mathcal{T}| > 1$: There exists more than one goal state in the search tree. Let $t_1, t_2 \in \mathcal{T}$ be the two goal states with $f(t_1) > f(t_2) = f^*$ and $depth(t_1) < depth(t_2)$. Since t_1 will be expanded first, $f(t_1)$ will be used as the pruning value during the next iterations. In case, there does not exists any state u in the search tree between t_1 and t_2 with $f(u) > f(t_2)$, $n = m$, else $m < n$.

                                                                            □

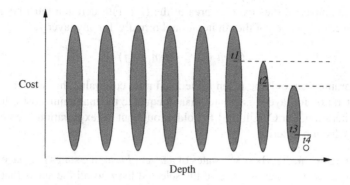

Fig. 5. A sample run of External Breadth First Branch-and-Bound; the t_i's represent different goals

The behaviour of External Breadth First Branch-and-Bound largely depends on how fast it reaches to some solution so that it can use that solution cost to further prune away the search space. Their exists a very trivial solution to this problem where the user provides some upper bound U on the solution cost that can be used for pruning. In case the upper bound U is actually equal to the optimal solution cost f^*, the algorithm is trivially *Cost-Optimal*.

Lemma 2. *External Breadth First Branch-and-Bound with $U = f^*$ is* Cost-Optimal.

Since the cost function f in our real-time domain is monotonically increasing, i.e., for all $(u, v) \in \mathcal{R}$, we have $f(u) \leq f(v)$, we will never prune any node that can ultimately take us to the goal node.

6 Iterative Broadening External Breadth First Branch-and-Bound

We observe that the efficiency of External Breadth First Branch-and-Bound is inversely proportional to the factor $U - f^*$. The more realistic the upper bound is, the bigger the pruning and, hence, the lesser the number of expansions. This observation guides us to an iterative strategy to find a good upper bound. We suggest to use only the first $k\%$ of the states when sorted with respect to the increasing cost value and discard the rest of the states in the layer. Hopefully, the algorithm will terminate with a solution, giving us a good upper bound on the optimal solution cost. Using the found solution cost as the upper bound for an increased value of k, we hope to converge to optimal solution cost when k approaches to 100. We will refer the parameter k as the beam width.

Unfortunately, there is an apparent problem with this approach. It is possible that for a particular iteration we arrive at a goal state, but at the next iteration we do not. This problem is more frequent in real-time domains, where there can be many different states with the same f-value, residing in a set that has no total order. The algorithm is not guaranteed to converge with increasing k (exception is when $k = 100\%$ and the whole state space is considered). Let k_i be the value of k in the ith iteration. For the algorithm to converge, the coverage area of the $(i + 1)$th iteration must be at least as large as the coverage area of the ith iteration. Formally, for any layer j,

$$Open_i(j) \subseteq Open_{i+1}(j) \tag{1}$$

Such a guarantee can only be given if the maximum cost value that was chosen in the $(i+1)$th iteration for layer j is greater than or equal to the maximum cost value chosen in the i-th iteration. For Condition 1 to hold throughout the exploration, we propose the following selection criterion.

Selection Criterion. The best $k\%$ states of a layer *plus* all the states that have the same f-value as that of the last state of the selected list *plus* all the states that have the smaller f-value as that of the maximum selected f-value of the last iteration.

With this selection criterion, for a particular cost f', we either choose all the states with a f value equal to f' or choose none.

Figure 6 shows the pseudo-code for the actual exploration involving upper bound pruning and the above mentioned selection criteria. The parameters of the algorithms are the beam width k (in percent), the upper bound U and the vector $F_{\max}$ of maximal f-values from the last iteration. With successive iterations, the value of k is increased and the solution cost value of the previous iteration is used as an upper bound. The set *Open* denotes the search frontier, sliced into layers as before. The sets A, A' and A'' are temporary sets, to construct the search frontier for the next iteration. Both the new *Cost* and the new vector of maximal f-values are returned. We use π_n to denote the n-th element in the sorted permutation of a set.

6.1   Correctness

Let U'_i be the cost of the solution found by Iterative Broadening External Breadth First Branch-and-Bound in the ith iteration with $k = k_i$ and $U = U_i$ as the arguments. In the following, we show that the algorithm converges for increasing value of k.

Lemma 3. *The selection criterion for Iterative Broadening External Breadth First Branch-and-Bound guarantees the coverage condition for every iteration i.*

Proof. We prove it by induction on the layer j. For $j = 0$, $Open_i(0) \subseteq Open_{i+1}(0)$. Assume that it holds for layer $j - 1$ i.e, $Open_i(j - 1) \subseteq Open_{i+1}(j - 1)$. Generating the successor sets for both sides of the relation yields $Succ(Open_i(j - 1)) \subseteq Succ(Open_{i+1}(j - 1))$. Removing duplicates from the successor sets on both sides does not change the subset condition. Now we turn to pruning. The selection criteria guarantees that the values $F^j_{\max}$ increase monotonically for increasing value of i, i.e., $F^j_{i,\max} \leq F^j_{i+1,\max}$. Moreover cost plateaux are completely searched. Therefore, pruning does not change the subset condition, so that $Open_i(j) \subseteq Open_{i+1}(j)$. $\qquad\square$

Lemma 4. *For all iterations i in Iterative Broadening External Breadth First Branch-and-Bound, we have $U'_{i+1} \leq U'_i$.*

Procedure Iterative Broadening External Breadth First Branch-and-Bound$(k, U, F_{\max})$
Input: A linearly priced timed automaton $\mathcal{A} = (\mathcal{S}, l_0, \mathcal{R}, \mathit{Inv}, P, \mathcal{T})$;
  A symbolic initial state $(l_0, \mathcal{Z}_0)$.
begin
  $Cost \leftarrow U; \ j \leftarrow 1$;; BEST GOAL COST IS U
  $Open(0) \leftarrow \{(l_0, \mathcal{Z}_0)\}$;; ALWAYS SART WITH THE INITIAL STATE
  while $(Open(j-1) \neq \emptyset)$
   $A(j) \leftarrow Succ(Open(j-1))$
   forall $(l, \mathcal{Z}) \in A(j)$;; ITERATE ON ALL SUCCESSORS
    if $(l \cap \mathcal{T} \neq \emptyset \wedge f(\mathcal{Z}) < Cost)$;; ANOTHER GOAL FOUND
     $Cost \leftarrow f(\mathcal{Z})$;; COST OF THE NEW GOAL
   $A'(j) \leftarrow A(j) \setminus \{(l, \mathcal{Z}) \in A(j) \mid f(\mathcal{Z}) \geq Cost\}$;; PRUNE THE EXPENSIVE STATES
   $A''(j) \leftarrow$ remove redundant zones within $A'(j)$;; DUPLICATES WITHIN THE LAYER
   for $loc \leftarrow 1$ **to** $locality(\mathcal{A})$;; DUPLICATES SEEN IN PREVIOUS LAYERS
    $A''(j) \leftarrow A''(j) \setminus$
     $\{(l, \mathcal{Z}') \in Open(j - loc) \mid (l, \mathcal{Z}) \in A''(j), \mathcal{Z} \subseteq \mathcal{Z}' \wedge f(\mathcal{Z}) \geq f(\mathcal{Z}')\}$
   $A''(j) \leftarrow$ External-sort $A''(j)$ w.r.t the cost function f
   $n \leftarrow \lfloor (k \cdot |A''(j)|)/100 \rfloor$;; THERE ARE n MANY STATES IN THE BEST $k\%$
   $(l_n, \mathcal{Z}_n) \leftarrow \pi_n(A''(j))$;; PICK THE n-TH STATE
   $F_{\max}^j \leftarrow \max\{F_{\max}^j, f(\mathcal{Z}_n)\}$;; COMPUTE THE NEW MAX F VALUE FOR THE LAYER
   $Open(j) \leftarrow \{(l, \mathcal{Z}) \in A''(j) \mid f(\mathcal{Z}) \leq F_{\max}^j\}$;; KEEP ONLY THE *best* STATES
   $j \leftarrow j + 1$
  if $(Cost < U)$;; IF THE BOUND HAS IMPROVED CONSTRUCT THE SOLUTION
   $ConstructSolution()$
  return $Cost, F_{\max}$;; RETURN NEW UPPER BOUND
end

Fig. 6. Iterative Broadening External Breadth First Branch-and-Bound. k represents beam width, U the upper bound, and $F_{\max}$ represents the maximum cost used in each layer during the last iteration. $(l_0, \mathcal{Z}_0)$ is the symbolic initial state of the priced timed automata $\mathcal{A}$ and $\mathcal{T}$ are the desired goal states.

Proof. Since the coverage area of iteration $i + 1$ is larger than the coverage area of iteration i, in the worst case it does not improve on the solution quality i.e., $U'_{i+1} = U'_i \leq U_i$, else we have $U'_{i+1} \leq U'_i \leq U_i$. In both cases, $U'_{i+1} \leq U'_i$.   □

Theorem 3. *Iterative Broadening External Breadth First Branch-and-Bound converges to the optimal solution.*

Proof. Lemma 3 provides the necessary ground for the coverage of whole state space, which implies the completeness of the algorithm and Lemma 4 provides the convergence to the optimal solution cost that proves its optimality.   □

7 Experiments

We have implemented the algorithms External Breadth First Branch-and-Bound, and Iterative Broadening External Breadth First Branch-and-Bound on top of UPPAAL CORA.

Table 1. ALS with 1 runway and 10 planes (left), and with 2 runways and 20 planes (right)

k	U	U'	Expanded		k	U	U'	Expanded
1	∞	970	91		0.1	∞	1940	1,060
20	970	970	91		20	1940	1940	1,285
40	970	810	125		40	1940	1420	18142
60	810	710	281		60	1420	1410	69,341
80	710	700	439		80	1410	1410	147,128
100	700	700	577		100	1410	1400	195,145
100	∞	700	31,458		100	∞	—	—

Our implementation also extends UPPAAL making it capable to perform External Breadth First Search in timed automata. The main memory requirements are kept constant.[4] Hash tables are replaced by files on harddisk with a small internal buffer for I/O efficiency. As the maximum file size on most file systems is 2GB, we also provide large file support, that splits files if they become too large. Trails for found solutions are reconstructed by saving the predecessor together with every state, by using backtracking along the stored files, and by looking for matching predecessors. This results in a I/O complexity that is at most linear to the number of stored states.

A limited functionality (which nonetheless does not compromise the correctness of the approach) of the current implementation is on the duplicate detection scope and on external sorting. We remove duplicates from the internal buffer before flushing it but the duplicates within different flushed buffers are not merged. All experiments are run on a Pentium-4 with 150 GB of harddisk space and 2GB RAM running Linux. We chose different instances of aircraft landing scheduling (ALS), for which [5] presented a UPPAAL CORA model. It involves considering a timed automaton for each of the airplane and runways.

We start with a smaller instance involving just 1 runway and 10 planes. Table 1 (left) provides the results of running Iterative Broadening External Breadth First Branch-and-Bound. Here k denotes the coverage, U the initial bound and U' the optimal solution obtained. The behaviour of pruning on the number of expanded states is quite evident. We also see a converging behaviour of the algorithm. In the last row we report the results for External Breadth First Branch-and-Bound to show the effect of pruning on the search space. Our result matches with the one found by UPPAAL CORA. Table 1 (right) illustrates the results for the instance, where we created two independent automata for runways and planes. We then instantiated 1 runway and 10 planes from the first type and 1 runway and 10 planes from the other. UPPAAL CORA with internal BnB cannot solve the instance because of memory requirements. Being an exact dual, the solution has to be 1400, which validates our implementation. With Iterative Broadening, we were able to find an optimal solution. On the other hand, External Breadth First Branch-and-Boundcould not finalize its execution in two hours consuming about 3 GB with 280 bytes per state, while expanding depth 19 - optimal solution lies at depth 40. The process was manually killed.

---

[4] Up to a leak of at most 100 MB per hour.

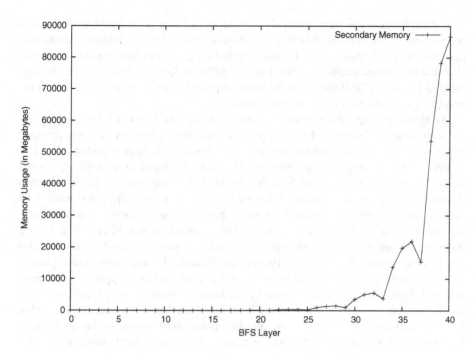

Fig. 7. Space consumption for each BFS Layer

For the third instance, we chose another instance of aircraft scheduling problem that was obtained by a translation from PDDL planning models [7]. The internal version of UPPAAL CORA failed to reach any solution for 3 planes and after quickly consuming about 1.6 GB of main memory started to swap on harddisk. For this instance just for 3 planes a total of 13 clocks were used. Our iterative broadening strategy, for $k <$ 100 didn't produce any solution. For $k = 100$, the algorithm ran for about 12 hours consuming a total of 311 GB and ran out of harddisk space using a mere 2KB per state. On a harddisk with just 150 GB available, this was achieved by removing the previous layers manually. Up till the 40th layer there was no solution. In Fig. 7, we depict the graph where space consumption for each layer is shown. The internal size of the program remained under 1.8 GB.

8 Conclusion

We have seen an approach for large scale scheduling based on external exploration on priced timed automata. We contributed two algorithms: *External Breadth First Branch-and-Bound* and *Iterative Broadening External Breadth First Branch-and-Bound*. Both algorithms perform an external Breadth First Search on the search space and preserve optimality of the computed cost values. Having performed an exploration of more than a quarter of a Terabyte, we believe to have pushed the limits of practical scheduling and model-checking in real-time domains.

The exploration can be performed on multiple disks, as sorting and searching can be distributed with optimal I/O efficiency. As external exploration realizes a controlled streamed access to states, there is also potential for a parallel implementation. A parallel and distributed reachability checking algorithm of UPPAAL based on the *Message Passing Interface* (MPI) partitions the list of explored states using a simple hash function [4]. It restricts itself to blind exploration.

We have not talked about heuristic search, although the UPPAAL CORA models incorporate hand-coded search heuristics to accelerate the exploration. A recent proposal to generate heuristics for UPPAAL automatically has recently been provided by [19].

Iterative Broadening has been introduced by [10]. The Breadth First BnB approach is related to Breadth-First Heuristic Search (BFHS) [26], a frontier search method that was designed to save internal memory. It is based on the observation that the Breadth First Search frontier is often much smaller than the best-first search frontier. A recent extension of BFHS is its integration with beam search known as Beam-Stack Search [28]. As it iterates on different beams, this algorithm is a natural competitor for Iterative Broadening External Breadth First Branch-and-Bound. This algorithm is also guaranteed to continously converge. There are several differences to our approach. The beam width in Beam-Stack Search is driven by the limits of main memory (previous layers can be flushed to the harddisk). Such a limit is not needed in our case, as we exploit the secondary storage. Therefore, we introduce parameter k to control the beam width. Moreover, a backtracking strategy is employed to pick more elements from the previous layer in case the upper bound is not improved.

The approach we are currently working on, splits the layer that is being expanded, into several ones, and distributes the work among different processors. As states can be expanded independently of each other, a speedup is expected.

References

1. Aggarwal, A., Vitter, J.S.: The input/output complexity of sorting and related problems. Journal of the ACM 31(9), 1116–1127 (1988)
2. Alur, R., Dill, D.L.: A theory of timed automata. Theoretical Computer Science 126(2), 183–235 (1994)
3. Arge, L., Knudsen, M., Larsen, K.: Sorting multisets and vectors in-place. In: Dehne, F., Sack, J.-R., Santoro, N. (eds.) WADS 1993. LNCS, vol. 709, pp. 83–94. Springer, Heidelberg (1993)
4. Behrman, G., Fehnker, A., Vaandrager, F.: Distributed timed model checking - how the search order matters. In: Emerson, E.A., Sistla, A.P. (eds.) CAV 2000. LNCS, vol. 1855, Springer, Heidelberg (2000)
5. Behrmann, G., Larsen, K.G., Rasmussen, J.I.: Optimal scheduling using priced timed automata. In: ICAPS Workshop on Verification and Validation of Model-Based Planning and Scheduling Systems (2005)
6. Cassez, F., David, A., Fleury, E., Larsen, K.G., Lime, D.: Efficient on-the-fly algorithms for the analysis of timed games. In: Abadi, M., de Alfaro, L. (eds.) CONCUR 2005. LNCS, vol. 3653, Springer, Heidelberg (2005)
7. Dierks, H.: Finding optimal plans for domains with restricted continuous effects with cora. In: ICAPS Workshop on Verification and Validation of Model-Based Planning and Scheduling Systems (2005)

8. Edelkamp, S., Jabbar, S.: Large-scale directed model checking LTL. In: Valmari, A. (ed.) Model Checking Software. LNCS, vol. 3925, pp. 1–18. Springer, Heidelberg (2006)
9. Edelkamp, S., Jabbar, S., Schroedl, S.: External A*. In: German Conference on Artificial Intelligence (KI), pp. 226–240 (2004)
10. Ginsberg, M., Harvey, W.: Iterative broadening. Artificial Intelligence, pp. 367–383 (1992)
11. Henzinger, T.A., Kopke, P.W., Puri, A., Varaiya, P.: What's decidable about hybrid automata? In: ACM STOC, pp. 373–381 (1995)
12. Hirschberg, D.S.: A linear space algorithm for computing common subsequences. Communications of the ACM 18(6), 341–343 (1975)
13. Jabbar, S., Edelkamp, S.: I/O efficient directed model checking. In: Cousot, R. (ed.) VMCAI 2005. LNCS, vol. 3385, pp. 313–329. Springer, Heidelberg (2005)
14. Jabbar, S., Edelkamp, S.: Parallel external directed model checking with linear I/O. In: Emerson, E.A., Namjoshi, K.S. (eds.) VMCAI 2006. LNCS, vol. 3855, pp. 237–251. Springer, Heidelberg (2006)
15. Korf, R.E.: Divide-and-conquer bidirectional search: First results. In: IJCAI, pp. 1184–1191 (1999)
16. Korf, R.E., Schultze, P.: Large-scale parallel breadth-first search. In: AAAI, pp. 1380–1385 (2005)
17. Korf, R.E., Zhang, W.: Divide-and-conquer frontier search applied to optimal sequence allignment. In: AAAI, pp. 910–916 (2000)
18. Kristensen, L., Mailund, T.: Path finding with the sweep-line method using external storage. In: Dong, J.S., Woodcock, J. (eds.) ICFEM 2003. LNCS, vol. 2885, pp. 319–337. Springer, Heidelberg (2003)
19. Kupferschmid, S., Hoffmann, J., Dierks, H., Behrmann, G.: Adapting an AI planning heuristic for directed model checking. In: Valmari, A. (ed.) Model Checking Software. LNCS, vol. 3925, pp. 35–52. Springer, Heidelberg (2006)
20. Larsen, K.G., Behrmann, G., Brinksma, E., Fehnker, A., Hune, T.S., Petterson, P., Romijn, J.: As cheap as possible: Efficient cost-optimal reachability for priced timed automata. In: Berry, G., Comon, H., Finkel, A. (eds.) CAV 2001. LNCS, vol. 2102, pp. 493–505. Springer, Heidelberg (2001)
21. Larsen, K.G., Larsson, F., Petterson, P., Yi, W.: Efficient verification of real-time systems: Compact data structures and state-space reduction. In: IEEE Real Time Systems Symposium, pp. 14–24 (1997)
22. Munagala, K., Ranade, A.: I/O-complexity of graph algorithms. In: SODA, pp. 687–694 (1999)
23. Rasmussen, J.I., Larsen, K.G., Subramani, K.: Resource-optimal scheduling using priced timed automata. In: Jensen, K., Podelski, A. (eds.) TACAS 2004. LNCS, vol. 2988, pp. 220–235. Springer, Heidelberg (2004)
24. Sanders, P., Meyer, U., Sibeyn, J.F.: Algorithms for Memory Hierarchies. Springer, Heidelberg (2002)
25. Stern, U., Dill, D.: Using magnetic disk instead of main memory in the murphi verifier. In: Vardi, M.Y. (ed.) CAV 1998. LNCS, vol. 1427, pp. 172–183. Springer, Heidelberg (1998)
26. Zhou, R., Hansen, E.: Breadth-first heuristic search. In: ICAPS, pp. 92–100 (2004)
27. Zhou, R., Hansen, E.: External-memory pattern databases using structured duplicate detection. In: AAAI (2005)
28. Zhou, R., Hansen, E.A.: Beam-stack search: Integrating backtracking with beam search. In: ICAPS, pp. 90–98 (2005)

Checking Liveness Properties of Concurrent Systems by Reinforcement Learning

Tadashi Araragi[1] and Seung Mo Cho[2]

[1] NTT Communication Science Laboratories, Nippon Telegraph and Telephone
Corporation, Japan
[2] Division of Computer Science, Samsung Electronics Co., Korea
araragi@cslab.kecl.ntt.co.jp

Abstract. In this paper, we propose a new method of testing concurrent systems by using an artificial intelligence technique: reinforcement learning. In particular, the method verifies the liveness properties given in temporal logic formulas and dynamically controls a target system in runtime monitoring to efficiently reveal possible error against specification. In this control, the learning method accumulates necessary information by monitoring the running system. We built a simulator to evaluate this idea and conducted experiments with simple examples. As a result we showed the effectiveness of this approach for solving the difficult problem of testing the liveness properties of concurrent systems.

1 Introduction

The rapid development of the Internet has increased the need to foster more distributed concurrent systems for creating new services. Such systems provide services to a huge number of clients, and sometimes these independently developed systems use each other. Therefore, bugs in one system may have serious consequences on a wide range of clients and other systems. On the other hand, guaranteeing the correctness of concurrent systems is very difficult, since an enormous number of executions are possible depending on the timing of asynchronous communication between processes in the systems. Therefore, much work has been conducted to achieve assurance.

Formal methods and testing, the two major techniques used to guarantee the correctness of concurrent systems, have both advantages and disadvantages. Formal methods allow high-level abstract requirement specifications and fully verify them against a given protocol of concurrent systems using logical calculations. However, this technique can only be applied to systems of limited size, because it requires much computational power and resources. Testing, in contrast, can deal with large-scale systems by using runtime monitoring of instrumented systems. On the other hand, requirement specifications can be system-dependent, and the method cannot verify all possible executions of the systems. Therefore, it may miss some crucial exceptions.

A third approach has emerged that combines both techniques to overcome weaknesses. Specification-based monitoring (e.g., [6]) can deal with high-level

S. Edelkamp and A. Lomuscio (Eds.): MoChart IV, LNAI 4428, pp. 84–94, 2007.

requirement specifications for runtime monitoring. Moreover, model checking techniques of formal methods can be introduced to such runtime monitoring, especially for checking the liveness property of a system, which is usually more difficult than safety property in testing ([5]).

In this paper, we adopt this third approach and focus on finding rare but crucial exceptions while checking liveness properties. This overcomes one weakness of testing that has been neglected. In our method, when a requirement specification is given in a restricted LTL formula, we dynamically control the execution of concurrent systems by using a well-known AI technique, a reinforcement learning method to produce evidence of specification violations. In particular, in the produced evidential traces, fair execution among the processes in the system must be guaranteed. By coding the likeliness of violating a given specification and fairness among processes in the framework of reinforcement learning, we can find a fair execution that invalidates the specification.

This paper is organized as follows. In Section 2, we briefly explain requirement specifications and reinforcement learning, especially Q-learning. In Section 3, we show the basic framework of our method as well as the design of our learning algorithm and its implementation. In Section 4, we show two example models and experimental results along with some of their implications. In Section 5, we present discussion and a conclusion.

2   Research Background

2.1   Testing of Liveness Properties in Temporal Formulas

Two types of previous works share similarity with ours. The first is the field of the dynamic analysis of concurrent systems (e.g., [4], [6]). Given a temporal logic specification, such analyses execute the systems under tests and monitor the resulting execution traces to find a specification violation. However, all currently available dynamic analysis systems can only analyze safety properties. Because dynamic analysis is expected to produce results from the traces of finite executions, it is commonly believed that the scope of the analysis is inevitably limited to safety properties.

The second similar approach is the concept recently developed by Holzmann [5] in which liveness properties can also be the target of dynamic analysis. Using Büchi automata translated from LTL specifications representing liveness properties, we can detect the occurrence of a cycle of Büchi automata in the trace. This means that the system at least has the possibility of falling into a cycle that violates liveness requirements. Consequently, we can report an alarm once we detect the occurrence of such a cycle. Although fascinating, this idea is just at the stage of pseudocode and has not been verified by experiments. Moreover, this approach seems passive for obtaining counterexample traces.

Our approach addresses the verification of liveness properties. Although the class of temporal logic specification we deal with is currently limited, we can actively control the execution of systems to quickly produce a rare trace that violates specification. Such ability is the main contribution of our approach.

In the case of a finite state system, we verify whether, in that trace, there is a loop (cycle) that violates specification and includes all expected nondeterministic executions, especially turns of processes in fairly interleaving all executions. In the case of an infinite system, our verification system controls the running to produce a specified length of a long fair trace that violates specification.

2.2   Reinforcement Learning and the Q-Learning Algorithm

The framework of reinforcement learning [9] is one branch of artificial intelligence. One of its goals is training an agent to maximize the total number of rewards it receives when interacting with an environment. In a reinforcement learning framework, the agent learns how to react with the environment based on the rewards it has received so far. The collected knowledge is used to tune the *action-value* function, which is used to choose an agent's action expected to maximize the total gain.

We give an overview of the Q-learning method. Q-learning is the most representative algorithm of reinforcement learning. In this learning, we assume a probabilistic state transition system (Markov model), which describes the behavior of agents and the environment. At each state, enabled actions are given with the probabilities of resulting state transitions, when an action is chosen from them. A *reward* 0 or a positive real value is also given to each state transition. The aim of Q-learning is to find a path from the initial state that maximizes the sum of rewards of its state transitions. When there is an infinite length of state transition path, such as reactive concurrent systems, the sum is defined as $\sum_i \gamma^{i-1} r_i$, where r_i is a reward of each transition and γ is a parameter with $0 < \gamma < 1$, called a *discount value*. In Q-learning, the action-value function is realized by Q-value $Q(s, a)$, where s is a state and a is an action enabled at s. $Q(s, a)$ denotes an expected maximal sum of rewards on paths from s, when action a is chosen at s. The Q-value is updated as follows.

From state s_t, executing action a_t results in next state s_{t+1}, and the controller is given a reward of r_{t+1} and then

$$Q(s_t, a_t) \leftarrow Q(s_t, a_t) + \alpha \big[r_{t+1} + \gamma \max Q(s_{t+1}, a) - Q(s_t, a_t) \big].$$

This means that the value of action-value function $Q(s_t, a_t)$ is adjusted to become closer to the sum of reward (r_{t+1}) and the expected maximum action-value function from next state ($\max Q(s_{t+1}, a)$). Parameter α is introduced so that learning converges. Parameters α and γ are used to fine-tune the learning process.

Another point of learning is that, during its early period, we should not only try maximum value but also other actions at a state to explore many choices to find the optimal action. Otherwise, there is a risk of being caught in a local maximum. Therefore, we generally adopt another parameter ϵ to control the algorithm. With the possibility of ϵ, we randomly choose the next action. This value is decreased as analysis proceeds.

The algorithmic process of Q-learning is as follows.

1. Let s_t be the current state
2. Generate a random number between 0 and 1, and compare it with ϵ
   (a) if below ϵ, let a_t be chosen randomly
   (b) if not, let a_t be an action with maximum $Q(s_t, a_t)$
3. Execute action a_t
   (a) the state becomes s_{t+1}
   (b) the reward for executing a_t is r_{t+1}
4. Choose a maximum action-value among enabled actions at state s_{t+1}, i.e., max $Q(s_{t+1}, a)$
5. Update the action-value of $Q(s_t, a_t)$ with the following formula.
6. Repeat from step 1

Therefore, the design of a solution using Q-learning involves carefully devising the reward function and determining parameters α, γ, ϵ, and the rate of decrease in ϵ. Each of these variables should be tuned by repeated experiments.

Here, note that in our Q-learning application, state transitions are not probabilistic. That is, when an enabled action is chosen at a state, then the resulting next state is uniquely determined.

3 Control in Runtime Monitoring

In this section, we explain our problem more concretely and then show how to apply the reinforcement learning method to solve it.

3.1 Problem: Finding a Counterexample of Response Property

Because our method is based on monitoring, we assume that a target concurrent system can be inspected to display its current state and execution. Moreover, it's also possible to control the system's nondeterministic behaviors such as those caused by the turns of the execution of each process in the system. This assumption can be confirmed by many concurrent systems if we properly instrument them. By monitoring the execution of a system, we gain information that can be used to control its execution. Here we let the obtained information dynamically affect control so that we can efficiently uncover possible errors in the system.

The requirement specification is given in a temporal formula that expresses the liveness property. Our goal is to produce an execution trace that invalidates specification by using the control.

To simplify the explanation of our method, here, we restrict the goal of analysis to one specific temporal property: the *response property* [8]. A typical liveness property argues that if event p happens, then event q should happen in the future. In linear temporal logic, it can be specified as $\Box$ ($p \rightarrow \Diamond q$). Given a response property, i.e., predicates p and q, our analysis seeks an execution trace showing that the system violates the response property. Theoretically speaking, such a sequence should be an infinite sequence that contains a state satisfying p (*p-state*), and thereafter, no state satisfying a q (*q-state*) event should occur. In a finite system, we produce a trace with a loop that invalidates specification and includes fair turns for the processes. In an infinite system, it may be impossible to provide such a loop as evidence. Accordingly, our method provides an invalidating fair execution with a sufficient length such that an invalidation suspect arises.

3.2   Applying Q-Learning

We use Q-learning to find an execution trace that is evidence (or possible evidence) of the violation of a response property.

Now, we explain the theoretical framework of the application of Q-learning and later mention how the framework is implemented efficiently. In this framework, the following must be done: modification of the original state transition of concurrent systems and design of a reward function. The execution trace we are deriving has to satisfy two requirements: invalidating a given response property and maintaining fairness among the processes. We show the above modification and design for these two requirements.

3.2.1 Invalidating Response Properties

We explain the basic idea of invalidation. The counterexample of response property $\Box\,(\,p \rightarrow \Diamond\,q\,)$ is an execution trace where p is true sometimes and q is never true after that time. To find such a trace, the controller explore the transition system in the following guideline.

(1) if p has not been achieved, take an action that may lead to a state where p is true in the future.
(2) once p becomes true, try to keep taking actions whose resulting state invalidates q.
(3) if q happens to be true in (2), then reset the achievement of p and go to (1).

In the case of finite state systems, we try to find a loop in stage (2), and in the case of infinite state systems, we try to remain at stage (2) as long as possible. To realize this control in the exploration, we encode the achievement of p in the state transition and give a reward for remaining at stage (2).

Modification of state transition

We create two states from original state s: $\langle s, before\text{-}p \rangle$ and $\langle s, after\text{-}p \rangle$. $before\text{-}p$ means that p has not been achieved, while $after\text{-}p$ means that p has. For the transition, assume that $S1$ transits to $S2$ in the original state transition, then we have the followings. If $S2$ is a p-state and a non q-state, $\langle S1, before\text{-}p \rangle$ transits $\langle S2, after\text{-}p \rangle$. If $S2$ is a non q-state, and $\langle S1, after\text{-}p \rangle$ transits $\langle S2, after\text{-}p \rangle$. If $S2$ is a non p-state, $\langle S1, before\text{-}p \rangle$ transits $\langle S2, before\text{-}p \rangle$. If $S2$ is a q-state, $\langle S1, after\text{-}p \rangle$ transits $\langle S2, before\text{-}p \rangle$.

Reward design

We give a reward to transition $\langle S1, before\text{-}p \rangle$ transits $\langle S2, after\text{-}p \rangle$ and $\langle S1, after\text{-}p \rangle$ transits $\langle S2, after\text{-}p \rangle$ so that the execution trace stays at stage (2).

3.2.2 Maintaining Fairness

We use a similar encoding of states as invalidation. State value is extended with a set of recently executed process identifiers that is reset when all processes are executed. The basic guideline of finding a fair execution trace is as follows.

(1) if there is a process which has not been given a execution turn, try to take an action of the process.
(2) when every process is given a turn, reset the record of turns and go to (1).

Fairness will be achieved if the control visits (2) infinitely often. So the reward is given to this transition.

Modification of state transition

For simplicity, we explain modification when there are two processes. Assume two processes, $p1$ and $p2$, and three states, $S0$, $S1$, and $S2$. From $S0$, executing $p1$ makes the next state $S1$, and executing $p2$ makes the next state $S2$. By extending state value for fairness, the state transition diagram is changed, as shown in Figure 1.

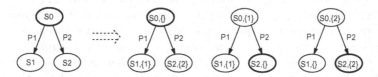

Fig. 1. Extended State Encoding for Fairness

Here, for example, state $\langle S0, \{1\}\rangle$ means that the original state is $S0$ and process $P1$ has recently been executed. The second part of the state encoding represents the set of processes that have been recently executed. Therefore, from that state, re-executing $P1$ doesn't change the second part. However, if $P2$ is executed, all processes have been given turns for execution, and we can reset the information for checking fairness. Thus, we satisfy the second part of state encoding, which will result in reset state $\langle S2, \{\}\rangle$.

Reward design

We assign a reward of 1 to transitions reaching those states having an empty set as the second part of state encoding, $< S, \{\} >$.

3.2.3 Combination of Invalidation and Fairness

We have to find an execution trace satisfying invalidation requirement and fairness requirement at the same time. There are two possible ways of this combination. One is a simple combination of the two extended states. For example, $< s, after\text{-}p >$ and $< s, \{p1\} >$ are combined to be $< s, after\text{-}p, \{p1\} >$. Actions are applied to each component of the state to derive the next state. The combined reward is a sum of those for invalidation and fairness. This combination is simple and works fast, but there is a small possibility that only one of invalidation and fairness would be satisfied. Our experiments in section 4 are based on this reward.

The other is a little complicated. After the simple combination of the states, we introduce another state-variable, whose value is *invalid*, *fair* or *reset*. Initially, the value is *reset* and if an action gain a reward of invalidation or fairness, then the value becomes *invalid* or *fairness* respectively. When the current value is *invalid* and the executed action gain a reward of fairness, then the value becomes *reset*. Similarly, if the value is *fair* and the action is rewarded by invalidation, then it becomes *reset*. Finally, combined reward is only given to the transition from *invalid* or *fair* state to *reset* state. This idea comes form intersection of Büchi Automata [1].

3.3   Other LTL Formulas

In a similar way, we can also apply this method to LTL formulas for such liveness properties as $\Diamond$ ($p \wedge \Box q$), $\Diamond$ ($p \wedge \Diamond q$), $\Box$ ($\Box p \vee \Diamond q$), $\Box$ ($p \vee \Diamond\Box q$), and $\Box$ ($p \vee \Box\Diamond q$). Here, they cover a wide class of LTL formulas for liveness properties if we note the following. $\Box$ ($p \vee \Diamond q$) is the response property, $\Box$ ($p \vee \Box q$) is a safety property, and they are not listed above. $\Box$ ($p \wedge \Diamond q$) is equivalent to $\Box p \wedge \Box\Diamond q$, $\Box\Diamond\Box p$ is equivalent to $\Diamond\Box p$, and they are reduced to a Boolean combination or a special case of some of the listed formulas.

For the counterexample, in the case of $\Diamond$ ($p \wedge \Box q$), for example, we have to find an execution trace where if there is a p-state, there is always a non q-state after that. For a finite system, we have to find a loop satisfying this condition, and the Q-learning application is designed similar to the response property formula. Formally, for $\Diamond$ ($p \wedge \Box q$), we can extend the state in the same way, but the transition rules and rewards are different. If $S2$ is a p-state and a q-state, $\langle S1, before\text{-}p \rangle$ transits $\langle S2, after\text{-}p \rangle$ and $\langle S1, after\text{-}p \rangle$ transits $\langle S2, after\text{-}p \rangle$. If $S2$ is a non q-state, $\langle S1, before\text{-}p \rangle$ transits $\langle S2, before\text{-}p \rangle$ and $\langle S1, after\text{-}p \rangle$ transits $\langle S2, before\text{-}p \rangle$. Otherwise, $\langle S1, before\text{-}p \rangle$ transits $\langle S2, before\text{-}p \rangle$ and $\langle S1, after\text{-}p \rangle$ transits $\langle S2, after\text{-}p \rangle$. Here, the actions that make transitions to $\langle S, before\text{-}p \rangle$ are rewarded. The formal description of other cases is similar.

3.4   Implementation

In 3.2, we introduced extended state transition systems where the number of states is multiplied. Because Q-learning updates Q-value $Q(s, a)$, the table size grows and the learning becomes inefficient with this extension. Actually, in its implementation, we introduce global variables instead of local variable for *after-p/before-p*, the set of executed processes and so on. Then we update the value of this global variable, use it to decide a reward and modify Q-value $Q(s, a)$ where s is not extended but original one. This simplification is allowed because original state and the corresponding extended state have a kind of bisimulation relation in their transition systems.

4   Experiments

In this section, we present two intermediate trials and then provide example models and results. Using the design of Q-learning just explained, we conducted experiments to test the feasibility and performance of the algorithm. We implemented the analysis algorithm and target models using the same language Allegro CL Common LISP v6.1 (compiled). The reflective features of LISP enable easy execution control of behavior models.

The two models are classical N-process versions of the mutual exclusion and dining philosopher problems. We slightly changed the solution model of the dining philosopher to seed liveness errors in it.

Mutual exclusion: We used Dijkstra's mutual exclusion algorithm, as presented in textbooks [7], that uses a *turn* variable to check whether it has the right to enter a critical section. When a process seeks entry, it first checks whether the turn variable refers to itself. If not, it waits and keeps trying to change the turn variable. After this checking is done, there is another checking right before entering the critical section to assure that no other process has simultaneously cleared the checking of the turn variable. In such cases, the process returns to the initial state. The model is parametric to the number of processes, and each process has 9+(n-1) states, where n is the number of processes. (n-1) states result from checking other processes' flags. Moreover, one shared variable *turn* has n states. This algorithm assures mutual exclusion but doesn't guarantee the response property of *lockoutfreeness*; that is, there is a possibility that a process can be repeatedly denied access to the critical section, even though it is constantly trying to enter.

Dining philosopher: The model for the dining philosopher problem is simple. N philosophers are sitting around a table with N forks among them. At a philosopher's initial state, he can choose the fork on his right if it hasn't been taken by the philosopher to his right. After taking the fork, he checks the availability of the fork on his left. If unavailable, he concedes and releases the fork on his right and returns to the initial state. If available, he picks it up and enters the eating state. After finishing his meal, he releases the two forks and returns to the initial state. The model is parametric to the number of philosophers, where each philosopher model has seven states and each link between the two philosophers in the ring has three states. If all philosophers follow this scheme, some may starve by repeating a loop of getting and releasing the fork on the right.
We analyzed the following response properties.

- Mutual exclusion: Once process 0 has tried to enter the critical section, it should eventually be permitted to enter.
- Dining philosopher: Once philosopher A picks up the first fork, he should eventually be eating.

We used Q-learning, as explained in 3.2. The results shown in Tables 1 and 2 illustrate the number of transitions required to find a fair execution loop that

Table 1. Number of transitions required to report mutual exclusion error

N of proc.	4	6	8	10	12	14	16	18	20
trial 1	288	520	1400	1794(1299)	7068	1514	24913	53578	168563(17731)
trial 2	267	1132	1323	1085 (352)	1996	4747	26237	38963	56886 (6794)
trial 3	153	567	2355	939 (589)	2479	5711	6763	25238	143491(14367)
trial 4	99	427	944	1557 (841)	1373	4490	19055	45806	55356(14472)*
trial 5	473	3339	1930	1804 (486)	3764	9270	8361	5469	35003(11539)

Table 2. Number of transitions required to report error for dining philosopher

N of proc.	20	50	100	150	200	250
trial 1	123	702	1657(880)	8652	3332	6518(1811)*
trial 2	497	456	1507(789)	1945	4695	5114(3635)
trial 3	273	1565	2094(938)	3826	19422	14876(2561)
trial 4	82	3351	4498(634)	6093	6281	10129(2625)
trial 5	286	1695	1591(746)	15241	3425	18269(1870)

violates the response property for the targeted models. The size of the system, i.e., the number of processes, is used as a parameter indicating the size of the problem. We show the length of the obtained loop in parentheses: n=10 and 20 in the mutual exclusion model and n=100 and 250 in the dining philosopher model. As the Q-learning parameter, we set α 0.5, γ 0.9, and ϵ 0.2 and reduce ϵ by multiplying 0.99 for every 3000 transitions (ϵ-interval). We executed these experiments with 512 Mb memory and a Pentium 3 866 MHz CPU notebook PC running a Red Hat Linux 8.0 OS. In both cases the runtime to get the desired loop is almost linear to the number of transitions. For example, Trial 4 at n=20 for mutual exclusion and Trial 1 at n=250 for the dining philosopher, both of which are marked with *, took about 5 minutes of practical time, respectively. All of these experiments were successfully conducted within the allocated 20 Mb of memory. As seen in Table 3, runtime may widely vary for a fixed n, depending on the trials because Q-learning behaves probabilistically. In particular, a probabilistic decision based on the value of ϵ (2. (a) step in the Q-learning algorithm) may reset a promising current trace. We can check the dining philosopher problem for a large number of n because it has a simple relation among its processors and is likely to produce counterexamples. On the other hand, looking at the * marked entries in the tables, the dining philosopher model seems to take much time to produce the same length of execution sequences compared with the mutual exclusion scheme. This reflects our implementation in LISP. Since the dining philosopher model encounters many more new states in creating the sequence, it spends a lot of time in data allocation. Even in the case of mutual exclusion, our method is applicable for much larger-sized models than those possible with automated formal methods such as model checking.

5   Discussion

In this paper, we proposed a new method of testing concurrent systems for the liveness properties given in restricted temporal logic formulas. Instead of simply providing test cases as those used in conventional testing methods, we chose an active approach by controlling nondeterminism while executing concurrent systems under verification. A reinforcement learning method is applied to accumulate information used to dynamically control analysis. To our knowledge, this is the first attempt to apply the AI reinforcement learning technique to computer programs. We believe this approach has demonstrated its effectiveness in solving the difficult problem of testing liveness properties. Actually, before applying this Q-learning method, we introduced an ad hoc method to explore the execution path, where we performed two operations: dynamically ranking the transition to find paths likely to violate specification and randomizing the turns of execution of the involved processes to realize fair executions. These two operations were dynamically managed by adjusting the parameters that affect the weight of usage of these operations. However, we never successfully created a balanced trace with either operation. However, the Q-learning method did enable the compatibility of two key properties: violation and liveness.

As a first step, we conducted experiments with relatively simple examples. In future work, three important tasks remain to expand this method so that it is applicable to a wide range of systems. First, in the experiments here, we used fixed parameter values, α, γ, and ϵ-interval for Q-learning. We must thoroughly investigate how these values affect the ability to efficiently derive the desired trace, depending on the size and structures of the targeted systems. Next, to deal with large-sized or infinite state systems, we have to manage the state explosion problem. Although in our experiments we memorized all encountered states to deduce counterexamples, the mutual exclusion experiment showed that memory is soon exhausted in complex and large systems. One candidate solution is abstraction, as in the case of formal verification. However, in our method, it seems too difficult to store the crucial information needed to control execution in this framework. We believe that another approach, partial order reduction, might provide a good strategy to decide which information can be discarded to properly control execution.

The last problem is to elaborate the specification form. In the current method, we restricted our attention to a limited class of LTL formulas of liveness properties: response properties and those with similar structure in LTL formulas. We would like to introduce a systematic way of dealing with a wider class of LTL formulas of liveness properties.

Acknowledgments

We would like to thank Prof. Kazuteru Miyazaki for valuable discussion about Q-learning.

References

1. Clarke, E.M., Grumberg, O., Peled, D.: Model Checking. MIT Press, Cambridge, MA (2000)
2. Dwyer, M.B., Avrunin, G.S., Corbett, J.C.: Patterns in Property Specification for Finite-state Verification. The 21st ICSE, pp. 411–420 (1999)
3. Harel, D.: On Visual Formalism. Comm. of ACM, pp. 514–530 (1988)
4. Havelund, K., Rosu, G.: Testing Linear Temporal Logic Formulae on Finite Execution Traces. RIACS Technical Report TR 01-08 (2001)
5. Holzmann, G.: Software Analysis and Model Checking. In: Proc. Computer Aided Verification, pp. 1–16 (2002)
6. Kim, M., Kannan, S., Lee, I., Sokolsky, O., Viswanathan, M.: Java-MaC: a Runtime Assurance Tool for Java Programs. In: Proc. First Workshop on Runtime Verification (RV'01), July 2001 (2001)
7. Lynch, N.: Distributed Algorithms. Morgan Kaufmann, San Francisco (1997)
8. Manna, Z., Pnueli, A.: The Temporal Logic of Reactive and Concurrent Systems - Specification. Springer, Heidelberg (1992)
9. Sutton, R.S., Barto, A.G.: Reinforcement Learning: An introduction. MIT Press, Cambridge, MA (1998)

Bounded Model Checking Real-Time Multi-agent Systems with Clock Differences: Theory and Implementation

Alessio Lomuscio[1,*], Bożena Woźna[2,**], and Andrzej Zbrzezny[2,***]

[1] Department of Computing, Imperial College London, London SW72BZ, UK
A.Lomuscio@doc.imperial.ac.uk
[2] IMCS, Jan Długosz University. Al. Armii Krajowej 13/15, 42-200 Częstochowa, Poland
{b.wozna,a.zbrzezny}@ajd.czest.pl

Abstract. We present a methodology for verifying epistemic and real-time temporal properties of multi-agent systems. We introduce an interpreted systems semantics based on diagonal timed automata and use a real-time temporal epistemic language to describe properties of multi-agent systems. We develop a bounded model checking algorithm for this setting and present experimental results for a real-time version of the alternating bit-transmission problem obtained by means of a preliminary implementation of the technique.

1 Introduction

Reasoning about knowledge has always been a core concern in AI and in multi-agent systems. This is no surprise given that knowledge is a key concept to model intelligent, rational activities, human or artificial. A plethora of formalisms have been proposed and refined over the years, many of them based on logic. One of the most widely studied is based on variants of modal logics and is commonly referred to as epistemic logic [10]. Rather than providing a computational engine for artificial agents' reasoning, epistemic logic, at least in this line, is seen as a specification language for modelling and reasoning about systems, much in common with formal methods in computer science.

Specification languages are most useful when they can be verified automatically. In this effort both theorem proving and model checking techniques and tools have been made available for epistemic logic. In particular, model checking techniques based on BDD [18,20], bounded model checking [16], unbounded model checking [11] have been developed and their implementation either publicly released [18,12] or made available via a web-interface [15].

---

   * The author acknowledge support from the EPSRC (grant GR/S49353).
  ** The research presented here was conducted while B. Woźna was at University College London supported by EPSRC (grant GR/S49353). The author also acknowledges support from the Ministry of Science and Information Society Technologies under grant number 3 T11C 011 28.
*** The author acknowledges partial support from the Ministry of Science and Information Society Technologies under grant number 3 T11C 011 28.

S. Edelkamp and A. Lomuscio (Eds.): MoChart IV, LNAI 4428, pp. 95–112, 2007.
© Springer-Verlag Berlin Heidelberg 2007

Given the above, one may be forgiven for thinking that verification via model checking of temporal epistemic logic has now become of age; however, in many respects the area is still lacking support for many essential functionalities. One of these is *real-time*. While the formalisms above deal with discrete sequence of events, it is often of both theoretical and practical interest to refer to a temporal model that assumes a dense sequence of events and use operators able to represent dense temporal intervals. The only work in this line we are aware of is [21], where a bounded model checking algorithm for TECTLK was suggested. In this paper we aim to extend two key limitations of that work in that: 1) we assume a computationally more expressive underlying semantical model (diagonal timed automata), 2) we report on an in-house implementation of this technique and discuss experimental results. Further, to exemplify the use of the techniques described in the paper we present a real-time version of the alternating bit transmission problem — a key requirement of this example is the expressive power of a semantics based on diagonal timed automata as the one presented here.

The rest of the paper is organised as follows. In Section 2 we present real-time interpreted systems, a semantics for knowledge and real-time, based on diagonal timed automata. In Section 3 we present syntax and semantics for TECTLK, the logic for which the verification method is defined. In Section 4 we define a bounded model checking algorithm for the logic; given the state-spaces in question are infinite the method involves a tailored discretisation process. Finally we test these techniques on a novel real-time variant of the alternating bit protocol.

2   Diagonal Real-Time Interpreted Systems

In [21] a semantics for real-time and knowledge based on non-diagonal timed automata was proposed. Automata are given as the finer grained semantics on which real-time interpreted systems are defined. In that framework the only clock conditions that can be used are of the form $x \sim c$, where x is a clock, c a constant and $\sim$ an equality/inequality relation. While this is appropriate for some scenarios (like the "railroad crossing system"), it is known that in others more expressive tests are required. Crucially, we may need to *compare two clocks of the system as an enabling condition for a transition*. Aim of this paper is to analyse this setting for the case of real-time and epistemic properties by means of diagonal automata.

Of course from a theoretical point of view, every diagonal timed automaton can be transformed into non-diagonal timed automaton [3], but the transformation suffers from an exponential blow up in the size of the automaton's clocks. However the approach presented here is known to generate considerable complications in the verification methodology [5] and results in a loss of completeness in the resulting bounded model checking technique [14].

To define diagonal real-time interpreted systems we first recall the definitions of diagonal timed automata and their composition. We refer to [19] for discussion and more details.

We assume a finite set X of real variables, called *clocks*, and for $x, y \in X$, $\sim \in \{<, \leq, =, >, \geq\}$, $c \in \mathbb{N}$, where $\mathbb{N} = \{0, 1, \ldots\}$ is a set of natural numbers, we define a set of *clock constraints* over X, denoted by $C(X)$, by means of the following grammar:

$$cc ::= \ true \mid x \sim c \mid x - y \sim c \mid cc \wedge cc$$

A *clock valuation* v is a total function from X into the set of non-negative real numbers $\mathbb{R}$; $\mathbb{R}^X$ denotes the set of all the clock valuations. For $cc \in C(X)$, $[\![cc]\!]$ denotes the set of all the clock valuations that satisfy cc. The clock valuation that assigns the value 0 to all clocks is denoted by v^0. For $v \in \mathbb{R}^X$ and $\delta \in \mathbb{R}$, $v + \delta$ is the clock valuation that assigns the value $v(x) + \delta$ to each clock x. For $v \in \mathbb{R}^X$ and $Y \subseteq X$, $v[Y]$ denotes the clock valuation of X that assigns the value 0 to each clock in Y and leaves the values of the other clocks unchanged.

Definition 1 (Diagonal timed automaton). *Let $\mathcal{PV}$ be a set of propositional variables. A* diagonal timed automaton *is a tuple $\mathcal{A} = (\Sigma, L, l^0, X, I, R, \mathcal{V})$, where Σ is a nonempty finite set of actions, L is a nonempty finite set of locations, $l^0 \in L$ is an initial location, $\mathcal{V} : L \mapsto 2^{\mathcal{PV}}$ is a function assigning to each location a set of atomic propositions true in that location, X is a finite set of clocks, $I : L \mapsto C(X)$ is a state invariant function, and $R \subseteq L \times \Sigma \times C(X) \times 2^X \times L$ is a transition relation.*

An element $(l, \sigma, cc, Y, l') \in R$ represents a transition from location l to location l' labelled with an action σ. The invariant condition states that the automaton is allowed to remain in location l only as long as the constraint $I(l)$ is satisfied. The guard cc has to be satisfied to enable the transition. The transition resets all clocks in the set Y to the value 0.

As usual, the semantics of diagonal timed automata is defined by associating *dense models* to them.

Definition 2 (Dense model). *Let $\mathcal{A} = (\Sigma, L, l^0, X, I, R, \mathcal{V})$ be a diagonal timed automaton, and $C(\mathcal{A}) \subseteq C(X)$ a set of all the clock constrains occurring in any enabling condition used in the transition relation R or in a state invariant of $\mathcal{A}$. A* dense model *for $\mathcal{A}$ is a tuple $\mathcal{G}(\mathcal{A}) = (\Sigma \cup \mathbb{R}, Q, q^0, \rightarrow, \widetilde{\mathcal{V}})$, where $\Sigma \cup \mathbb{R}$ is a set of labels, $Q = L \times \mathbb{R}^X$ is a set of states, $q^0 = (l^0, v^0)$ is an initial state, $\widetilde{\mathcal{V}} : Q \mapsto 2^{\mathcal{PV}}$ is a valuation function such that $\widetilde{\mathcal{V}}((l, v)) = \mathcal{V}(l)$, and $\rightarrow \subseteq Q \times (\Sigma \cup \mathbb{R}) \times Q$ is a time/action transition relation defined by:*

- *Time transition: $(l, v) \xrightarrow{\delta} (l, v + \delta)$ iff $(\forall 0 \leq \delta' \leq \delta)\ v + \delta' \in [\![I(l)]\!]$*
- *Action transition: $(l, v) \xrightarrow{\sigma} (l', v')$ iff $(\exists cc \in C(\mathcal{A}))(\exists Y \subseteq X)$ such that $v' = v[Y]$, $(l, \sigma, cc, Y, l') \in R$, $v \in [\![cc]\!]$, and $v' \in [\![I(l')]\!]$.*

In this paper we take diagonal timed automata to provide the lower level, fine-grained description for the agents; the composition of these defines a multi-agent systems. So the computations of a multi-agent system are simply the traces generated by the executions of a network of diagonal timed automata that communicate through shared actions. We model this communication via the standard notion of the parallel composition [19], as defined below.

Consider a network of m diagonal timed automata $\mathcal{A}_i = (\Sigma_i, L_i, l^0_i, X_i, I_i, R_i, \mathcal{V}_i)$, for $i = 1, \ldots, m$, such that $L_i \cap L_j = \emptyset$ for all $i, j \in \{1, \ldots, m\}$ and $i \neq j$, and denote by $\Sigma(\sigma) = \{1 \le i \le m \mid \sigma \in \Sigma_i\}$ the set of indexes of the automata performing action σ. The *parallel composition* of m diagonal timed automata $\mathcal{A}_i$ is a diagonal timed automaton $\mathcal{A} = (\Sigma, L, l^0, X, \mathcal{I}, R, \mathcal{V})$, where $\Sigma = \bigcup_{i=1}^m \Sigma_i$, $L = \prod_{i=1}^m L_i$, $l^0 = (l_1^0, \dots, l_m^0)$, $X = \bigcup_{i=1}^m X_i$, $\mathcal{I}((l_1, \dots, l_m)) = \bigwedge_{i=1}^m \mathcal{I}_i(l_i)$, $\mathcal{V}((l_1, \dots, l_m)) = \bigcup_{i=1}^m \mathcal{V}_i(l_i)$, and a transition $((l_1, \dots, l_m), \sigma, cc, Y, (l_1', \dots, l_m')) \in R$ iff $(\forall i \in \Sigma(\sigma)) (l_i, \sigma, cc_i, Y_i, l_i') \in R_i$, $cc = \bigwedge_{i \in \Sigma(\sigma)} cc_i$, $Y = \bigcup_{i \in \Sigma(\sigma)} Y_i$, and $(\forall j \in \{1, \dots, m\} \setminus \Sigma(\sigma)) \, l_j' = l_j$.

Observe that, given the above, transitions in which actions are not shared are interleaved, whereas the transitions caused by shared action are synchronised.

To give a definition of real-time interpreted systems that supports clock constraints of the form $x - y \sim c$, we first define the notion of *weak region equivalence* [22].

Definition 3 (Weak Region Equivalence). *Assume a set of clocks X, and for any $t \in \mathbb{R}$ let $\langle t \rangle$ denote the fractional (respectively integral) part of t (respectively $\lfloor t \rfloor$). The weak region equivalence is a relation $\cong \subseteq \mathbb{R}^X \times \mathbb{R}^X$ defined as follows. For two clock valuations u and v in $\mathbb{R}^X$, $u \cong v$ iff all the following conditions hold:*

(E1.) $\lfloor u(x) \rfloor = \lfloor v(x) \rfloor$*, for all $x \in X$.*
(E2.) $\langle u(x) \rangle = 0$ *iff* $\langle v(x) \rangle = 0$*, for all $x \in X$.*
(E3.) $\langle u(x) \rangle < \langle u(y) \rangle$ *iff* $\langle v(x) \rangle < \langle v(y) \rangle$*, for all $x, y \in X$.*

We will use Z, Z', and so on to denote the equivalence classes induced by the relation $\cong$. As customary, we call these classes zones, and the set of all the zones we denote by $Z(|X|)$.

Definition 4 (Diagonal real-time interpreted system). *Consider m diagonal timed automata and their parallel composition. A diagonal real-time interpreted system (or a model) is a tuple $M = (\Sigma \cup \mathbb{R}, Q, q^0, \to, \sim_1, \dots, \sim_m, \widetilde{\mathcal{V}})$ such that $\Sigma \cup \mathbb{R}$, Q, q^0, $\to$, and $\widetilde{\mathcal{V}}$ are defined as in Definition 2, and for each agent i, $\sim_i \subseteq Q \times Q$ is a relation defined by: $(l, v) \sim_i (l', v')$ iff $l_i((l, v)) = l_i((l', v'))$ and $v \cong v'$, where $l_i : Q \mapsto L_i$ is a function returning the location of agent i from a global state.*

As in [10] we consider two (global) states to be epistemically indistinguishable for agent i if its local state (i.e., its location) is the same in the two global states. Additionally we assume the agents' clocks to be globally visible, although only privately resettable. For two states to be indistinguishable we further assume the clocks of the states belong to the same zone. This is not dissimilar from [21].

3 TECTLK

In this section we introduce the logic TECTLK(Timed Existential CTL with Knowledge). While the logic is the same as the one described in [21], satisfaction is here defined on diagonal real-time interpreted systems.

Syntax. Let $\mathcal{PV}$ be a set of propositional variables containing the symbol $\top$, $\mathcal{AG}$ a set of m agents, and I an interval in $\mathbb{R}$ with integer bounds of the form $[n, n']$, $[n, n')$, $(n, n']$, (n, n'), (n, ∞), and $[n, \infty)$, for $n, n' \in \mathbb{N}$. For $p \in \mathcal{PV}$, $i \in \mathcal{AG}$, and $\Gamma \subseteq \mathcal{AG}$, the *set of* TECTLK *formulae* is defined by the following grammar:

$$\varphi := p \mid \neg p \mid \varphi \wedge \varphi \mid \varphi \vee \varphi \mid E(\varphi U_I \varphi) \mid E(\varphi R_I \varphi) \mid \overline{K}_i \varphi \mid \overline{D}_\Gamma \varphi \mid \overline{C}_\Gamma \varphi \mid \overline{E}_\Gamma \varphi$$

The other temporal modalities are defined as usual: $\perp \overset{def}{=} \neg \top$, $EG_I \varphi \overset{def}{=} E(\perp R_I \varphi)$, $EF_I \varphi \overset{def}{=} E(\top U_I \varphi)$. Moreover, $\alpha \Rightarrow \beta \overset{def}{=} \neg \alpha \vee \beta$.

Semantics. Let $M = (\Sigma \cup \mathbb{R}, Q, q^0, \rightarrow, \sim_1, \ldots, \sim_m, \widetilde{\mathcal{V}})$ be a *model*. We define a q_0-*run* ρ as a sequence of states: $q_0 \overset{\delta_0}{\rightarrow} q_0 + \delta_0 \overset{\sigma_0}{\rightarrow} q_1 \overset{\delta_1}{\rightarrow} q_1 + \delta_1 \overset{\sigma_1}{\rightarrow} q_2 \overset{\delta_2}{\rightarrow} \ldots$, where $q_i \in Q$, $\sigma_i \in \Sigma$ and $\delta_i \in \mathbb{R}_+$ for each $i \in \mathbb{N}$, and by $f_{\mathcal{A}}(q_0)$ we denote the set of all such q_0-runs. We say that a state $q \in Q$ is reachable if there is a q^0–run ρ such that there exists a state in ρ equal to q. Finally, in order to give a semantics to TECTLK, we introduce the notation of a *dense path* π_ρ corresponding to a run ρ. A dense path π_ρ corresponding to ρ is a mapping from $\mathbb{R}$ to a set of states Q such that $\pi_\rho(r) = q_i + \delta$ for $r = \Sigma_{j=0}^{i} \delta_j + \delta$ with $i \in \mathbb{N}$ and $0 \le \delta < \delta_i$. Moreover, we define the following epistemic relations: $\sim_{\Gamma}^{E} = \bigcup_{i \in \Gamma} \sim_i$, and $\sim_{\Gamma}^{C} = (\sim_{\Gamma}^{E})^+$ (the transitive closure of $\sim_{\Gamma}^{E}$), and $\sim_{\Gamma}^{D} = \bigcap_{i \in \Gamma} \sim_i$, where $\Gamma \subseteq \mathcal{A}\mathcal{G}$.

Definition 5. *Let M be a model such that the set Q contains reachable states only. $M, q \models \alpha$ denotes that α is true at state q in M. The satisfaction relation $\models$ is defined inductively as follows:*

$M, q \models p \quad \text{iff } p \in \widetilde{\mathcal{V}}(q), \quad M, q \models \alpha \vee \beta \text{ iff } q \models \alpha \text{ or } q \models \beta,$

$M, q \models \neg p \quad \text{iff } p \notin \widetilde{\mathcal{V}}(q), \quad M, q \models \alpha \wedge \beta \text{ iff } q \models \alpha \text{ and } q \models \beta,$

$M, q \models E(\alpha U_I \beta) \text{ iff } (\exists \rho \in f_{\mathcal{A}}(q))(\exists r \in I)[M, \pi_\rho(r) \models \beta \text{ and } (\forall r' < r)M, \pi_\rho(r') \models \alpha],$

$M, q \models E(\alpha R_I \beta) \text{ iff } (\exists \rho \in f_{\mathcal{A}}(q))(\forall r \in I)[M, \pi_\rho(r) \models \beta \text{ or } (\exists r' < r)M, \pi_\rho(r') \models \alpha],$

$M, q \models \overline{K}_i \alpha \qquad \text{iff } (\exists q' \in Q)(q \sim_i q' \text{ and } M, q' \models \alpha),$

$M, q \models \overline{D}_\Gamma \alpha \qquad \text{iff } (\exists q' \in Q)(q \sim_{\Gamma}^{D} q' \text{ and } M, q' \models \alpha),$

$M, q \models \overline{E}_\Gamma \alpha \qquad \text{iff } (\exists q' \in Q)(q \sim_{\Gamma}^{E} q' \text{ and } M, q' \models \alpha),$

$M, q \models \overline{C}_\Gamma \alpha \qquad \text{iff } (\exists q' \in Q)(q \sim_{\Gamma}^{C} q' \text{ and } M, q' \models \alpha).$

We say a TECTLK formula φ is *valid in M* (denoted by $M \models \varphi$) iff $M, q^0 \models \varphi$, i.e., φ is true at the initial state of the model M. In the rest of the paper we are concerned with devising and implementing an automatic model checking algorithm for checking whether a formula φ is valid in a given model M.

4   Bounded Model Checking for TECTLK

Bounded model checking (BMC) is a popular model checking technique for the verification of reactive systems [4,7]. On discrete-time, it is supported by nuSMV [6] and in its epistemic extension by Verics [15]. Verifying whether a system S satisfies a property P amounts to checking $M_S \models \phi_P$, where M_S is a model capturing S and ϕ_P is a property representing P. In BMC this check is turned into the propositional satisfiability test (ultimately performed by ad-hoc highly-efficient SAT solvers) of $[M_S] \wedge [\phi_P]$, where $[M_S]$, $[\phi_P]$ are appropriate Boolean formulae representing a truncated portion of the model M_S and the modal formula ϕ_P. We refer to [16] for a description of the technique for the case of discrete-time epistemic properties.

To define a BMC method for diagonal real-time interpreted systems, we adapt the BMC technique for TECTLK and non-diagonal automata presented in [21]. We first translate the BMC problem from TECTLK into the BMC problem for ECTLK$_y$, and then we define BMC for ECTLK$_y$. We do not report full details and proofs in this abstract. These can be found in [14].

4.1 Translation from TECTLK to ECTLK$_y$

When dealing with real-time one can use DBMs [8], CDDs [2], or a discretisation technique [1,17,22] to represent zones. In the BMC settings for branching real-time logics it is customary to discretise zones. In particular, here we take the discretisation scheme introduced in [22], which uses the following set of discretised clock's values and labels as primitives. Let $\mathbb{Q}$ be a set of rational numbers, and $D_m = \{d \in \mathbb{Q} \mid (\exists k \in \mathbb{N}) \, d \cdot 2^m = k\}$ and $E_m = \{e \in \mathbb{Q} \mid (\exists k \in \mathbb{N}) \, e \cdot 2^m = k \text{ and } e > 0\}$ for every $m \in \mathbb{N}$. Then, $D = \bigcup_{m=0}^{\infty} D_m$ defines the set of discretised clock's values, and $E = \bigcup_{m=1}^{\infty} E_m$ defines the set of labels. We use this technique to define a discretised model, which is crucial for the translation of the model checking problem for TECTLK to the model checking problem for ECTLK$_y$ as described below.

Definition 6 (Discretised model). *Let $\mathcal{A} = (\Sigma, L, l^0, X, I, R, \mathcal{V})$ be a diagonal timed automaton resulting from the parallel composition of m diagonal timed automata (agents). A discretised model for $\mathcal{A}$ is a tuple $M_d = (\Sigma \cup E, S, s^0, \rightarrow_d, \sim_1^d, \ldots, \sim_m^d, \widetilde{\mathcal{V}}_d)$, where $S = L \times D^X$ is a set of states, $s^0 = (l^0, v^0)$ is the initial state, $\sim_i^d \subseteq S \times S$ is an relation defined by $(l, v) \sim_i^d (l', v')$ iff $l_i((l, v)) = l_i((l', v'))$ and $v \cong v'$, for each agent i, $\widetilde{\mathcal{V}}_d : S \mapsto 2^{\mathcal{PV}}$ is a valuation function defined by $\widetilde{\mathcal{V}}_d((l, v)) = \mathcal{V}(l)$, and $\rightarrow_d \subseteq S \times (\Sigma \cup E) \times S$ is a time/action transition relation defined by:*

- *Time transition: for any $\delta \in E$, $(l, v) \xrightarrow{\delta}_d (l, v + \delta)$ iff $(l, v) \xrightarrow{\delta} (l, v + \delta)$ in $\mathcal{G}(\mathcal{A})$ and $(\forall \delta' \leq \delta) \, v + \delta' \cong v$ or $v + \delta' \cong v + \delta$,*
- *Action transition: for any $\sigma \in \Sigma$, $(l, v) \xrightarrow{\sigma}_d (l', v')$ iff $(\exists \delta)(\exists v'')$ such that $(l, v) \xrightarrow{\delta}_d (l, v'')$ and $(l, v'') \xrightarrow{\sigma} (l', v')$ in $\mathcal{G}(\mathcal{A})$.*

The general idea of the translation is the same as the one in [21], but obviously given the different capabilities there are differences. In particular, the discretised model used here is infinite; so while the procedure in [21] is sound and complete, the one here is only sound.[1]

Specifically, given a multi-agent system modelled by a network of diagonal timed automata $\mathcal{A}_i = (\Sigma_i, L_i, l_i^0, X_i, I_i, R_i, \mathcal{V}_i)$ and a TECTLK formula φ, we extend each automaton $\mathcal{A}_i$ by a new clock y, an action σ_y, and transitions to obtain a new automaton $\mathcal{A}_i^{\varphi} = (\Sigma_i \cup \{\sigma_y\}, L_i, l_i^0, X_i', I_i, R_i', \mathcal{V}_i)$ with $X_i' = X_i \cup \{y\}$ and $R_i' = R_i \cup \{(l, \sigma_y, true, \{y\}, l) \mid l \in L\}$. The clock y corresponds to all the timing intervals appearing in φ, and special transitions are used to reset the new clock. We then construct the discretised model for the parallel composition of $\mathcal{A}_i^{\varphi}$, denoted by $\mathcal{A}_{\varphi}$, and augment its valuation function with the set of propositional variables containing a new proposition $p_{y \in I}$ for every interval I appearing in φ, and a new proposition p_b representing that a state s is boundary, i.e., at least one clock from the original automata has to have the fractional part of its valuation

---

[1] Note though that because of the complexity in the SAT translation and satisfiability checks, BMC is never complete in practice when the system is sufficiently complex, so this is not a real concern.

equal to zero in s. Finally, we translate the TECTLK formula φ into an ECTLK$_y$ formula $\psi = \text{cr}(\varphi)$ such that model checking of φ over the model for the parallel composition of $\mathcal{A}_i$ can be reduced to the model checking of ψ over the discretised model for $\mathcal{A}_\varphi$. Before we define the final part of the above construction, we will first introduce the syntax and semantics for ECTLK$_y$.

Let $p \in \mathcal{PV}' = \mathcal{PV} \cup \{p_b\} \cup \{p_{y \in I} \mid I$ is an interval in $\varphi\}$. The set of ECTLK$_y$ formulae is defined by the following grammar:

$$\alpha := p \mid \neg p \mid \alpha \wedge \alpha \mid \alpha \vee \alpha \mid E_y(\alpha U \alpha) \mid E_y(\alpha R \alpha) \mid \overline{K}_i \alpha \mid \overline{D}_\Gamma \alpha \mid \overline{C}_\Gamma \alpha \mid \overline{E}_\Gamma \alpha$$

The satisfaction relation for ECTLK$_y$ is defined with respect to a discretised model M_d. Namely, assume that s is a state, α, β formulae of ECTLK$_y$, $\rightarrow_{\mathcal{A}}$ denotes the part of $\rightarrow_d$, where transitions are labelled with elements of $\Sigma \cup E$, and $\rightarrow_y$ denotes the transitions that reset the clock y. Next, define a *path* π in M_d to be a sequence $(s_0, s_1, \ldots)$ of states such that $s_i \rightarrow_{\mathcal{A}} s_{i+1}$ for each $i \in \mathbb{N}$, and denote the set of all the paths starting at s in M_d by $\Pi(s)$. Then, the satisfaction relation $\models$ for ECTLK$_y$ is defined as follows:

$M_d, s \models p$ iff $p \in \widetilde{\mathcal{V}}_d(s)$,

$M_d, s \models \neg p$ iff $p \notin \widetilde{\mathcal{V}}_d(s)$,

$M_d, s \models \alpha \vee \beta$ iff $M_d, s \models \alpha$ or $M_d, s \models \beta$,

$M_d, s \models \alpha \wedge \beta$ iff $M_d, s \models \alpha$ and $M_d, s \models \beta$,

$M_d, s \models E_y(\alpha U \beta)$ iff $(\exists s' \in S)(s \rightarrow_y s'$ and $(\exists \pi \in \Pi(s'))(\exists m \geq 0)$
$\qquad\qquad [M_d, \pi(m) \models \beta$ and $(\forall j < m)\, M_d, \pi(j) \models \alpha])$,

$M_d, s \models E_y(\alpha R \beta)$ iff $(\exists s' \in S)(s \rightarrow_y s'$ and $(\exists \pi \in \Pi(s'))(\forall m \geq 0)$
$\qquad\qquad [M_d, \pi(m) \models \beta$ or $(\exists j \leq m)\, M_d, \pi(j) \models \alpha])$,

$M_d, s \models \overline{K}_i \alpha$ iff $(\exists \pi \in \Pi(s^0))(\exists j \geq 0)(M_d, \pi(j) \models \alpha$ and $s \sim_i \pi(j))$,

$M_d, s \models \overline{D}_\Gamma \alpha$ iff $(\exists \pi \in \Pi(s^0))(\exists j \geq 0)(M_d, \pi(j) \models \alpha$ and $s \sim_\Gamma^D \pi(j))$,

$M_d, s \models \overline{E}_\Gamma \alpha$ iff $(\exists \pi \in \Pi(s^0))(\exists j \geq 0)(M_d, \pi(j) \models \alpha$ and $s \sim_\Gamma^E \pi(j))$,

$M_d, s \models \overline{C}_\Gamma \alpha$ iff $(\exists \pi \in \Pi(s^0))(\exists j \geq 0)(M_d, \pi(j) \models \alpha$ and $s \sim_\Gamma^C \pi(j))$.

Definition 7 (Validity). *An ECTLK$_y$ formula φ is valid in M_d (denoted $M_d \models \varphi$) iff $M_d, s^0 \models \varphi$, i.e., φ is true at the initial state of M_d.*

We can now translate inductively a TECTLK formula φ into the ECTLK$_y$ formula $\text{cr}(\varphi)$; note that for the propositional and epistemic part of ECTLK$_y$ the translation is defined as the corresponding translation in [16].

- $\text{cr}(p) = p$ for $p \in \mathcal{PV}'$,
- $cr(\neg p) = \neg cr(p)$ for $p \in \mathcal{PV}'$,
- $\text{cr}(\alpha \vee \beta) = \text{cr}(\alpha) \vee \text{cr}(\beta)$,
- $\text{cr}(\alpha \wedge \beta) = \text{cr}(\alpha) \wedge \text{cr}(\beta)$,
- $\text{cr}(E(\alpha U_I \beta)) = E_y(\text{cr}(\alpha) U (\text{cr}(\beta) \wedge p_{y \in I} \wedge (p_b \vee \text{cr}(\alpha))))$,
- $\text{cr}(E(\alpha R_I \beta)) = E_y(\text{cr}(\alpha) R (\neg p_{y \in I_i} \vee (\text{cr}(\beta) \wedge (p_b \vee \text{cr}(\alpha)))))$.
- $\text{cr}(\overline{K}_i \alpha) = \overline{K}_i \text{cr}(\alpha)$,
- $\text{cr}(\overline{D}_\Gamma \alpha) = \overline{D}_\Gamma \text{cr}(\alpha)$,
- $\text{cr}(\overline{E}_\Gamma \alpha) = \overline{E}_\Gamma \text{cr}(\alpha)$,
- $\text{cr}(\overline{C}_\Gamma \alpha) = \overline{C}_\Gamma \text{cr}(\alpha)$,

The following lemma shows that validity of the TECTLK formula φ over the model for $\mathcal{A}$ is equivalent to the validity of cr(φ) over the discretised model for $\mathcal{A}_\varphi$ with the extended valuation function.

Lemma 1 ([14]). *Let φ be a TECTLK formula, M a model, and M_d the discretised version of M. Further, let $(l, v) \downarrow X \overset{def}{=} (l, v \downarrow X)$. For any state $(l, v) \in Q$ there exists $(l, v') \in S$ such that $(l, v') \downarrow X \cong (l, v)$ and $M, (l, v) \models \varphi$ iff $M_d, (l, v') \models$ cr(φ).*

4.2 ECTLK$_y$ Bounded Model Checking

All the known BMC techniques are based on so called k-bounded semantics. In particular, BMC for ECTLK$_y$ is based on the k-bounded semantics for ECTLK$_y$, the definition of which we present below.

We start with some auxiliary notions. Let $M_d = (\Sigma \cup E, S, s^0, \rightarrow_d, \sim_1^d, \ldots, \sim_m^d, \widetilde{\mathcal{V}}_d)$ be a discretised model, and $k \in \mathbb{N}_+$ a bound. As before, we denote by $\rightarrow_{\mathcal{A}}$ the part of $\rightarrow_d$, where transitions are labelled with elements of $\Sigma \cup E$, and by $\rightarrow_y$ the transitions that reset the clock y. A k-*path* π in M_d is a finite sequence of states $(s_0, \ldots, s_k)$ such that $s_i \rightarrow_{\mathcal{A}} s_{i+1}$ for each $0 \leq i < k$, and $\Pi_k(s)$ denotes the set of all the k-paths starting at s in M_d. A k-*model* for M_d is a structure $M_k = (\Sigma \cup E, S, s^0, P_k, P_y, \sim_1^d, \ldots, \sim_m^d, \widetilde{\mathcal{V}}_d)$, where $P_k = \bigcup_{s \in S} \Pi_k(s)$ and $P_y = \{(s, s') \mid s \rightarrow_y s'$ and $s, s' \in S\}$.

The satisfaction of the temporal operator $E_y R$ on a k-path in the bounded case depends on whether or not π represents a loop. To indicate k-paths that can simulate loops, we define a function $loop : P_k \mapsto 2^{\mathbb{N}}$ by $loop(\pi) = \{i \mid 0 \leq i \leq k$ and $\pi(k) \rightarrow_{\mathcal{A}} \pi(i)\}$.

We can now define a bounded semantics for ECTLK$_y$ formulae. Let $k \in \mathbb{N}_+$, M_d be a discretised model, M_k its k-model, α, β ECTLK$_y$ formulae, and let $M_k, s \models \alpha$ denote that α is true at the state s of M_k. Then, the (bounded) satisfaction relation $\models$ for ECTLK$_y$ is defined as follows:

$M_k, s \models p$ iff $p \in \widetilde{\mathcal{V}}_d(s)$, $\quad M_k, s \models \alpha \vee \beta$ iff $M_k, s \models \alpha$ or $M_k, s \models \beta$,

$M_k, s \models \neg p$ iff $p \notin \widetilde{\mathcal{V}}_d(s)$, $\quad M_k, s \models \alpha \wedge \beta$ iff $M_k, s \models \alpha$ and $M_k, s \models \beta$,

$M_k, s \models \overline{K}_i \alpha \quad$ iff $(\exists \pi \in \Pi_k(s^0))(\exists 0 \leq j \leq k)(M_k, \pi(j) \models \alpha$ and $s \sim_i \pi(j))$,

$M_k, s \models \overline{D}_\Gamma \alpha \quad$ iff $(\exists \pi \in \Pi_k(s^0))(\exists 0 \leq j \leq k)(M_k, \pi(j) \models \alpha$ and $s \sim_\Gamma^D \pi(j))$,

$M_k, s \models \overline{E}_\Gamma \alpha \quad$ iff $(\exists \pi \in \Pi_k(s^0))(\exists 0 \leq j \leq k)(M_k, \pi(j) \models \alpha$ and $s \sim_\Gamma^E \pi(j))$,

$M_k, s \models \overline{C}_\Gamma \alpha \quad$ iff $(\exists \pi \in \Pi_k(s^0))(\exists 0 \leq j \leq k)(M_k, \pi(j) \models \alpha$ and $s \sim_\Gamma^C \pi(j))$,

$M_k, s \models E_y(\alpha U \beta)$ iff $(\exists s' \in S)((s, s') \in P_y$ and $(\exists \pi \in \Pi_k(s'))(\exists 0 \leq j \leq k)$
$\qquad (M_k, \pi(j) \models \beta$ and $(\forall 0 \leq i < j) \, M_k, \pi(i) \models \alpha))$,

$M_k, s \models E_y(\alpha R \beta)$ iff $(\exists s' \in S)((s, s') \in P_y$ and $(\exists \pi \in \Pi_k(s'))[(\exists 0 \leq j \leq k)$
$\qquad (M_k, \pi(j) \models \alpha$ and $(\forall 0 \leq i \leq j) M_k, \pi(i) \models \beta)$ or
$\qquad (\forall 0 \leq j \leq k)(M_k, \pi(j) \models \beta$ and $loop(\pi) \neq \emptyset)])$.

Note that for the propositional and epistemic part of ECTLK$_y$, the (bounded) satisfaction relation $\models$ is defined as the corresponding relation in [21].

Definition 8 (Validity). *An ECTLK$_y$ formula φ is valid in a k-model M_k (denoted $M_d \models_k \varphi$) iff $M_k, s^0 \models \varphi$, i.e., φ is true at the initial state of the k-model M_k.*

We can now describe how the model checking problem ($M_d \models \varphi$) can be reduced to the bounded model checking problem ($M_d \models_k \varphi$).

Theorem 1. *Let $k \in \mathbb{N}_+$, M_d be a discretised model, M_k its k-model, and φ an ECTLK$_y$ formula. For any s in M_d, $M_k, s \models \varphi$ implies $M_d, s \models \varphi$.*

Proof. By straightforward induction on the length of φ.

Note that both the discretised model and its k-model are infinite. So, to perform bounded model checking we have to consider a finite submodels of a k-model such that an ECTLK$_y$ formula ψ holds in M_d if and only if ψ holds in a finite submodel of M_k.

Definition 9. *An s-submodel of k-model $M_k = (\Sigma \cup E, S, s^0, P_k, P_y, \sim_1^d, \ldots, \sim_m^d, \widetilde{\mathcal{V}}_d)$ is a tuple $M'(s) = (\Sigma \cup E, S', s, P'_k, P'_y, \sim'_1, \ldots, \sim'_m, \widetilde{\mathcal{V}}'_d)$ such that $P'_k \subseteq P_k$, $S' = \{r \in S \mid (\exists \pi \in P'_k)(\exists i \leq k)\pi(i) = r\} \cup \{s\}$, $P'_y \subseteq P_y \cap (S' \times S')$, $\sim'_i = \sim_i^d \cap (S' \times S')$ for each $i \in \{1, \ldots, m\}$, and $\widetilde{\mathcal{V}}'_d = \widetilde{\mathcal{V}}_d \downarrow S'$.*

The bounded semantics for ECTLK$_y$ over a submodel $M'(s)$ is defined as for M_k. Moreover, the following theorem holds.

We now introduce a definition of a function f_k that gives a bound on the number of k-paths in the submodel $M'(s)$, and a function $f_{k,y}$ that gives a bound on the number of elements of the set P'_y in the submodel $M'(s)$. It can be shown that these bound guarantee that the validity of ψ in $M'(s)$ is equivalent to the validity of ψ in M_k (see Theorem 2). The function $f_k : \text{ECTLK}_y \to \mathbb{N}$ is defined by:

- $f_k(p) = f_k(\neg p) = 0$, where $p \in \mathcal{PV}'$,
- $f_k(\alpha \vee \beta) = max\{f_k(\alpha), f_k(\beta)\}$,
- $f_k(\alpha \wedge \beta) = f_k(\alpha) + f_k(\beta)$,
- $f_k(\text{E}_y(\alpha\text{U}\beta)) = k \cdot f_k(\alpha) + f_k(\beta) + 1$,
- $f_k(\text{E}_y(\alpha\text{R}\beta)) = (k+1) \cdot f_k(\beta) + f_k(\alpha) + 1$,
- $f_k(Y\alpha) = f_k(\alpha) + 1$, for $Y \in \{\overline{\text{K}}_i, \overline{\text{D}}_\Gamma, \overline{\text{E}}_\Gamma\}$,
- $f_k(\overline{\text{C}}_\Gamma\alpha) = f_k(\alpha) + k$.

The function $f_{k,y} : \text{ECTLK}_y \to \mathbb{N}$ is defined by:

- $f_{k,y}(p) = f_{k,y}(\neg p) = 0$, where $p \in \mathcal{PV}'$,
- $f_{k,y}(\alpha \vee \beta) = max\{f_{k,y}(\alpha), f_{k,y}(\beta)\}$,
- $f_{k,y}(\alpha \wedge \beta) = f_{k,y}(\alpha) + f_{k,y}(\beta)$,
- $f_{k,y}(\text{E}_y(\alpha\text{U}\beta)) = k \cdot f_{k,y}(\alpha) + f_{k,y}(\beta) + 1$,
- $f_{k,y}(\text{E}_y(\alpha\text{R}\beta)) = (k+1) \cdot f_{k,y}(\beta) + f_{k,y}(\alpha) + 1$,
- $f_{k,y}(Y\alpha) = f_{k,y}(\alpha)$, for $Y \in \{\overline{\text{K}}_i, \overline{\text{D}}_\Gamma, \overline{\text{E}}_\Gamma, \overline{\text{C}}_\Gamma\}$.

Theorem 2 ([14]). *Let M_d be a discretised model, and ψ an ECTLK$_y$ formula. If there exist $k \in \mathbb{N}_+$ and s^0-submodel $M'(s^0)$ of k-model M_k with $P'_k \leq f_k(\psi)$ and $|P'_{k,y}| \leq f_{k,y}(\psi)$ such that $M'(s^0) \models_k \psi$, then $M_d \models \psi$.*

Given the above, note that both functions f_k and $f_{k,y}$ give the upper bound on the number of paths in P'_k and number of transitions in $P'_{k,y}$, respectively.

Having defined the bounded semantics, we can easily translate the model checking problem for ECTLK$_y$ to the problem of satisfiability of a Boolean formula that encodes all the discretised model for an ECTLK$_y$ formula under consideration and an appropriate fragments of the considered discretised models. The translation can be done in a similar way as the one in [21] and it is presented in the next section.

4.3 Translation to Boolean Formulae

The main idea of BMC for ECTLK$_y$ consists in translating the model checking problem for ECTLK$_y$ into the satisfiability problem of a propositional formula. Namely, given an ECTLK$_y$ formula ψ, a discretised model M_d, and a bound $k \in \mathbb{N}_+$, this proposition formula, denoted by $[M_d, \psi]_k$, is of the form: $[M_d^{\psi,s^0}]_k \wedge [\psi]_{M_k}$. The first conjunct represents possible submodels of M_d such that they consist of $f_k(\psi)$ k–paths of M_d and at least one of these submodels is an s^0-submodel. The second conjunct encodes a number of constraints that must hold on these submodels for ψ to be satisfied. Once this translation is defined, checking satisfiability of an ECTLK$_y$ formula can be done by means of a SAT-checker. In order to define $[M_d, \psi]_k$, we proceed as follows.

Let us assume that each state s of submodels of k-model M_k for the discretised model M_d is encoded by a bit-vector whose length, say b, depends on the number of locations, the number of clocks, and the bound $k \in \mathbb{N}_+$. So, each such a state s can be represented by a vector $w = (w[1], \ldots, w[b])$ (called *global state variable*), where each $w[i]$, for $i = 1, \ldots, b$, is a propositional variable (called *state variable*). Notice that we distinguish between states s encoded as sequences of 0s and 1s and their representations in terms of propositional variables $w[i]$. A finite sequence $(w_0, \ldots, w_k)$ of global state variables is called a *symbolic k-path*. In general, we need to consider not just one but a number of symbolic k-paths. This number depends on the formula ψ under investigation, and it is returned as the value $f_k(\psi)$ of the function f_k. The j-th symbolic k-path is denoted by $w_{0,j}, \ldots, w_{k,j}$, where $w_{i,j}$ are global state variables for $1 \leq j \leq f_k(\psi)$, $0 \leq i \leq k$. For two global state variables w, w', we define the following propositional formulae:

- $I_s(w)$ is a formula over w, which is true for a valuation s_w of w iff $s_w = s$.
- $p(w)$ is a formula over w, which is true for a valuation s_w of w iff $p \in \mathcal{V}_d(s_w)$, where $p \in \mathcal{PV}'$,
- $H_i(w, w')$ is a formula over two global state variables $w = (\mathfrak{l}, \mathfrak{v})$, $w' = (\mathfrak{l}', \mathfrak{v}')$, which is true for valuations $s_{\mathfrak{l}}$ of $\mathfrak{l}$, $s_{\mathfrak{l}'}$ of $\mathfrak{l}'$, $s_{\mathfrak{v}}$ of $\mathfrak{v}$, and $s_{\mathfrak{v}'}$ of $\mathfrak{v}'$ iff $l_i(s_{\mathfrak{l}}) = l_i(s_{\mathfrak{l}'})$ and $s_{\mathfrak{v}} \cong s_{\mathfrak{v}'}$ (encodes equality of local states of agent i).
- $\mathcal{R}(w, w')$ is a formula over w, w', which is true for two valuations s_w of w and $s_{w'}$ of w' iff $s_w \rightarrow_{\mathcal{A}} s_{w'}$ (encodes the non-resetting transition relation of M_d),
- $R_y(w, w')$ is a formula over w, w', which is true for two valuations s_w of w and $s_{w'}$ of w' iff $s_w \rightarrow_y s_{w'}$ (encodes the transitions resetting the clock y).

The propositional formula $[M_d, \psi]_k$ is defined over state variables $w_{0,0}, w_{n,m}$, for $0 \leq m \leq k$ and $1 \leq n \leq f_k(\psi)$. We start off with a definition of its first conjunct, i.e., $[M_d^{\psi,s^0}]_k$, which constrains the $f_k(\psi)$ symbolic k-paths to be valid k-path of M_k. Namely,

$$[M_d^{\psi,s^0}]_k := I_{s^0}(w_{0,0}) \wedge \bigwedge_{n=1}^{f_k(\psi)} \bigwedge_{m=0}^{k-1} \mathcal{R}(w_{m,n}, w_{m+1,n})$$

The second conjunct, i.e., the formula $[\psi]_{M_k} = [\psi]_k^{[0,0]}$, is inductively defined as follows:

$$[p]_k^{[m,n]} := p(w_{m,n}), \qquad\qquad [\alpha \wedge \beta]_k^{[m,n]} := [\alpha]_k^{[m,n]} \wedge [\beta]_k^{[m,n]},$$

$$[\neg p]_k^{[m,n]} := \neg p(w_{m,n}), \qquad\quad [\alpha \vee \beta]_k^{[m,n]} := [\alpha]_k^{[m,n]} \vee [\beta]_k^{[m,n]},$$

$$[E_y(\alpha U \beta)]_k^{[m,n]} := \bigvee_{i=1}^{f_k(\psi)} (R_y(w_{m,n}, w_{0,i}) \wedge \bigvee_{j=0}^{k} ([\beta]_k^{[j,i]} \wedge \bigwedge_{l=0}^{j-1} [\alpha]_k^{[l,i]})),$$

$$[E_y(\alpha R \beta)]_k^{[m,n]} := \bigvee_{i=1}^{f_k(\psi)} (R_y(w_{m,n}, w_{0,i}) \wedge (\bigvee_{j=0}^{k} ([\alpha]_k^{[j,i]} \wedge \bigwedge_{l=0}^{j} [\beta]_k^{[l,i]})$$
$$\vee \bigwedge_{j=0}^{k} [\beta]_k^{[j,i]} \wedge \bigvee_{l=0}^{k} \mathcal{R}(w_{k,i}, w_{l,i}))),$$

$$[\overline{K}_l \alpha]_k^{[m,n]} := \bigvee_{i=1}^{f_k(\psi)} (I_{s^0}(w_{0,i}) \wedge \bigvee_{j=0}^{k} ([\alpha]_k^{[j,i]} \wedge H_l(w_{m,n}, w_{j,i}))),$$

$$[\overline{D}_\Gamma \alpha]_k^{[m,n]} := \bigvee_{i=1}^{f_k(\psi)} (I_{s^0}(w_{0,i}) \wedge \bigvee_{j=0}^{k} ([\alpha]_k^{[j,i]} \wedge \bigwedge_{l \in \Gamma} H_l(w_{m,n}, w_{j,i}))),$$

$$[\overline{E}_\Gamma \alpha]_k^{[m,n]} := \bigvee_{i=1}^{f_k(\psi)} (I_{s^0}(w_{0,i}) \wedge \bigvee_{j=0}^{k} ([\alpha]_k^{[j,i]} \wedge \bigvee_{l \in \Gamma} H_l(w_{m,n}, w_{j,i}))),$$

$$[\overline{C}_\Gamma \alpha]_k^{[m,n]} := [\bigvee_{i=1}^{k} (\overline{E}_\Gamma)^i \alpha]_k^{[m,n]}.$$

Lemma 2. *Let M_d be discretised model, M_k its k-model, and ψ an ECTLK$_y$ formula. For each state s of M_d, the following holds: $[M_d^{\psi,s}]_k \wedge [\psi]_{M_k}$ is satisfiable iff there is a submodel $M'(s)$ of M_k with $|P'_k| \leq f_k(\psi)$ and $|P'_y| \leq f_{k,y}(\psi)$ such that $M'(s), s \models \psi$.*

Proof. (=>) Let $[M_d^{\psi,s}]_k \wedge [\psi]_{M_k}$ be satisfiable. By the definition of the translation, the propositional formula $[\psi]_{M_k}$ encodes all the sets of k-paths of size $f_k(\psi)$ which satisfy the formula ψ and all the sets of transitions resetting the clock y of size $f_{k,y}(\psi)$. By the definition of the unfolding of the transition relation, the propositional formula $[M^{\psi,s}]_k$ encodes $f_k(\psi)$ symbolic k-paths to be valid k-paths of M_k. Hence, there is a set of k-paths in M_k, which satisfies the formula ψ of size smaller or equal to $f_k(\psi)$, and there is a set of transitions resetting the clock y of size $f_{k,y}(\psi)$. Thus, we conclude that there is a submodel $M'(s)$ of M_k with $|P'_k| \leq f_k(\psi)$ and $|P'_y| \leq f_{k,y}(\psi)$ such that $M'(s), s \models \psi$.

(<=) The proof is by induction on the length of ψ. The lemma follows directly for the propositional variables and their negations. Consider the following cases:

- For $\psi = \alpha \vee \beta, \alpha \wedge \beta$, or the temporal operators the proof is like in [16].
- Let $\psi = \overline{K}_l \alpha$. If $M'(s), s \models \overline{K}_l \alpha$ with $|P'_k| \leq f_k(\overline{K}_l \alpha)$ and $|P'_y| \leq f_{k,y}(\overline{K}_l \alpha)$, then by the definition of bounded semantics we have that there is a k-path π such that $\pi(0) = s^0$ and $(\exists j \leq k)\ s \sim_l \pi(j))$ and $M'(s), \pi(j) \models \alpha$. Hence, by induction we obtain that for some $j \leq k$ the propositional formula $[\alpha]_k^{[0,0]} \wedge [M^{\alpha,\pi(j)}]_k$ is satisfiable. Let $ii = f_k(\alpha) + 1$ be the index of a new symbolic k-path which satisfies the formula $I_{s^0}(w_{0,ii})$. Therefore, by the construction above, it follows that the propositional formula $I_{s^0}(w_{0,ii}) \wedge \bigvee_{j=0}^{k} ([\alpha]_k^{[j,ii]} \wedge H_l(w_{0,0}, w_{j,ii})) \wedge [M^{\overline{K}_l \alpha, s}]_k$ is satisfiable. Therefore, the following propositional formula is satisfiable:

$$\bigvee_{1 \leq i \leq f_k(\overline{K}_l \alpha)} \left(I_{s^0}(w_{0,i}) \wedge \bigvee_{j=0}^{k} ([\alpha]_k^{[j,i]} \wedge H_l(w_{0,0}, w_{j,i})) \wedge [M^{\overline{K}_l \alpha, s}]_k \right).$$

Hence, by the definition of the translation of an ECTLK$_y$ formula, the above formula is equal to the propositional formula $[\overline{K}_l \alpha]_k^{[0,0]} \wedge [M^{\overline{K}_l \alpha, s}]_k$.

- The other proofs are similar.

Theorem 3. *Let M_d be a discretised model, and ψ an ECTLK$_y$ formula. If there exists $k \in \mathbb{N}_+$ such that $[\psi]_{M_k} \wedge [M_d^{\psi,s^0}]_k$ is satisfiable, then $M_d \models \psi$.*

Proof. Follows from Theorem 2 and Lemma 2.

5   A Real-Time Alternating Bit Transmission Problem

To exemplify the theoretical concepts of the previous sections we analyse a real-time version of one of the variants of the alternating bit protocol. In the original formulation [10] two agents attempt to transmit information over an unreliable communication channel, which they have access to. Sender S starts sending the bit to receiver R. R is initially silent but as soon as it receives the bit from S, it starts sending acknowledgments back to S. As soon as S receives one of these acknowledgments, it stops sending the bit, the system is reset and a new bit is sent. Under these conditions it can be checked automatically [18] that whenever S receives an acknowledgment it then knows (in the formal epistemic sense) that R knows the value of the bit (expressed by the formula $AG(\textbf{recack} \Rightarrow K_S K_R \textbf{recbit})$). Consider now one of the variants analysed in [13] where R may (erroneously) send acknowledgments without having received the bit first. Intuitively in this case, the property above will no longer hold; indeed this can also be checked automatically [18].

We extend the scenario above by adding the clock expressions. Assume that each agent has two possibly faulty communication channels to choose from to send bits or acknowledgments. In order to optimise the performance of the transmission both agents concurrently run a channel monitoring service in the background. To this aim they regularly send each other control bits and keep track of the time elapsed since the receipt of a control bit from the other party. The agents send the information bit on the channel that has demonstrated to be in the better working condition, i.e., the one that has recently been able to transmit the control bit from the other party.

To formalise the above we use a network of diagonal timed automata consisting of an automaton for S (see Figure 1) and an automaton for R (see Figure 2). S can be in 11 different local states: *Decide* ("S selects which bit will be sent"), 0-*ctr-bit* and 1-*ctr-bit* ("S sends a control bit and listens to R's control bit"), 0-*select* and 1-*select* ("S selects the channel to use to send bit 0 (1), or he sends a control bit"), 0-*channel*-1 and 0-*channel*-2 ("S sends bit 0 through channel 1 (2)"), 1-*channel*-1 and 1-*channel*-2, ("S sends bit 1 through channel 1 (2)"), 0-*ack* and 1-*ack* ("S has received an acknowledgment"). S can perform independently the following actions: 0-*bit*, 1-*bit* ("bit 0 (1) is sent"), *scbs*-1-*fail*, *scbs*-2-*fail* ("a control bit is sent to a faulty channel 1 (2)"), *s-send-fail* ("bit 0 or 1 is sent to a faulty channel"), *nothing*, and *next-bit* whose interpretation is obvious. The remaining actions are synchronised with R.

R can be in 10 different local states: *wait* ("R is listening to the channels"), *ctr-bit* ("R sends a control bit, or he sends a faulty acknowledgment"), *r0* and *r1* ("R has received bit 0 (1)"), 0-*select* and 1-*select* ("R selects the channel for the ack"), 0-*channel*-1, 0-*channel*-2, 1-*channel*-1 and 1-*channel*-2, ("R sends an ack on channel 1 (2).."). R can perform independently the following actions: *scbr*-1-*fail*, *scbr*-2-*fail* ("a control bit is sent to a faulty channel 1 (2)"), *r-send-fail* ("an ack is sent to a faulty channel"). We refer to Figures 1, 2 for a pictorial representation.

Further, S uses 3 clocks $(x, x_1, x_2,)$, and R three more (y, y_1, y_2). Control bits are sent at regular intervals: t_1 for channel 1 and t_2 for channel 2; the clocks x and y are used for this purpose. Clocks x_i and y_i measure the time since a control bit has been received; x_i gets reset when S receives a control bit on channel i, likewise for y_i for R. When sending bits (either information bits of acknowledgments) each agent evaluates

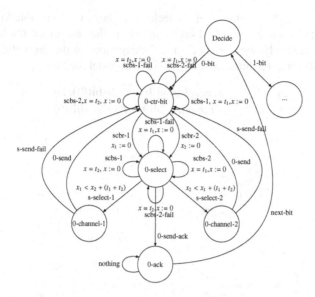

Fig. 1. An automaton for Sender - the part for bit 0. The part for bit 1 is symmetric.

the following two clock expressions $z_1 - z_2 < (t_1 + t_2)$ and $z_2 - z_1 < (t_1 + t_2)$ for $z \in \{x, y\}$. When the former expression is true, channel 1 is chosen, when the latter is true, channel 2 is chosen. Intuitively the above guarantees that the channel that has been demonstrated to be alive more recently gets selected. Using the threshold $t_1 + t_2$ enables an agent not to switch channel unnecessarily often (for instance simply because they are desynchronised). Note that ease with which the use of a clock difference allows us to implement real-time channel selection without having a large state space for the automata in question.

The automata run in parallel and synchronise through the actions: *scbs*-1, *scbs*-2, *scbr*-1, and *scbr*-2 ("send a control bit via channel 1 (2)"), 0-*send*, and 1-*send* ("send bit 0 (1)"), 0-*send-ack*, and 1-*send-ack* (" send an acknowledgment to bit 0 (1)").

Given the above, one can construct the automaton $\mathcal{A}_{BTP}$ that describes the whole alternating bit protocol running in real time as well as the set of traces generated by it. In our approach this is done automatically by the bounded model checking implementation.

Now, assume the following set of propositional variables: $\mathcal{PV} = \{\textbf{recack}, \textbf{bit0}\}$, and the following usual interpretation for the proposition variables in $\mathcal{PV}$: $\mathcal{V}_S(0\text{-}channel\text{-}1) = \mathcal{V}_S(0\text{-}channel\text{-}2) = \mathcal{V}_S(0\text{-}ack) = \textbf{bit0}$, and $\mathcal{V}_S(0\text{-}ack) = \mathcal{V}_S(1\text{-}ack) = \textbf{recack}$.

The typical specification properties that one may be interested in checking for the example above are the following: 1) "forever in the future from t_1 if an acknowledgment has been received by S and the value of the bit is 0, then R knows the bit is equal to 0" and 2) "forever in the future from t_1 if an acknowledgment has been received by S and the value of the bit is 0, then S knows that R knows the bit is equal to 0."

By means of an implementation of the technique above we were able to check that the properties above are not satisfied (as intuitively is the case given $\mathcal{R}$'s possible behaviour). More precisely, we can check that the negations of the properties above are true, i.e., the following formulae are satisfied on the model for $\mathcal{A}_{BTP}$:

$$\varphi_1 = \text{EF}_{[t_1,\infty]}(\textbf{recack} \wedge \textbf{bit0} \wedge \overline{\text{K}}_{\mathcal{R}}(\neg\textbf{bit0})), \text{ and}$$
$$\varphi_2 = \text{EF}_{[t_1,\infty]}(\textbf{recack} \wedge \textbf{bit0} \wedge \overline{\text{K}}_{\mathcal{S}}\overline{\text{K}}_{\mathcal{R}}(\neg\textbf{bit0})).$$

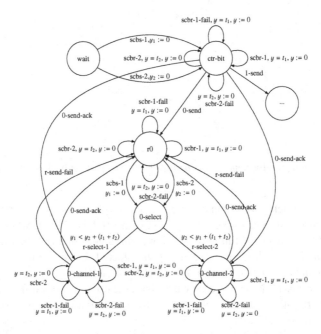

Fig. 2. An automaton for Receiver - the part for bit 0. The part for bit 1 is symmetric.

Tables 1 and 2 illustrate error traces for the above properties, i.e., it shows the witness for the formulae φ_1 and φ_2, respectively, which have been generated by our implementation.

To verify satisfaction of φ_1 over the model for $\mathcal{A}_{BTP}$, 2 paths of length 11 were required. To do this we checked satisfaction of the Boolean formula encoding the translation of the formula φ_1 and the appropriate fragments of the model for $\mathcal{A}_{BTP}$ as described in [14]. The formula in question consists of 125260 variables and 258821 clauses; our implementation needed 19.6 second and 18.7 MB memory to produce it. Its satisfaction was checked by MiniSat [9], a mainstream SAT solver; 4.0 seconds and 19.9 MB of memory were needed to check this.

For what concerns the satisfaction of φ_2, the corresponding experimental results are presented in Table 3 and in Table 4. Table 3 refers to the search assuming 3 paths

Table 1. A witness for the property φ_1

depth	locations		clocks' valuation						
0	decide	wait	$0\frac{0}{8192}$	$0\frac{0}{8192}$	$0\frac{0}{8192}$	$0\frac{0}{8192}$	$0\frac{0}{8192}$	$0\frac{0}{8192}$	$0\frac{0}{8192}$
1	decide	wait	$0\frac{4608}{8192}$	$0\frac{4608}{8192}$	$0\frac{4608}{8192}$	$0\frac{4608}{8192}$	$0\frac{4608}{8192}$	$0\frac{4608}{8192}$	$0\frac{4608}{8192}$
2	0-ctr-bit	wait	$0\frac{4608}{8192}$	$0\frac{4608}{8192}$	$0\frac{4608}{8192}$	$0\frac{4608}{8192}$	$0\frac{4608}{8192}$	$0\frac{4608}{8192}$	$0\frac{4608}{8192}$
3	0-ctr-bit	wait	$1\frac{0}{8192}$	$1\frac{0}{8192}$	$1\frac{0}{8192}$	$1\frac{0}{8192}$	$1\frac{0}{8192}$	$1\frac{0}{8192}$	$1\frac{0}{8192}$
4	0-ctr-bit	wait	$1\frac{7168}{8192}$	$1\frac{7168}{8192}$	$1\frac{7168}{8192}$	$1\frac{7168}{8192}$	$1\frac{7168}{8192}$	$1\frac{7168}{8192}$	$1\frac{7168}{8192}$
5	0-ctr-bit	wait	$2\frac{0}{8192}$	$2\frac{0}{8192}$	$2\frac{0}{8192}$	$2\frac{0}{8192}$	$2\frac{0}{8192}$	$2\frac{0}{8192}$	$2\frac{0}{8192}$
6	0-ctr-bit	ctr-bit	$2\frac{0}{8192}$	$2\frac{0}{8192}$	$2\frac{0}{8192}$	$2\frac{0}{8192}$	$2\frac{0}{8192}$	$2\frac{0}{8192}$	$2\frac{0}{8192}$
7	0-ctr-bit	ctr-bit	$2\frac{7524}{8192}$	$2\frac{7524}{8192}$	$2\frac{7524}{8192}$	$2\frac{7524}{8192}$	$2\frac{7524}{8192}$	$2\frac{7524}{8192}$	$2\frac{7524}{8192}$
8	0-ctr-bit	ctr-bit	$3\frac{0}{8192}$	$3\frac{0}{8192}$	$3\frac{0}{8192}$	$3\frac{0}{8192}$	$3\frac{0}{8192}$	$3\frac{0}{8192}$	$3\frac{0}{8192}$
9	0-select	ctr-bit	$3\frac{0}{8192}$	$3\frac{0}{8192}$	$3\frac{0}{8192}$	$3\frac{0}{8192}$	$3\frac{0}{8192}$	$3\frac{0}{8192}$	$3\frac{0}{8192}$
10	0-select	ctr-bit	$3\frac{1}{8192}$	$3\frac{1}{8192}$	$3\frac{1}{8192}$	$3\frac{1}{8192}$	$3\frac{1}{8192}$	$3\frac{1}{8192}$	$3\frac{1}{8192}$
11	0-ack	0-channel-1	$3\frac{1}{8192}$	$3\frac{1}{8192}$	$3\frac{1}{8192}$	$3\frac{1}{8192}$	$3\frac{1}{8192}$	$3\frac{1}{8192}$	$3\frac{1}{8192}$

Table 2. A witness for the property φ_2

depth	locations		clocks' valuation						
0	decide	wait	$0\frac{0}{8192}$	$0\frac{0}{8192}$	$0\frac{0}{8192}$	$0\frac{0}{8192}$	$0\frac{0}{8192}$	$0\frac{0}{8192}$	$0\frac{0}{8192}$
1	decide	wait	$0\frac{4608}{8192}$	$0\frac{4608}{8192}$	$0\frac{4608}{8192}$	$0\frac{4608}{8192}$	$0\frac{4608}{8192}$	$0\frac{4608}{8192}$	$0\frac{4608}{8192}$
2	0-ctr-bit	wait	$0\frac{4608}{8192}$	$0\frac{4608}{8192}$	$0\frac{4608}{8192}$	$0\frac{4608}{8192}$	$0\frac{4608}{8192}$	$0\frac{4608}{8192}$	$0\frac{4608}{8192}$
3	0-ctr-bit	wait	$1\frac{0}{8192}$	$1\frac{0}{8192}$	$1\frac{0}{8192}$	$1\frac{0}{8192}$	$1\frac{0}{8192}$	$1\frac{0}{8192}$	$1\frac{0}{8192}$
4	0-ctr-bit	wait	$1\frac{7168}{8192}$	$1\frac{7168}{8192}$	$1\frac{7168}{8192}$	$1\frac{7168}{8192}$	$1\frac{7168}{8192}$	$1\frac{7168}{8192}$	$1\frac{7168}{8192}$
5	0-ctr-bit	wait	$2\frac{0}{8192}$	$2\frac{0}{8192}$	$2\frac{0}{8192}$	$2\frac{0}{8192}$	$2\frac{0}{8192}$	$2\frac{0}{8192}$	$2\frac{0}{8192}$
6	0-ctr-bit	ctr-bit	$2\frac{0}{8192}$	$2\frac{0}{8192}$	$2\frac{0}{8192}$	$2\frac{0}{8192}$	$2\frac{0}{8192}$	$2\frac{0}{8192}$	$2\frac{0}{8192}$
7	0-ctr-bit	ctr-bit	$2\frac{7524}{8192}$	$2\frac{7524}{8192}$	$2\frac{7524}{8192}$	$2\frac{7524}{8192}$	$2\frac{7524}{8192}$	$2\frac{7524}{8192}$	$2\frac{7524}{8192}$
8	0-ctr-bit	ctr-bit	$3\frac{0}{8192}$	$3\frac{0}{8192}$	$3\frac{0}{8192}$	$3\frac{0}{8192}$	$3\frac{0}{8192}$	$3\frac{0}{8192}$	$3\frac{0}{8192}$
9	0-select	ctr-bit	$3\frac{0}{8192}$	$3\frac{0}{8192}$	$3\frac{0}{8192}$	$3\frac{0}{8192}$	$3\frac{0}{8192}$	$3\frac{0}{8192}$	$3\frac{0}{8192}$
10	0-select	ctr-bit	$3\frac{1}{8192}$	$3\frac{1}{8192}$	$3\frac{1}{8192}$	$3\frac{1}{8192}$	$3\frac{1}{8192}$	$3\frac{1}{8192}$	$3\frac{1}{8192}$
11	0-ack	0-channel-2	$3\frac{1}{8192}$	$3\frac{1}{8192}$	$3\frac{1}{8192}$	$3\frac{1}{8192}$	$3\frac{1}{8192}$	$3\frac{1}{8192}$	$3\frac{1}{8192}$

are needed (this is the upper bound is given by the function f_k); Table 4 summarises the result for a search of only 1 path. The tables show the following data: the first column represents the bound on the model for $\mathcal{A}_{BTP}$; the next two show the number of variables and clauses generated by BMC during the translation of φ_2 into a Boolean formula; the next two show the time and memory needed by BMC to generate the set of clauses; the next two columns give the time and the memory required by MiniSat to check satisfaction, and the last column shows the answer given by MiniSat.

For reference, all the above experiments were performed on an AMD Athlon XP 1800 (1544 MHz), 768 MB main memory, running Linux with Kernel 2.6.15.

Table 3. The computation of the witness - 3 paths

	BMC				MiniSat		
k	variables	clauses	sec	MB	sec	MB	satisfiable
2	12243	28811	2.7	4.5	< 0.1	5.1	NO
3	20771	48413	8.8	5.7	< 0.1	6.2	NO
4	35589	85115	24.0	8.0	0.2	8.1	NO
5	49967	117551	55.2	9.8	0.6	10.1	NO
6	66952	154829	115.7	11.9	1.1	11.9	NO
7	86688	197030	206.1	14.9	2.4	14.2	NO
8	120067	278552	356.9	19.2	12.9	20.2	NO
9	147687	337205	587.3	23.9	9.9	24.1	NO
10	178628	401492	922.3	27.5	20.5	28.6	NO
11	213034	471494	1364.4	31.4	320.0	81.8	YES

Table 4. The computation of the witness - 1 path

	BMC				MiniSat		
k	variables	clauses	sec	MB	sec	MB	satisfiable
2	3570	7706	0.2	3.2	< 0.1	3.7	NO
3	6021	12877	0.5	3.5	< 0.1	4.2	NO
4	10164	22320	1.3	4.2	< 0.1	4.7	NO
5	14213	30551	2.5	4.6	< 0.1	5.2	NO
6	18997	39934	4.8	5.3	< 0.1	5.8	NO
7	24564	50496	8.4	6.0	0.1	6.2	NO
8	33578	70301	14.4	7.0	0.2	7.5	NO
9	41277	84625	23.6	8.3	0.4	8.5	NO
10	49925	100281	33.7	9.2	0.4	9.4	NO
11	59570	117296	54.0	10.2	0.9	10.3	YES

Unfortunately we are not able to compare these results to other tools as we are not aware of any other implementation available that is capable of a real-time epistemic check for (diagonal and non-diagonal) automata.

6   Conclusions

Model checking real-time in AI and MAS is still in its infancy. In [21] a first proposal was made for a bounded model checking algorithm for real-time epistemic properties based on non-diagonal automata semantics. In this paper we have tried to extend that work by allowing the expressivity of clock differences. We have proposed a syntax, semantics for the logic, as well as a bounded model checking method, and showed experimental results of a preliminary implementation for a real-time version of the alternating bit protocol.

References

1. Asarin, E., Bozga, M., Kerbrat, A., Maler, O., Pnueli, A., Rasse, A.: Data-structures for the verification of Timed Automata. In: Maler, O. (ed.) HART 1997. LNCS, vol. 1201, pp. 346–360. Springer, Heidelberg (1997)
2. Behrmann, G., Larsen, K., Pearson, J., Weise, C., Yi, W.: Efficient Timed Reachability Analysis Using Clock Difference Diagrams. In: Halbwachs, N., Peled, D.A. (eds.) CAV 1999. LNCS, vol. 1633, pp. 341–353. Springer, Heidelberg (1999)
3. Bérard, B., Petit, A., Diekert, V., Gastin, P.: Characterization of the expressive power of silent transitions in timed automata. Fundamenta Informaticae 36(2-3), 145–182 (1998)
4. Biere, A., Cimatti, A., Clarke, E., Zhu, Y.: Symbolic model checking without BDDs. In: Cleaveland, W.R. (ed.) ETAPS 1999 and TACAS 1999. LNCS, vol. 1579, pp. 193–207. Springer, Heidelberg (1999)
5. Bouyer, P., Laroussinie, F., Reynier, P.: Diagonal constraints in timed automata: Forward analysis of timed systems. In: Pettersson, P., Yi, W. (eds.) FORMATS 2005. LNCS, vol. 3829, pp. 112–126. Springer, Heidelberg (2005)
6. Cimatti, A., Clarke, E.M., Giunchiglia, E., Giunchiglia, F., Pistore, M., Roveri, M., Sebastiani, R., Tacchella, A.: NuSMV2: An open-source tool for symbolic model checking. In: Brinksma, E., Larsen, K.G. (eds.) CAV 2002. LNCS, vol. 2404, pp. 359–364. Springer, Heidelberg (2002)
7. Dembiński, P., Janowska, A., Janowski, P., Penczek, W., Półrola, A., Szreter, M., Woźna, B., Zbrzezny, A.: VerICS: A tool for verifying Timed Automata and Estelle specifications. In: Garavel, H., Hatcliff, J. (eds.) ETAPS 2003 and TACAS 2003. LNCS, vol. 2619, pp. 278–283. Springer, Heidelberg (2003)
8. Dill, D.: Timing assumptions and verification of finite state concurrent systems. In: Sifakis, J. (ed.) Automatic Verification Methods for Finite State Systems. LNCS, vol. 407, pp. 197–212. Springer, Heidelberg (1990)
9. Eén, N., Sörensson, N.: MiniSat,
http://www.cs.chalmers.se/Cs/Research/FormalMethods/MiniSat/
10. Fagin, R., Halpern, J.Y., Moses, Y., Vardi, M.Y.: Reasoning about Knowledge. MIT Press, Cambridge (1995)
11. Kacprzak, M., Lomuscio, A., Penczek, W.: Verification of multiagent systems via unbounded model checking. In: Jennings, N.R., Sierra, C., Sonenberg, L., Tambe, M. (eds.) Proceedings of the Third International Conference on Autonomous Agents and Multiagent Systems (AAMAS'04), July 2004, vol. II, pp. 638–645. ACM, New York (2004)
12. Lomuscio, A., Raimondi, F.: MCMAS: A model checker for multi-agent systems. In: Hermanns, H., Palsberg, J. (eds.) TACAS 2006 and ETAPS 2006. LNCS, vol. 3920, pp. 450–454. Springer, Heidelberg (2006)
13. Lomuscio, A., Sergot, M.: A formalisation of violation, error recovery, and enforcement in the bit transmission problem. Journal of Applied Logic 2(1), 93–116 (2004)
14. Lomuscio, A., Woźna, B., Zbrzezny, A.: Bounded model checking real-time multi-agent systems with clock differences: theory and implementation. Technical Report RN/06/03, Department of Computer Science, University College London, Gower Street, London WC1E 6BT, United Kingdom (2006)
15. Nabialek, W., Niewiadomski, A., Penczek, W., Półrola, A., Szreter, M.: VerICS 2004: A model checker for real time and multi-agent systems. In: Proceedings of the International Workshop on Concurrency, Specification and Programming (CS&P'04), Informatik-Berichte,Humboldt University, vol. 170, pp. 88–99 (2004)
16. Penczek, W., Lomuscio, A.: Verifying epistemic properties of multi-agent systems via bounded model checking. Fundamenta Informaticae 55(2), 167–185 (2003)

17. Penczek, W., Woźna, B., Zbrzezny, A.: Towards bounded model checking for the universal fragment of TCTL. In: Damm, W., Olderog, E.-R. (eds.) FTRTFT 2002. LNCS, vol. 2469, pp. 265–288. Springer, Heidelberg (2002)
18. Raimondi, F., Lomuscio, A.: Automatic verification of multi-agent systems by model checking via OBDDs. Journal of Applied Logic, 2007. To appear in Special issue on Logic-based agent verification (2007)
19. Tripakis, S., Yovine, S.: Analysis of timed systems using time-abstracting bisimulations. Formal Methods in System Design 18(1), 25–68 (2001)
20. van der Meyden, R., Su, K.: Symbolic model checking the knowledge of the dining cryptographers. In: Proceedings of the 17th IEEE Computer Security Foundations Workshop (CSFW'04), pp. 280–291. IEEE Computer Society Press, Washington, DC, USA (2004)
21. Woźna, B., Lomuscio, A., Penczek, W.: Bounded model checking for knowledge over real time. In: Proceedings of the 4st International Conference on Autonomous Agents and Multi-Agent Systems (AAMAS'05), July 2005, vol. 1, pp. 165–172. ACM Press, New York (2005)
22. Zbrzezny, A.: SAT-based reachability checking for timed automata with diagonal constraints. Fundamenta Informaticae 67(1-3), 303–322 (2005)

Symbolic Model Checking of Logics with Actions

Charles Pecheur[1,*] and Franco Raimondi[2,**]

[1] Université catholique de Louvain
charles.pecheur@uclouvain.be
[2] University College London
f.raimondi@cs.ucl.ac.uk

Abstract. Reasoning about agents and modalities such as knowledge and belief leads to models where different relations over states co-exist, or equivalently, where information (labels, actions) is associated to state transitions. This paper discusses how to augment classical CTL symbolic model-checking to support logics with actions such as A-CTL (action-CTL), and how this can be implemented using BDDs in tools such as the SMV/NuSMV package. Considering general action-state structures, we first propose a natural extension of CTL to actions, called Action-Restricted CTL (ARCTL) and adapt classical results from CTL to express model checking based on three functions *eax*, *eau* and *eag*. On these grounds, we present two different implementations of symbolic model checking with actions. The first approach encodes action-state models and logics into pure state-based models and logics, that can be checked with existing model-checkers. The second approach consists in a native implementation of the three extended operators. We report on our prototype implementation of both approaches based on NuSMV and give an overview of how this is used to model-check the temporal epistemic logic CTLK.

1 Introduction

In the domains of artificial intelligence and multi-agent systems, it is natural to reason about both actions *and* states. Moreover, a number of modalities, such as epistemic or deontic, can be formalized in terms of relations over the states of a system or model. In this setting, it is desirable to have analysis techniques and tools where information can be associated to both states and transitions of the model, or more generally where more than one relation over states can be considered within the same model.

Symbolic model checking, and the SMV tool in particular, have adopted a state-based view of the systems to be verified, expressed mathematically as Kripke structures. Meanwhile, another large body of work has developed based on an observable, action-based view of systems, where the state itself is abstracted away and models are characterized by the visible actions they can perform, and expressed mathematically as Labeled Transition Systems (LTS). These

---

* With RIACS at NASA Ames while performing this work.
** On internship with MCT at NASA Ames while performing this work.

S. Edelkamp and A. Lomuscio (Eds.): MoChart IV, LNAI 4428, pp. 113–128, 2007.

two views can be, and have been, combined. In this paper, we designate as *mixed* the models and logics that combine state-based and action-based reasoning. However, to the best of our knowledge, there is no widely available tool that allows to apply the power of BDD-based symbolic model checking of branching-time logics to mixed models and logics.

This paper discusses how BDD-based symbolic model checking for mixed logics can be achieved, and presents two different implementations:

1. by reducing the mixed-logic model-checking problem to a state-based model-checking problem that can be solved with existing tools;
2. by extending existing model-checkers to support mixed models and logics natively.

To this end, after reviewing the prominent existing state-based and action-based models (Kripke structures, labeled transition systems) and logics (CTL, A-CTL) in Section 2, we set our formal definition of mixed models, introduce a mixed logic, ARCTL, that cleanly generalizes CTL with actions, and extend symbolic model checking from CTL to ARCTL in Section 3. In Section 4, we describe how mixed models and logics can be reduced to Kripke structures and CTL while preserving validity. In Section 5, we describe a prototype implementation of both approaches based on the NuSMV tool [1]. In Section 6, we give an overview of how a model checker for the temporal epistemic logic CTLK [2] has been built on top of these implementations. Finally, Section 7 discusses related work and Section 8 draws conclusions and perspectives.

2   Background

2.1   State-Based Logics

Computation Tree Logic (CTL) [3,4] is the classical branching-time logic used in symbolic model checking. Given a set of propositional atoms $\mathcal{P}$, a CTL formula is interpreted over a *Kripke Structure* (KS) $\mathcal{K} = \langle \mathcal{S}, \mathcal{S}_0, \mathcal{R}, \mathcal{V} \rangle$, where $\mathcal{S}$ is a non-empty set of states, $\mathcal{S}_0 \subseteq \mathcal{S}$ is a set of possible initial states, $\mathcal{R} \subseteq \mathcal{S} \times \mathcal{S}$ is a transition relation, denoted $s \longrightarrow s'$, and $\mathcal{V} : \mathcal{S} \to 2^{\mathcal{P}}$ is an interpretation function.

The syntax of CTL is given by the following grammar, where $p \in \mathcal{P}$ and ϕ and γ range respectively over CTL (state) formulae and path formulae:

$$\phi ::= \mathsf{true} \mid p \mid \neg\phi \mid \phi \wedge \phi \mid \mathsf{E}\gamma \mid \mathsf{A}\gamma$$
$$\gamma ::= \mathsf{X}\,\phi \mid \phi\,\mathsf{U}\,\phi$$

with the usual derived Boolean operators and the following derived temporal operators:

$$\mathsf{EF}\,\phi = \mathsf{E}[\mathsf{true}\,\mathsf{U}\,\phi] \quad \mathsf{AF}\,\phi = \mathsf{A}[\mathsf{true}\,\mathsf{U}\,\phi]$$
$$\mathsf{EG}\,\phi = \neg\mathsf{AF}\,\neg\phi \quad \mathsf{AG}\,\phi = \neg\mathsf{EF}\,\neg\phi$$

Note that temporal logic operators take precedence over Boolean connectives: $\mathsf{EX}\,\phi \vee \phi' = (\mathsf{EX}\,\phi) \vee \phi' \neq \mathsf{EX}\,(\phi \vee \phi')$. The semantics of a CTL formula ϕ is defined as a satisfaction relation $s \models \phi$ over states $s \in \mathcal{S}$, see for example [4]. We postpone the detailed definition of semantics to mixed logics in Section 3.2.

All CTL operators can be reduced to EX, EU and EG. Symbolic model checking of CTL over finite models, as implemented in the SMV family of tools, works by providing BDD-based evaluation functions $ex(S)$, $eu(S, S')$ and $eg(S)$, where S, S' are Boolean encodings of sets of states, that compute the semantics of the corresponding operators. In the case of eu and eg, this means computing fixpoints over ex (which are guaranteed to converge thanks to finiteness of the model), for example $eg(S) = \nu Z.S \cap ex(Z)$ [4].

CTL symbolic model checking has been extended to support *fairness*, in the form of a set of conditions that characterize fair computations. Fairness is not taken into consideration within the scope of this paper, but the issue is nevertheless discussed in Section 3.4.

2.2 Action-Based Logics

In contrast to state-based logics such as CTL, *action-based logics* focus on the actions that a system can perform. These logics are interpreted over *labeled transition systems* (LTS). A LTS is a structure $\mathcal{L} = \langle \mathcal{S}, \mathcal{S}_0, \mathcal{A}, \mathcal{T} \rangle$, where $\mathcal{S}$ and $\mathcal{S}_0$ are as in Kripke structures, $\mathcal{A}$ is a set of actions and $\mathcal{T} \subseteq \mathcal{S} \times \mathcal{A} \times \mathcal{S}$ is a labeled transition relation. We write $s \xrightarrow{a} s'$ for $(s, a, s') \in \mathcal{T}$, $s \not\xrightarrow{a}$ when no such s' exists and $s \not\rightarrow$ when no such a and s' exist.

For example, *Action CTL*, or A-CTL [5], is an adaptation of CTL to labeled transition systems.[1] A-CTL extends CTL operators with action formulae α interpreted over actions $a \in \mathcal{A}$. For example, the A-CTL formula $\mathsf{A}[\phi_\alpha \mathsf{U}_{\alpha'} \phi']$ holds if all paths are of the form

$$s_0 \xrightarrow{a_1} s_1 \cdots \xrightarrow{a_k} s_k \xrightarrow{a'} s'$$

for some k, where all s_i, all a_i, s' and a' respectively satisfy ϕ, α, ϕ' and α'. The full syntax and semantics of A-CTL, defined over LTS, can be found in [5]. [6] provides a comprehensive survey of temporal logics with actions, and A-CTL in particular, including fixpoint characterizations of A-CTL operators.

Note that classical action-based models also feature a distinguished internal action. We do not deal explicitly with internal actions in the scope of this paper; our definitions correspond to a "strong" interpretation that treats all actions uniformly.

3 Mixing States and Actions

In this section, we set our formalisation of mixed models and formulae, that combine state-based and model-based reasoning.

---

[1] Action CTL is usually abbreviated ACTL, but that could be confused with the universal fragment of CTL, unfortunately also referred to as ACTL, for example in [4].

3.1   Mixed Transition Systems

We can generalize both state-based models (Kripke structures, KS) and action-based models (Labeled Transition Systems, or LTS) into a common super-structure that we call *mixed transition system* (MTS). Given two sets of propositional atoms $\mathcal{P}_S$ and $\mathcal{P}_A$, respectively over states and actions, a *mixed transition system* over $\mathcal{P}_S$ and $\mathcal{P}_A$ is a structure $\mathcal{M} = \langle S, S_0, A, T, V_S, V_A \rangle$, where

- S is a non-empty set of states;
- $S_0 \subseteq S$ is the set of possible initial states;
- A is a non-empty set of actions;
- $T \subseteq S \times A \times S$ is the transition relation;
- $V_S : S \to 2^{\mathcal{P}_S}$ is the interpretation function on states;
- $V_A : A \to 2^{\mathcal{P}_A}$ is the interpretation function on actions.

MTS combine actions over transitions from LTS and propositional atoms over states from KS, and add propositional atoms over actions that allow for a generalized and more uniform presentation of logic formulae over MTS models.

An MTS can be projected to a KS sub-structure $\langle S, S_0, \mathcal{R}, V_S \rangle$, where $\mathcal{R} = \{(s, s') \mid (s, a, s') \in T\}$, or an LTS sub-structure $\langle S, S_0, A, T \rangle$, and thus both state-based and action-based logics can be interpreted over an MTS.

A *path* π of $\mathcal{M}$ is a finite or infinite sequence of connected transition steps $(s_{i-1}, a_i, s_i) \in T$, denoted as $s_0 \xrightarrow{a_1} s_1 \xrightarrow{a_2} s_2 \ldots$. In particular, a zero-length path consists of a single state. Let T^* (resp. T^ω) be the set of finite (resp. infinite) paths of $\mathcal{M}$. Given a finite (resp. infinite) path $\pi = s_0 \xrightarrow{a_1} s_1 \xrightarrow{a_2} s_2 \ldots \xrightarrow{a_n} s_n$ $(\xrightarrow{a_{n+1}} \ldots)$, we define:

- $|\pi| = n$ (resp. ω), the length of a path;
- $\pi(i) = s_i$, the i-th state of π ($0 \leq i \leq |\pi|$);
- $\pi(\bullet i) = a_i$, the i-th action of π ($1 \leq i \leq |\pi|$).

A *full-path* is a path that is either infinite or ends in a terminal state. We define $\Pi(\mathcal{M})$ (or just Π) as the set of full-paths of $\mathcal{M}$, and $\Pi(\mathcal{M}, s)$ (or $\Pi(s)$) as the set of full-paths from state s.

$$\Pi(\mathcal{M}) := T^\omega \cup \{\pi \in T^* \mid (|\pi| = n \wedge \pi(n) \not\longrightarrow)\}$$
$$\Pi(\mathcal{M}, s) := \{\pi \in \Pi(\mathcal{M}) \mid \pi(0) = s\}$$

Note that unlike classical definitions of CTL model-checking, we do not enforce the transition T to be serial; deadlocks or refused actions are in general possible and full-paths need not be infinite. Even if T were required to be serial, action-based logics have to consider cases where some action a is not allowed ($s \not\xrightarrow{a}$), so deadlock states where no action is allowed ($s \not\longrightarrow$) arise as a particular case anyway.

3.2   Action-Restricted CTL

As a logic over mixed state-action models, we introduce a generalization of CTL, called *Action-Restricted CTL*, or ARCTL. ARCTL has the same temporal operators as CTL, except that they can be restricted to paths whose actions satisfy a given action formula α. The syntax of ARCTL is given by the following grammar, where $p \in \mathcal{P}_S$, $b \in \mathcal{P}_A$, and ϕ, γ and α range respectively over ARCTL (state) formulae, path formulae and action formulae:

$$\phi ::= \text{true} \mid p \mid \neg\phi \mid \phi \wedge \phi \mid \mathsf{E}_\alpha\gamma \mid \mathsf{A}_\alpha\gamma$$
$$\alpha ::= \text{true} \mid b \mid \neg\alpha \mid \alpha \wedge \alpha$$
$$\gamma ::= \mathsf{X}\,\phi \mid \phi\,\mathsf{U}\,\phi$$

Derived forms such as $\mathsf{E}_\alpha\mathsf{F}\,\phi$ are defined as for CTL. Intuitively, given an ARCTL formula $\mathsf{E}_\alpha\gamma$, the path formula γ is evaluated over full α-prefixes of full-paths of the model. To formalize that, we define the α-restriction of a MTS $\mathcal{M} = \langle \mathcal{S}, \mathcal{S}_0, \mathcal{A}, \mathcal{T}, \mathcal{V}_S, \mathcal{V}_A \rangle$ as the structure $\mathcal{M}|_\alpha = \langle \mathcal{S}, \mathcal{S}_0, \mathcal{A}, \mathcal{T}|_\alpha, \mathcal{V}_S, \mathcal{V}_A \rangle$, where $\mathcal{T}|_\alpha = \{(s, a, s') \in \mathcal{T} \mid a \models \alpha\}$. For conciseness we write $\Pi|_\alpha$ for $\Pi(\mathcal{M}|_\alpha)$ and $\Pi|_\alpha(s)$ for $\Pi(\mathcal{M}|_\alpha, s)$. Note that, by construction, any path (or full-path) of $\mathcal{M}|_\alpha$ is a prefix of a path (or full-path) of $\mathcal{M}$. A_α and E_α are interpreted over the full-paths of $\mathcal{M}|_\alpha$, and the path formulae are defined as in standard CTL. We define the semantic relation $(\mathcal{M}, s) \models \phi$, or concisely $s \models \phi$, as follows (we omit the natural semantics of Boolean connectives and propositional atoms):

$$s \models \mathsf{A}_\alpha\gamma \text{ iff } \forall\pi \in \Pi|_\alpha(s) \cdot \pi \models \gamma$$
$$s \models \mathsf{E}_\alpha\gamma \text{ iff } \exists\pi \in \Pi|_\alpha(s) \cdot \pi \models \gamma$$
$$\pi \models \mathsf{X}\,\phi \text{ iff } \underline{|\pi| \geq 1} \wedge \pi(1) \models \phi$$
$$\pi \models \phi\,\mathsf{U}\,\phi' \text{ iff } \exists i \geq 0 \cdot \underline{|\pi| \geq i} \wedge \pi(i) \models \phi' \wedge \forall k \in [0, i-1] \cdot \pi(k) \models \phi$$

The underlined terms pertain to finite paths. In particular, if $s \not\xrightarrow{\alpha}$ (i.e. $s \not\xrightarrow{a}$ for any $a \models \alpha$), then $\Pi|_\alpha(s) = \{s\}$, containing a single zero-length trace, and both $\mathsf{E}_\alpha\mathsf{X}\,\phi$ and $\mathsf{A}_\alpha\mathsf{X}\,\neg\phi$ are false for any ϕ, whereas $\neg\mathsf{E}_\alpha\mathsf{X}\,\text{true}$ is true. For any ϕ, α and s, we have that one and only one of $\mathsf{E}_\alpha\mathsf{X}\phi$, $\mathsf{A}_\alpha\mathsf{X}\neg\phi$ and $\neg\mathsf{E}_\alpha\mathsf{X}\text{true}$ holds in s. Also note that $\mathsf{E}_\alpha\mathsf{G}\,\phi$ also holds in s if there is a *finite* α-full-path from s where ϕ holds. In contrast, we can define $\mathsf{E}_\alpha\mathsf{G}^\omega\,\phi$ that holds only for infinite α-full-paths, with

$$\mathsf{E}_\alpha\mathsf{G}^\omega\,\phi = \mathsf{E}_\alpha\mathsf{G}\,(\phi \wedge \mathsf{E}_\alpha\mathsf{X}\,\text{true})$$

If we restrict action formulae to $\alpha = \text{true}$ and consider the Kripke substructure in $\mathcal{M}$, we obtain a semantics for CTL with finite and infinite traces. One can easily check that this semantics is consistent with the classical one for infinite traces.

Note that A-CTL can be extended to mixed models in the same manner. We chose instead to introduce ARCTL because it offers a more uniform interpretation of the action conditions: for all path formulae γ, $\mathsf{A}_\alpha\gamma$ means "for all α-full-paths, γ holds". In contrast, in A-CTL, $\mathsf{AF}_\alpha\phi$ is co-variant in α ("all paths do remain α-paths *until* they eventually reach ϕ") while $\mathsf{AG}_\alpha \phi$ is contra-variant ("all paths, *as long as* they remain α-paths, maintain ϕ"). Besides its structural simplicity, this also makes ARCTL appropriate for cases where actions denote transition relations of a different nature, such as temporal and epistemic modalities: if some action t is used for temporal transitions, temporal properties can be expressed as t-restricted ARCTL formulae, with their usual CTL interpretation. This was indeed the initial motivation for formulating this logic, as illustrated in section 6. On the other hand, it must be noted that A-CTL is more expressive than ARCTL on pure action models: $\mathsf{A}(\phi \,_\alpha\mathsf{U}_{\alpha'} \phi')$ cannot be translated to ARCTL (unless α and α' are disjoint).

3.3   Model Checking of ARCTL

Symbolic model-checking can be applied to ARCTL in the same way as to CTL, with two extensions: (i) transitions are constrained by action formulae, and (ii) additional conditions are set to deal with finite paths. For (i), the pre-image computation embodied in the function $ex(S)$ is extended to deal with actions. For (ii), we modify the computations to deal specifically with finite paths.

Given $S, S' \in 2^S$ and $A \in 2^A$, we define functions $eax(A, S)$, $eau(A, S, S')$ and $eag(A, S)$ as follows:

$$eax(A, S) = \{s \mid \exists a, s' \cdot s \xrightarrow{a} s' \wedge a \in A \wedge s' \in S\}$$
$$eau(A, S, S') = \mu Z \cdot S' \cup (S \cap eax(A, Z))$$
$$eag(A, S) = \nu Z \cdot S \cap eax(A, Z)$$

where we write $\mu Z.F(Z)$ (resp. $\nu Z.F(Z)$) for the least (resp. greatest) fixpoint of F. For convenience, we also define $eax(A) = eax(A, S)$. Whereas eax and eau exactly capture the ARCTL operators $\mathsf{E}_\alpha\mathsf{X}$ and $\mathsf{E}_\alpha\mathsf{U}$, note that eag accepts infinite paths only; it corresponds to $\mathsf{E}_\alpha\mathsf{G}^\omega$ and not $\mathsf{E}_\alpha\mathsf{G}$. These functions are immediate translations of fixpoint characterizations of the corresponding operators:

$$\mathsf{E}_\alpha[\phi \,\mathsf{U}\, \phi'] = \mu Z \cdot \phi' \vee (\phi \wedge \mathsf{E}_\alpha\mathsf{X}\, Z)$$
$$\mathsf{E}_\alpha\mathsf{G}^\omega\, \phi = \nu Z \cdot \phi \wedge \mathsf{E}_\alpha\mathsf{X}\, Z$$

These characterizations can be proven through a simple adaptation of similar results on CTL, see for example [4]. As an aside, they also imply that ARCTL, like CTL, belongs to the alternation-free fragment of modal μ-calculus, that can be checked in linear time w.r.t. the size of the model and formula.

As in CTL, all ARCTL operators can be expressed in terms of the three primitive computations above, as follows (where $\neg S$ stands for $\mathcal{S} \setminus S$, the complement of S). Note the underlined $eax(A)$ terms, needed for finite traces.

$$[\![\mathsf{E}_\alpha\mathsf{X}\, \phi]\!] = eax([\![\alpha]\!], [\![\phi]\!])$$
$$[\![\mathsf{A}_\alpha\mathsf{X}\, \phi]\!] = \underline{eax([\![\alpha]\!])} \cap \neg eax([\![\alpha]\!], \neg[\![\phi]\!])$$
$$[\![\mathsf{E}_\alpha(\phi \,\mathsf{U}\, \phi')]\!] = eau([\![\alpha]\!], [\![\phi]\!], [\![\phi']\!])$$
$$[\![\mathsf{A}_\alpha(\phi \,\mathsf{U}\, \phi')]\!] = \neg eau([\![\alpha]\!], \neg[\![\phi']\!], \neg[\![\phi']\!] \cap (\neg[\![\phi]\!] \cup \underline{\neg eax([\![\alpha]\!])})) \cap \neg eag([\![\alpha]\!], \neg[\![\phi']\!])$$

The evaluation functions eax, eau and eag can be implemented in a BDD-based model checker like NuSMV, based on a Boolean encoding of $\mathcal{S}$ and $\mathcal{A}$, in a very similar way to CTL model-checking as implemented in SMV [7]. A prototype of such an implementation is described in Section 5.3.

3.4   Fairness

CTL symbolic model checking can also handle *fairness conditions*, in the form of a set of sets of states $\mathcal{F} \in 2^{2^{\mathcal{S}}}$. A path is *fair* if it visits every set in $\mathcal{F}$ infinitely often. The functions ex, eg and eu have variants ex_F, eg_F and eu_F restricted to fair paths.

This approach can be extended to mixed models and ARCTL, by considering fair α-full-paths when evaluating α-restricted operators. In that setting, fairness conditions can be extended to sets of states-action pairs $\mathcal{F} \in 2^{2^{\mathcal{S} \times \mathcal{A}}}$ (this is indeed already implemented in NuSMV).

However, by their very definition, fair paths are necessarily infinite, so fair model checking does not work well at all with finite paths. If a state has no infinite path from it, then there is no fair path either, and all E formulae are false and all A formulae are true. As an extreme example, if $s \xrightarrow{a} s' \nrightarrow$, then $s \not\models \mathsf{EX}\,\langle\mathsf{true}\rangle$, because there is no fair path from s'.

Extending fair CTL model checking to action-based logics interpreted over finite α-full-paths is an important issue to be further investigated.

4   From Mixed to State-Based Logic

This section presents a transformation *post* from mixed transition systems to Kripke structures and from ARCTL to classical CTL, such that the combined transformation preserves validity. This provides a way to reduce action-based and mixed model-checking to standard CTL model checking, that can be performed using a tool such as SMV.

4.1   Post-Projection of Mixed Models

Given a MTS $\mathcal{M} = \langle \mathcal{S}, \mathcal{S}_0, \mathcal{A}, \mathcal{T}, \mathcal{V}_S, \mathcal{V}_A \rangle$ over $\mathcal{P}_S$ and $\mathcal{P}_A$, we define the *post-projection* as the KS $post(\mathcal{M}) = \langle \mathcal{S}', \mathcal{S}_0', \mathcal{R}', \mathcal{V}' \rangle$ over $\mathcal{P}' = \mathcal{P}_S \cup \mathcal{P}_A$, where

- $\mathcal{S}' = \mathcal{A} \times \mathcal{S}$,
- $\mathcal{S}_0' = \mathcal{A} \times \mathcal{S}_0$,
- $\mathcal{R}' = \{((a, s), (a', s')) \mid (s, a', s') \in \mathcal{T} \wedge a \in \mathcal{A}\}$,
- $\mathcal{V}'((a, s)) = \mathcal{V}_A(a) \cup \mathcal{V}_S(s)$.

In essence, transition labels are projected into the post-state, and $s \xrightarrow{a} s'$ becomes $(*, s) \longrightarrow (a, s')$, for any action $*$. By construction, the action atoms in $\mathcal{P}_A$ become state atoms in $\mathcal{P}'$.

4.2   Post-Projection of Action-Based Logics

As action atoms of a MTS $\mathcal{M}$ become state atoms in the KS $post(\mathcal{M})$, action-based formulae can be converted into plain CTL formulae on $post(\mathcal{M})$, with action conditions turning into state conditions. Formally, given an ARCTL state formula ϕ, we define the CTL formula $post(\phi)$ as follows:

$$post(\mathsf{E}_\alpha\mathsf{X}\,\phi) = \mathsf{EX}\,(\alpha \wedge post(\phi))$$
$$post(\mathsf{A}_\alpha\mathsf{X}\,\phi) = \mathsf{AX}\,(\alpha \Rightarrow post(\phi)) \wedge \mathsf{EX}\,\alpha$$
$$post(\mathsf{E}_\alpha(\phi\,\mathsf{U}\,\phi')) = post(\phi') \vee (post(\phi) \wedge \mathsf{EX}\,\mathsf{E}[\alpha \wedge post(\phi)\,\mathsf{U}\,\alpha \wedge post(\phi')])$$
$$post(\mathsf{A}_\alpha(\phi\,\mathsf{U}\,\phi')) = post(\phi') \vee (post(\phi) \wedge \mathsf{EX}\,\alpha$$
$$\wedge\,\mathsf{AX}\,\mathsf{A}[post(\phi) \wedge \mathsf{EX}\,\alpha\,\mathsf{U}\,\neg\alpha \vee post(\phi')])$$

Appropriately, the semantics is preserved by the transformation, in the sense of the generalized semantics of CTL with finite paths:

$$(\mathcal{M}, s) \models \phi \quad \text{iff} \quad (post(\mathcal{M}), s) \models post(\phi)$$

which can be proved by structural induction on ϕ. The details are tedious but the principle is straightforward.

Some sub-formulae get replicated in the transformation, so an exponential increase in the size of the transformed formula may result in the worst case. In practice however, the caching of BDD computation results largely mitigates the impact of this increase when performing symbolic model checking. In any case, this provides additional motivation for using a native implementation of action-based logics in the model checker, that avoids the redundant computations. This is the topic of the next section.

5   Action-Based Model-Checking in SMV

This section discusses how SMV has been extended to support logics with actions. We first give an overview of SMV, then we describe two different implementations of actions in SMV: the first one by implementing the *post* transformation as a pre-processing stage using the macro-processor M4, the second one by modifying the SMV tool itself to support mixed formulae in specifications.

5.1   Overview of SMV

SMV is a symbolic model checker that evaluates CTL specifications on a finite-state model described in a custom language. While SMV was initially developed at Carnegie Mellon [7], we have been using NuSMV, an open-source extended re-implementation of the tool [8]. NuSMV uses an efficient BDD library to perform symbolic model checking of formulae. (NuSMV also supports linear temporal logic and SAT-based bounded model checking.)

The latest version of NuSMV (2.2) provides partial support for action-style constructs, in the form of *input variables*. Input variables (IVARs) are not part of states, and they are used to represent input values for models (typically, they correspond to the input lines of a circuit). Technically, these variables are existentially quantified out when computing transitions. Input variables can appear in transition relations, but they are not allowed in CTL formulae.

NuSMV uses BDDs to perform model checking of CTL formulae: given encodings of state and input variables into Boolean arrays $\underline{s}$ and $\underline{a}$, respectively, the transition relation $\mathcal{T}$ and initial states $\mathcal{S}_0$ are compiled by NuSMV into BDDs $[\![\mathcal{T}]\!](\underline{s}, \underline{a}, \underline{s}')$ and $[\![\mathcal{S}_0]\!](\underline{s})$. Then, for any CTL formula ϕ, the BDD $[\![\phi]\!](\underline{s})$ corresponding to the set of states of the model in which the formula holds is computed inductively on the formula's structure, based on (fair) implementations of the functions ex, eg and eu described before.

SMV supports two styles for declaring transitions: the *assignment style* is based on non-deterministic assignments of initial and next values of each variable, whereas the *constraint style* allows arbitrary conditions over variable values in consecutive states. The former is safer and more convenient for human-written models, but the latter is more flexible, especially in the context of mechanically generated models.

5.2 Post-Projection to SMV

We have implemented the *post* mapping on SMV models, in the form of a macro library for M4, a generic macro-processor included in most UNIX distributions [9]. The library provides macros supporting the two sides of the *post* transformation: models and logic formulae. Our implementation currently supports ARCTL, but adaptation to similar logics such as A-CTL would be straightforward.

The mapping of logic formulae is a straightforward application of the equations of Section 4. For example, using the macro definition

```
define('EU_A','(((($2) & EX E[($1) & ($2) U ($1) & ($3)]) | ($3))')
```

$E_a[p \cup q]$ can be written as EU_A(a,p,q) and is expanded to

```
(((p) & EX E[(a) & (p) U (a) & (q)]) | (q))
```

Since input variables are forbidden in SMV specifications, state variables have to be used instead. It is up to the user to decide which (state) variables in the SMV model represent action and state variables of the mixed model, and consistently use them only in the appropriate parts of the ARCTL operator macros — this is not enforced by the macro package.

The expansion produces SMV constraint-style transition declarations: transitions are declared as **TRANS <tcond>**, where **<tcond>** is a transition condition with sub-terms of the form **next(<cond>)** to refer to the post-state. We provide a macro

```
define('TRANS_A','TRANS next($1) -> ($2)')
```

such that TRANS_A(a,t) defines a transition labeled by a and constrained by t, and expands to TRANS next(a) -> (t). Again, the user must make sure that the action and state parts (a and t) of TRANS_A(a,t) declarations contain only his chosen action and state variables, respectively.

5.3   Action Logics in SMV

We have extended NuSMV to support ARCTL formulae. We use NuSMV's existing input variables as actions, in the sense that any valuation of input variables correspond to a different action. In other words, the action set $\mathcal{A}$ is the cross-product of the ranges of all input variables. Correspondingly, action formulae correspond to conditions over these variables.

In particular, we modified the syntax of formulae accepted by NuSMV to include ARCTL operators, as follows:

$$
\begin{aligned}
ctlexpr ::= &\ldots \text{(existing CTL forms)} \\
| \;&\text{EAX} \;(\; simpleexpr \;)\; ctlexpr \\
| \;&\text{EAG} \;(\; simpleexpr \;)\; ctlexpr \\
| \;&\text{EA} \;(\; simpleexpr \;)\; [\; ctlexpr \;\text{U}\; ctlexpr \;] \\
| \;&\ldots \text{(others defined similarly)}
\end{aligned}
$$

where *simpleexpr* is a conditional expression, further restricted to contain only input variables. For example, EA(a)[p U q] is the concrete syntax for $E_a[p \cup q]$.

Here is an overview of the modifications that were performed on the NuSMV code base to evaluate these new operators:

- Action formulae can readily be evaluated as BDDs, in the same way as standard state formulae, without any code modification.
- We defined a new BDD function $eax(A, S)$ which implements the *eax* function of Section 3.3 over BDD-encoded sets of actions and states (A, S). This function is a fairly simple adaptation of the existing $ex(S)$ function for CTL. Technically, the function merges A and S into a (BDD-encoded) set of action-state pairs.
- Similarly, we defined BDD functions $eau(A, S, S')$ and $eag(A, S)$, implementing functions *eau* and *eag* of Section 3.3 over BDDs, based on fix-point computations using the function *eax*.
- These three BDD functions were used to compute the (BDD corresponding to the) set of states satisfying any ARCTL formula, by providing a corresponding evaluation function for each operator.
- Besides these core changes, support for the new operators had to be folded in several other modules, including of course the SMV model parser and CTL evaluation dispatch functions.

These modifications allow for the evaluation of ARCTL formulae, as illustrated in the example of Figure 1, involving two agents bob and alice who can non-deterministically select, at each time step, whether to perform an increment of their variable count or not. In this case, we have two Boolean input variables alice.move and bob.move, there are four possible actions corresponding to possible valuations of these variables, and action formulae are conditions on these variables. As illustrated at the end of the example, ARCTL formulae allow to reason about the consequences of actions.

```
MODULE agent
  IVAR move : boolean;
  VAR count : 0..10;
  ASSIGN
    init(count) := 0 ;
    next(count) := case
                     move & count < 10: count + 1;
                     1 : count;
                   esac;
  DEFINE win := (count=10);

MODULE main
  VAR alice : agent;
  VAR bob : agent;

SPEC !EAX (bob.move) bob.count = 0
SPEC AAX (bob.move & alice.move) (bob.count > 0 & alice.count > 0)
SPEC AAF (bob.move) bob.win
```

Fig. 1. NuSMV code with ARCTL specifications

Our implementation is at the prototype stage and still needs some improvements. In particular, the generation of witness traces for unsatisfied specifications is not yet supported for our new ARCTL operators.

Also, our implementation computes one monolithic BDD $[\![T]\!](\underline{s}, \underline{a}, \underline{s}')$ covering all possible actions. In some cases, separate transition relations could be computed for separate actions, potentially resulting in smaller BDDs and thus better scalability. Let us assume a finite action set $\mathcal{A} = \{a_1, \ldots, a_n\}$ (typically, the range of a unique input variable in the SMV model). Then for each $a_i \in \mathcal{A}$ we can define $\mathcal{T}_{a_i}(s, s') = \mathcal{T}(s, a_i, s')$ and pre-compute the BDDs for each action a_i

$$[\![\mathcal{T}_{a_i}]\!] = [\![\mathcal{T}]\!][\underline{a} := a_i]$$

and we have

$$[\![\mathsf{E}_\alpha \mathsf{X}\, \phi]\!](\underline{s}) = \exists \underline{s}'. \bigvee_{a \models \alpha} [\![\mathcal{T}_a]\!](\underline{s}, \underline{s}') \wedge [\![\phi]\!](\underline{s}')$$

6   Using ARCTL for Knowledge Logics

The material in this Section is presented in more details in a forthcoming companion article [10].

CTLK is a logic to reason about time and knowledge in a system of agents. Besides the temporal logic operators of CTL, CTLK offers *epistemic* (i.e. knowledge) operators, such as $\mathsf{K}_A\, \phi$, meaning that some agent A *knows* that ϕ holds. Intuitively, A knows ϕ if ϕ holds in all the states that A deems possible. Under certain hypotheses, this is formalized as an *epistemic* (equivalence) relation over states $\sim_A$ that equates states that are indistinguishable by A.

CTLK has been introduced in [2], extending the framework appearing in [11]. A model checking tool for CTLK and various examples have been presented in [12], showing that temporal-epistemic properties may offer a more efficient characterisation than temporal-only formulae.

6.1   From CTLK to ARTCL

The problem of model checking CTLK can be reduced to the problem of model checking ARCTL, as follows. In this setting, each agent Ag_i is associated with a set of "local" variables v_i, so that $s \sim_{Ag_i} s' \equiv (v_i(s) = v_i(s'))$, where $v_i(s)$ is the projection of s on v_i. Given a CTLK model $\mathcal{M}_K$ and a CTLK formula ϕ_K, a MTS $\mathcal{M} = F(\mathcal{M}_K)$ and an ARCTL formula $F(\phi_K)$ can be defined such that $\mathcal{M}_K \models \phi_K$ iff $F(\mathcal{M}_K) \models F(\phi_K)$. The MTS $\mathcal{M}$ includes two kind of action atoms: an atom RUN associated to temporal transitions, and atoms Ag_i (one for each agent) associated to each epistemic relation $\sim_{Ag_i}$. These atoms are used in the definition of two kinds of transitions of $\mathcal{M}$, either temporal or epistemic. $F(\phi_K)$ is generated as follows: standard CTL operators in ϕ_K are translated into their ARCTL extensions restricted to RUN actions, and epistemic operators are translated to ARCTL operators labelled with Ag_i. For instance

$$F(\mathsf{EX}\,\phi) = \mathsf{E}_{RUN}\mathsf{X}\,F(\phi)$$
$$F(\mathsf{K}_{Ag_i}\,\phi) = \mathsf{A}_{Ag_i}\mathsf{X}\,F(\phi)$$

We have implemented this translation as an M4 macro package that allows to write CTLK models and specifications, to be verified with the modified NuSMV presented in Section 5.3.

6.2   Experimental Results

We have conducted some early experiments using action-based model checking for verifying CTLK, in the context of analyzing *diagnosability* properties. Diagnosability is the ability of performing a diagnosis of a given system, knowing which variables (or events) of the system can be observed. Considering these variables as the observations of an agent D (the Diagnoser), diagnosability properties can be phrased as epistemic properties. For example, a fault condition *faulty* can be detected if and only if the diagnoser always knows whether the system is faulty or not:

$$AG(K_D(faulty) \vee K_D(\neg faulty))$$

We have carried out experiments on a simple cascaded power distribution model, illustrated in Figure 2, for various depths of the cascade. This models features a power source, circuit breakers (CBs) and LEDs (as power sinks), where the CBs can fail in different ways and only the commands applied to the CBs and the LED states are observable. We have been able to verify a fairly large model (240 variables, for a total state space of size $\approx 10^{70}$). Despite its size, this model can be verified in less than 10 minutes thanks to the BDD-based symbolic encodings used in NuSMV. Notice that the modification of the

NuSMV code and the verification of epistemic properties using the reduction to ARCTL do not affect the performance of NuSMV: the non-modified version of SMV obtains similar results in the verification of temporal-only properties for the CB example.

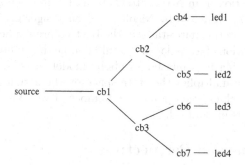

Fig. 2. Sample circuit

7   Related Work

Several authors have already described symbolic model checking algorithms for action-based logics, along very similar lines to what we describe here. In principle, after [7] it is sufficient to have a core set of temporal eventualities expressed as fixpoint formulae to provide the grounds for symbolic model checking.

- In [13,14], the authors present a variant of A-CTL with unless operators EW and AW and slightly different semantics (and syntax). That logic is more expressive than classic A-CTL. They give a fixpoint characterization using extended operators $EX[\{\alpha\}\phi \vee \{\alpha'\}\phi']$ and $AX[\{\alpha\}\phi \vee \{\alpha'\}\phi']$, which slightly extend our $E_\alpha X$ and $A_\alpha X$ and allow the increased expressivity, but otherwise follows the classical approach used as a basis for CTL and ARCTL model-checking. They have implemented their approach in the *Efficient Symbolic Tools* (EST) package [15], which offers symbolic A-CTL model-checking for a process-algebra language.
- [16] describe SAM, a symbolic model checker for μ-A-CTL, an extension of A-CTL with fixpoint operators. SAM uses a BDD-based Boolean system called BSP. SAM is part of the JACK toolset which uses the process algebra CCS/Meije to describe models.

Compared to those two systems, the work presented here is at a more preliminary stage but offers two significant contributions: firstly, it considers mixed systems, reconciling the state-based and action-based schools of formal methods; second, it is implemented in NuSMV, an open-source, feature-rich, efficient and widely distributed system with an expressive modelling language.

In a related topic, [17] discuss the encoding of CCS-style process algebras as BDDs. The authors envision that encoding as a way to enable efficient bisimilarity checking, but action-based temporal logic could equally be applied. [18]

brings this idea one level higher, by proposing a BDD encoding for any process-algebraic language whose structural operational semantics follow a given pattern (so-called *Simple GSOS Systems*).

Regarding the *post* reduction from mixed to state-based models and formulae, a similar reduction from A-CTL to CTL (and more generally from A-CTL* to CTL*) is already presented by Nicola and Vaandrager in [5]. That approach creates additional intermediate states in the KS to represent actions, which complicates the translation of formulae and would double the number of computation steps when computing fixpoints for symbolic model checking. In contrast, our *post* transformation multiplies the state space by the action space, but from a symbolic model checking standpoint, the number of variables and the depth of fixpoint iterations is unchanged.

8   Conclusions and Perspectives

Although symbolic model checking of action-based logics is well-understood in principle and has been implemented in several places, it has so far focused on pure action-based, process-algebra formalisms with a relatively limited distribution. This paper presents a step towards making mixed state-based and action-based reasoning capabilities more widely available, with two complementary contributions: at the theoretical level, a formulation of the model-checking problem for mixed models and an associated mixed logic, called ARCTL, that provides a clean generalization of CTL; at the practical level, two prototype implementations of mixed-logic model-checking in the mainstream symbolic model-checker NuSMV.

The initial motivation for this work arose from a need to perform model checking of logics with modalities for both the temporal evolution of the system and the knowledge (or beliefs) of agents in the system. Under some assumptions, this can be reduced to a mixed-logic model-checking problem. Our initial experiments in checking the epistemic temporal logic CTLK with NuSMV based on that reduction provided successful and encouraging results.

The work presented here can be extended in a number of ways:

- The treatment of internal (invisible) actions needs to be investigated. Essentially, this amounts to considering weak variants of temporal operators that ignore a distinguished τ action. This should not cause major technical issues, as fixpoint characterizations for such operators are well-known (see e.g. [6]), but the precise formalization and implementation need to be worked out.
- Fairness needs to be reconsidered. As we have seen in Section 3.4, the notion of *fair path* used for CTL is not appropriate with finite traces. Instead, action-based theories commonly define fairness in terms of not indefinitely refusing enabled actions [19]. How this can be addressed in symbolic model checking is a matter to be investigated.
- On the implementation side, support for generation of counter-examples needs to be addressed, which should require minimal technical changes in NuSMV. Partitioning the transition relation between a set of actions is a more significant and more involved change that we would also like to address.

- We are currently investigating the feasibility of bounded model checking for action-based logics, which offers a very efficient technique for finding counter-examples, but it is currently supported by NuSMV for the verification of linear temporal logic (LTL) only.
- Support for other action-based logics such as A-CTL could easily be added, either as additional macro packages or as native extensions of SMV. Game-theoretic logics such as ATL [20] would be a very valuable addition but would require a deeper analysis and more involved changes to NuSMV.

A more thorough experimental assessment of the current prototype and its future extensions is also desirable, but, as mentioned in Section 6.2 the first results obtained from the CTLK application are quite encouraging.

Acknowledgements

The authors would like to thank anonymous referees of successive versions of this paper for their useful feedback, as well as the NuSMV development team at IRST for their technical support. The modified version of NuSMV supporting ARCTL operators is available from the authors upon request.

References

1. Cimatti, A., Clarke, E., Giunchiglia, F., Roveri, M.: NuSMV: a new symbolic model verifier. In: Proc. of International Conference on Computer-Aided Verification (1999)
2. Penczek, W., Lomuscio, A.: Verifying epistemic properties of multi-agent systems via bounded model checking. Fundamenta Informaticae 55, 167–185 (2003)
3. Clarke, E.M., Emerson, E.A., Sistla, A.P.: Automatic verification of finite-state concurrent systems using temporal logic specifications. ACM Transactions on Programming Languages and Systems 8, 244–263 (1986)
4. Clarke, E.M., Grumberg, O., Peled, D.: Model Checking. MIT Press, Cambridge (1999)
5. Nicola, R.D., Vaandrager, F.: Action versus state based logics for transition systems. In: Guessarian, I. (ed.) Semantics of Systems of Concurrent Processes. LNCS, vol. 469, pp. 407–419. Springer, Heidelberg (1990)
6. Mateescu, R.: Logiques temporelles basées sur actions pour la vérification des systèmes asynchrones. Rapport de recherche 5032, INRIA (2003)
7. Burch, J.R., Clarke, E.M., McMillan, K.L., Dill, D.L., Hwang, J.: Symbolic model checking: 10^{20} states and beyond. Information and Computation 98, 142–170 (1992)
8. Cimatti, A., Clarke, E., Giunchiglia, F., Roveri, M.: NuSMV: a new symbolic model verifier. In: Proc. of International Conference on Computer-Aided Verification (1999)
9. Kernighan, B., Ritchie, D.: The M4 Macro Processor. Bell Laboratories (1977)
10. Lomuscio, A., Pecheur, C., Raimondi, F.: Automatic verification of knowledge and time with NuSMV. In: Proceedings of IJCAI'07, Hyderabad, India (to appear) (2007)
11. Fagin, R., Halpern, J.Y., Moses, Y., Vardi, M.Y.: Reasoning about Knowledge. MIT Press, Cambridge (1995)

12. Raimondi, F., Pecheur, C., Lomuscio, A.: Applications of model checking for multi-agent systems: verification of diagnosability and recoverability. In: Proceedings of Concurrency, Specification & Programming (CS&P), Warsaw University, pp. 433–444 (2005)

13. Meolic, R., Kapus, T., Brezocnik, Z.: An action computation tree logic with unless operator. In: Proceedings of the 1st South-East European workshop on formal methods SEEFM 2003, pp. 100–114 (2003)

14. Meolic, R., Kapus, T., Brezocnik, Z.: Verification of concurrent systems using ACTL. In: Hamza, M.H., (ed.) Applied informatics: proceedings of the IASTED international conference AI'2000, IASTED/ACTA Press, pp. 663–669 (2000)

15. Meolic, R., Kapus, T., Brezocnik, Z.: The Efficient Symbolic Tools package. In: 8th International Conference Software, Telecommunications and Computer Networks (SoftCOM 2000), pp. 147–156 (2000)

16. Fantechi, A., Gnesi, S., Mazzanti, F., Pugliese, R., Tronci, E.: A symbolic model checker for ACTL. In: Hutter, D., Traverso, P. (eds.) Applied Formal Methods - FM-Trends 98. LNCS, vol. 1641, pp. 228–242. Springer, Heidelberg (1999)

17. Enders, R., Filkorn, T., Taubner, D.: Generating BDDs for symbolic model checking in CCS. In: Larsen, K.G., Skou, A. (eds.) CAV 1991. LNCS, vol. 575, Springer, Heidelberg (1992)

18. Dsouza, A., Bloom, B.: Generating BDD models for process algebra terms. In: Proceedings of the 7th International Conference on Computer Aided Verification, London, UK, pp. 16–30. Springer, Heidelberg (1995)

19. Brinksma, E., Rensink, A., Vogler, W.: Fair testing. In: Lee, I., Smolka, S.A. (eds.) CONCUR 1995. LNCS, vol. 962, pp. 313–327. Springer, Heidelberg (1995)

20. Alur, R., Henzinger, T.A., Kupferman, O.: Alternating-time temporal logic. J. ACM 49, 672–713 (2002)

A Framework for Model Checking Institutions *

Francesco Viganò

Università della Svizzera italiana, via G. Buffi 13, 6900 Lugano, Switzerland
francesco.vigano@lu.unisi.ch

Abstract. To increase positive expectations in the outcome of open multiagent systems, institutions have been put forward to regulate agents' behaviour. To *model* and to *verify* such institutions, we propose to adopt the notion of status function, which provides for a unified approach to ontological and deontic aspects regulated by an institution. Also, to enhance the development of *functional* and *rational* institutions, we propose a language amenable to model checking to describe them and their properties. Finally, we present our tool and an evaluation of our approach.

1 Introduction

To increase positive expectations in the outcome of systems composed by autonomous agents, *norms* have been put forward to regulate and to make more predictable agents' behaviour [20,8,9,24,5]. While in [20] norms (also named *social laws*) are assumed to be respected by agents because they are designed and encoded by a single organization, in [8,9,24,5] norms are *defined* by *institutions* and *enforced* by *organizations* to regulate *open* multiagent systems, where it is unrealistic to expect that agents implemented by different parties with interests in conflict will always behave according to a system of norms.

Our research is motivated on one hand by the fact that deontic aspects and institutional facts need a unified treatment, while so far they have been regarded separately [8,5,9,10,22]. Following [23], in [27] we have proposed to model institutions in terms of a single concept, that is, *status function*, which provides for a unified approach to ontological and deontic aspects regulated by an institution. Roughly speaking, status functions are positions imposed on agents to perform certain actions (institutional actions), which cannot be executed without the recognition of their effects by a community of agents (see [27] for more details). In fact, the effects of such actions essentially consist in the imposition or revocation of other status functions, which may confer to agents new authorizations or obligations to perform other institutional actions. For instance, in an English auction, when the auctioneer declares a new current price, participants are authorized only to make higher bids. For this reason, we think that our approach better clarify the interdependence existing among agents' deontic positions (authorizations, obligations, etc.) and the ontology of the context in which agents interact, while in [8,5,9,10,22] such relation is ignored.

---

* Supported by Swiss National Science Foundation project 200020-109525, "Artificial Institutions: specification and verification of open distributed interaction frameworks."

S. Edelkamp and A. Lomuscio (Eds.): MoChart IV, LNAI 4428, pp. 129–145, 2007.

On the other hand, our research is motivated by the lack of formal support for the verification of institutions. For instance, as observed in [25], certain aspects of the language proposed in [8] to model institutions lack of a formal semantics. For example, the meaning of labels used in [8] "is not clear from the notation only" [25]. This fact has negatively influenced the application of automated techniques to verify such formalism: in [4] and [13] the authors propose two frameworks to model check electronic institutions, but, due to the aforementioned limitations, only properties regarding their syntactic structure can be defined and verified. As a consequence, ISLANDER [7], a tool for modelling institutions according to the formalism introduced in [8], only checks syntactical aspects and does not integrate any support for the automatic verification of electronic institutions. Also, in [22], where agent societies are described with a formalism inspired by the Event-Calculus [15], the authors must rely on "systematic runs" to guarantee the correctness of their protocol. Given that institutions are introduced to increase the reliability of agents interactions by ensuring that agents have at their disposal all the needed powers to fulfill their objectives and that they will not be subject to contradictory or undesired norms, the aid of automated techniques it is necessary to foresee all possible evolutions and states in which an institution may evolve.

To allow designers to describe institutions in terms of status functions and to offer them the support of a tool that provides for their automatic verification, in [27] we have introduced FIEVeL (*Functions for Institutionalized Environ-ments Verification Language*), which is an institution definition language amenable to model checking [2]. In this paper we extend FIEVeL to allow a designer to express desirable properties that should be satisfied by his or her models in terms of the concepts defined in our meta-model [27], ignoring the actual translation of FIEVeL into the input language of the model checker.

The remainder of this paper is structured as follows. In Section 2 we briefly resume the main legal and philosophical concepts that we perceive as essential to specify institutions. In particular, since institutions have been applied to define protocols [9,22], we will ground our discussion with examples taken by a widely used interaction protocol, the English auction. Section 3 introduces certain critical aspects of the translation of FIEVeL models into Promela, the input language of SPIN [12]. In Section 4 we present how we have extended FIEVeL to specify domain-dependent properties, while Section 5 discusses an initial library of domain-independent properties. A key aspect of domain-dependent properties is that they can be automatically translated, while an important aspect of domain-independent properties is that they can be automatically generated by our tool, which is briefly presented and evaluated in Section 6. Finally, in Section 7 we provide a comparison of our approach with related works.

2   Modelling Institutions

The key concept that characterizes our approach to the description of an institution is the notion of *agent status function*, that is, a status imposed on an agent and recognized as existing by a set of agents [23]. Typical examples of status functions are not only the concept of auctioneer or winner of an auction, but also being the owner of a good, being the husband or the wife of somebody. Although there exist several similarities among the concepts of status function and role as it has been discussed in the literature [17], we prefer to use the term status function because it better represents the fact that we are concerned with statuses assigned to agents to perform several functions and whose existence depends on those agents that recognize them as existing.

Status functions are defined as possibly empty aggregates of *deontic positions* that can be expressed in terms of two main concepts, *authorizations* (also named *institutionalized power* [14,22]) and *obligations*. An obligation is characterized by certain expressions which are used to specify conditional obligations and when an obligation should be considered fulfilled or violated (more details can be found in [27]). An obligation is created because a status function is imposed, changes its state when its conditions are satisfied, and eventually reaches a final state (*inactive*) either because its expressions are evaluated to true or because it is associated to a revoked status function. In particular, when an obligation reaches the inactive state, we consider that it has been *fulfilled* if its fulfillment expression is satisfied, otherwise if the violation expression is satisfied we say that the agent has violated it. Obligations can be also used to express prohibitions by specifying suitable violation expressions, while we do not define a specific construct to explicitly represent the fact that an agent is permitted to perform an action as in [5,10,22]. Instead, as in [9] we consider that every action, if it is not prohibited, is also permitted.

Interdependent status functions are declared within *institutional entities* which enforce on a group of status functions a set of *constraints* (e.g. an auctioneer cannot be also a participant). Moreover, institutional entities define cardinality constraints, like "an auction is composed by an auctioneer and a set of participants".

FIEVeL allows to model two kinds of events, *base-level events* and *institutional events*. There exists an ontological difference among them: while the former exist because they correspond to certain physical changes or are relative to lower level institutions, like *time* events and *message-exchange* events, the latter exist because they are recognized as existing by a community of agents. Therefore, institutional events are not directly produced by the environment or by an agent thanks to its own capabilities, because their effects need to be recognized by a set of agents. Instead, institutional events happen because agents accept that when certain base-level events occur, if certain contextual conditions are satisfied, they *count as* institutional events. As it can be noticed in Figure 1, FIEVeL models institutional events by describing their preconditions in terms of the existence or absence of certain status functions, while their effects are expressed by *assigning* (or *revoking*) several status functions.

In [27] we extended the treatment of the count-as relation as it was presented in [9] by describing what kind of contextual conditions are relevant to model that a base-level event counts as an institutional event. In particular, we single out the following conditions: (i) there must exist a convention binding the base-level event to the institutional event; (ii) a precondition, expressed in terms of the existence or absence of certain status functions, must be satisfied; (iii) in the case of institutional actions, the agent must be authorized to perform the institutional action. If all these conditions are satisfied, a base-level event counts as an institutional event and its effects take place, which means that certain status functions will be assigned or revoked.

FIEVeL models status functions, base-level events, and institutional events as complex types defined in terms of certain *basic types*, which can be specified as subsets of built-in basic types or by enumerating their elements (see Figure 1). FIEVeL defines few built-in basic types, like integers (*int*), agent identifiers (*AID*), and objects identifiers (*OID*).

Figure 1 reports a few fragments of our specification of the English Auction institution, showing that an auctioneer that has opened an auction (represented by INSESSION status function) is not only authorized to close the auction if certain conditions

```
basic-types:
  priceD subtype-of int;
    . . .
base-events :
  message openRound();
    . . .
institution EnglishAuctionInstitution {
  institutional-entity englishAuction {
    . . .
    [0,ALL] status-function INSESSION() {
      authorizations:
        . . .
        newRound n <- exists[>=2] p in PARTICIPANT [true];
      deontic-specification:
        obligation(done(open,subject),
          (exists [<2] x in PARTICIPANT [true] or
          done(newRound,subject)),activation-time>1);
        . . .
    }// INSESSION
      . . .
    constraints:
      AUCTIONEER disjoint PARTICIPANT;
  }// entity
  conventions:
    exch-Msg(openRound ()) =c=> newRound();
    time() =c=> endRound();
      . . .
  institutional-events:
      . . .
    institutional-action newRound():
    pre: ((not exists x in INROUND [true] and
          not exists o in OFFERED[true])
          and not exists x in ENDAUCTION [true]) ;
    eff: p in PARTICIPANT -X->
          assign(p.subject, INROUND())[true],
        a in AUCTIONEER -X->
          assign(a.subject, INROUND()[true];
      . . .
}// institution
    . . .
model-definition:
  basic-domains:
    AID={aid_0,aid_1,aid_2};
      . . .
  initial-state:
    assign(aid_0,AUCTIONEER());
      . . .
```

Fig. 1. Fragments of the English Auction institution

hold, but thereafter it is also obliged to do so before the next time instant has elapsed. An auctioneer is also authorized to open a new round if there are at least two participants by performing the institutional action *newRound*, which is conventionally bound to the exchange of a message of type *openRound* and, if the previous round has been closed with at least two offers, a new round is open and participants can make their bids.

3 Institutional Models and Computational Models

Every institution described with FIEVeL corresponds to an *ideal* transition system characterized by a *many sorted first-order signature* [18] where every transition represents all institutional effects (institutional events, fulfillment of obligations, etc) associated with a base-level event. Intuitively, every transition is caused by a base-level event, which may also count-as an institutional event if certain conditions are met, and, as a consequence, institutional reality is modified by the imposition and revocation of certain status functions. Also, since expressions that regulate the evolution of agents' obligations refer to both events and institutional states, certain obligations may update their state. Ideally, all these changes correspond to a single transition of the base-level and institutional transition system.

Actually, the generation of such transition system is not only computationally expensive, but also its encoding into Promela, the input language of the SPIN model checker [12], would also lead to a huge number of code lines. In fact, due to several limitations of SPIN, we should generate a transition for each possible combination of base-level events, institutional-events, and obligation-state changes. For this reason, instead of calculating the ideal transition system, we prefer to derive a *computational* transition system, such that each transition partially represents the institutional effects of an event, so that summing the effects of a sequence of transitions we can reach the same institutional state.

To demonstrate that we can build a computational transition system which simulates the ideal system, that is, satisfies the same properties, let M be a Kripke structure over a set AP of atomic propositions such that V is a valuation function associating a value in $\{0, 1\}$ at each atomic proposition p in AP for each state, Π is the set of all paths and Π_0 represents the set of all initialized paths in M. In the sequel we write π_k for the k-th state of path $\pi = s_0, s_1, s_2, \ldots, \pi^k$ for the suffix of π starting at state π_k, that is, the sequence $s_k, s_{k+1}, s_{k+2}, \ldots$, and finally $M, \Pi_0 \models \varphi$ to mean that for each $\pi \in \Pi_0$, $M, \pi \models \varphi$.

Given two Kripke structures M and $\widehat{M}$, we define a relation $Z_{inst} \subseteq \Pi \times \widehat{\Pi}$ such that $(\pi, \widehat{\pi}) \in Z_{inst}$ if and only if for each proposition $p \in AP$:

1. $V(\pi_0, p) = \widehat{V}(\widehat{\pi}_0, p)$;
2. $\widehat{V}(\widehat{\pi}_0, inst) = 1$;
3. there exists a $k > 1$ such that:
   (a) $V(\pi_1, p) = \widehat{V}(\widehat{\pi}_k, p)$;
   (b) for every $0 < r < k$
       i. $V(\pi_0, p) = \widehat{V}(\widehat{\pi}_r, p)$;
       ii. $\widehat{V}(\widehat{\pi}_r, inst) = 0$;
   (c) $(\pi^1, \widehat{\pi}^k) \in Z$.

where *inst* is an atomic proposition belonging to $\widehat{AP}$ but which does not appear in AP.

Intuitively, we can imagine building a path $\hat{\pi}$ by taking path π, adding a set of atomic propositions which do not belong to AP, by marking every state of π such that the valuation function of $inst$ is *true*, and finally by inserting between two consecutive states (π_i, π_{i+1}) a new set of intermediate states which are characterized by the same valuation function of state π_i with respect to propositions AP and which valuate the proposition $inst$ to *false*. Path $\hat{\pi}$ is therefore emulating the behavior of path π by simulating each transition on path π with a finite sequence of transitions, such that it keeps unchanged the truth values of common atomic propositions until it changes them in a single step.

Z_{inst} has been introduced to guarantee that an institution described with FIEVeL can be verified with SPIN and that every property regarding the institutional state holding in the ideal institution also holds in the Promela model, and vice versa. While in [27] we presented a relation which preserves all temporal properties of the ideal system which do not contain the *next* temporal operator, Z_{inst} preserves all temporal formulas which are satisfied in the institutional system. To obtain such result, we first introduce a transformation τ defined as follows:

$$\tau[p] = p$$
$$\tau[\neg\chi] = \neg\tau[\chi]$$
$$\tau[\chi \wedge \psi] = \tau[\chi] \wedge \tau[\psi]$$
$$\tau[\mathbf{X}\chi] = inst\mathbf{U}(\neg inst \wedge (\neg inst)\mathbf{U}(inst \wedge \tau[\chi]))$$
$$\tau[\chi\mathbf{U}\psi] = (inst \rightarrow \tau[\chi])\mathbf{U}(inst \wedge \tau[\psi])$$

where p represents any atomic proposition in AP, and χ and ψ represent any formula. It can be demonstrated [1] the following Lemma:

Lemma 1. *If $(\pi, \hat{\pi}) \in Z_{inst}$ and φ is a temporal formula composed by atomic propositions belonging to AP, then $M, \pi \models \varphi$ if and only if $\widehat{M}, \hat{\pi} \models \tau[\varphi]$.*

From Lemma 1 it follows the subsequent theorem:

Theorem 1. *If for each $\pi \in \Pi_0$ there exists a $\hat{\pi} \in \widehat{\Pi}_0$ such that $(\pi, \hat{\pi}) \in Z_{inst}$, and for each $\hat{\pi} \in \widehat{\Pi}_0$ there exists a $\pi \in \Pi_0$ such that $(\pi, \hat{\pi}) \in Z_{inst}$, for each temporal formula φ composed by atomic propositions belonging to AP, $M, \Pi_0 \models \varphi$ if and only if $\widehat{M}, \widehat{\Pi}_0 \models \tau[\varphi]$.*

This result means that given an *ideal* transition system which corresponds to a FIEVeL model, we can build a *computational* transition system which preserves all temporal properties of the *ideal* system.

Before briefly introducing how we proceed to translate FIEVeL institutions into Promela models, it is worth discussing how we model *time*. FIEVeL regards time aspects in two distinct ways: (i) as in classical temporal logic, to define *qualitative* properties (e.g. it is always the case that an auctioneer cannot win an auction), and (ii) as in RTTL [21] to express *quantitative* properties (e.g. the auctioneer must open the auction before two minutes since now). Two consecutive time events t_i and t_{i+1} may be separated by a sequence (possible empty) of other base level events, which are assumed to

---

[1] For proofs of Lemma 1 and Theorem 1 refer to [26].

occur at time t_i. Hence the institutional state may change due, for instance, to message-exchange events even if the time does not change. In principle, there may be an infinite number of time ticks, while in [27] we considered only finite time intervals. The main drawback of the approach discussed in [27] is that certain formulas may (not) hold in a system because they refer to time instants that have not been considered by the model checker [19].

To solve this problem, we have slightly changed FIEVeL syntax by allowing only time expressions which assume a truth value that will not longer change after a fixed number of clock ticks have elapsed from the occurrence of a certain event. As a consequence, we have also changed our encoding of time references defined by an institution, which are substituted by suitable counters. In doing so, we are simulating an infinite number of time instants with a finite structure that is verifiable by a model checker. Therefore, we can ensure that a property holds in a Promela model if and only if it holds in the institution which is characterized by an infinite number of time tick. As a consequence, the number of possible events that the model checker should consider, and how they can be interleaved, has been increased, which means that we have increased the memory and time required to verify an institution.

To model check FIEVeL models we have defined an automatic translation of FIEVeL into Promela. A Promela model is composed by a set of *processes* and *global variables* that can be described by defining new *process types* and *record structures*. Essentially a Promela process is constituted by a set of statements (also named *guarded commands* in [6]), which can be *simple statements*, like assignments, or *compound statements*, like selection (`if`) and repetition (`do`). Each statement is characterized by an *enabling condition* and a *postcondition*. Promela imposes severe restrictions on what can be specified in a precondition, therefore, to overcome such limitations and to increase the expressiveness of FIEVeL without producing an huge number of intermediate states, we chose to use embedded C code to evaluate preconditions of transitions and to compute reachable states. The SPIN model checker adopts an interleaving semantics, which means that when several processes have executable statements, it randomly chooses one of them and executes it. When all enabling conditions are evaluated to false, two special preconditions (also named guards) `timeout` and `else`, are evaluated to *true*. In particular, `else` is enabled only if all transitions at the process level cannot be executed, while `timeout` is evaluated to true only if no process has an enabled transition. In this brief overview we have just introduced a few concepts that are necessary for the sake of the present discussion, while further details can be found in [12].

When we translate FIEVeL, status functions, institutional entities, obligations, base events, and institutional events are encoded as a set of type definitions, which are then used to declare two set of variables, one representing the *current institutional state* and another which is exploited to generate the *next institutional state*. Each institution is then translated into a new process definition according to the pattern represented in Figure 2. For sake of simplicity, we can imagine that every process representing an institution consists of a main loop which is enabled whenever a new base event is generated and contains an inner loop where each guard represents an institutional event or an obligation-state transition. Actually, to further reduce the number of intermediate

```
proctype institutionProc(int id) {
  do
  :: (nextEvent.analyzed[id]==FALSE) ->
    do
    :: ((condition_inst_event_x1 || condition_inst_event_x2) &&
        !(effects_x)) ->
         apply_effects(next_event);
    ...
    :: ((next_obligation.state==inactive) &&
       (start_obligation && obligation.state==inactive) ->
         next_obligation.state=active;
    ::else -> break;
    od
    nextEvent.analyzed[id]=TRUE;
  od
}

   ...

proctype eventGenerator(){
  do
  :: timeout ->
    curr_state=next_state; inst=true;
    inst=false; updateConditions();
    if
    :: true                 -> next_event = time_event;
    :: condition_event1 -> next_event = event1;
    :: condition_event2 -> next_event = event2;
    ...
    fi
  od
}
```

Fig. 2. Translation pattern for processes representing institutions and the structure of an event-Generator process

transitions and to generate a more compact Promela code, our current implementation introduces several improvements that have not been reported in Figure 2.

As discussed above, institutional states evolve because base-level events happen and they count-as institutional events. To model base-level events, we define a new process, named *eventGenerator*, which generates actions and events as if they were produced by agents or the environment. Agents therefore are not modelled as processes as in [28], while we reduce them as parameters of base-level events. This choice is motivated by the fact that in open multiagent systems agents' internal states are not accessible and therefore we must assume an external point of view. The process structures presented in Figure 2 ensures that the *eventGenerator* is activated only when all institution instances have generated the next institutional state by considering all possible institutional transitions (counts-as, institutional-event effects, and obligation transitions), such that current state variables can be updated with the new calculated values. Therefore, when an *eventGenerator* is activated, we consider reached the next institutional state and thereafter we start to compute the following institutional state by choosing the next base-level event. In doing so, events are modelled as if they were perceived and analyzed by a centralized *institution manager*, which manages the state of the system and updates it when an event occurs. Although such an assumption would be unrealistic in the implementation of a distributed system, we introduce it to reduce the complexity of the verified model. Also, it can be noticed that several prototypes of institutions, for example [10], consider a single centralized component which makes the institutional state evolve.

Finally we declare an *init* process to generate the initial state. Due to values assigned by default to variables that compose complex types, we cannot always build a computational path $\widehat{\pi}$ whose valuation function at the initial state simulates the valuation function of the institutional path π at its initial state such that $(\pi, \widehat{\pi}) \in Z_{inst}$. To overcome this problem, we consider a computational path such that: (i) $V(inst, \widehat{\pi}_i) = 0$ for each $i < 2$ and (ii) $(\pi, \widehat{\pi}^2) \in Z_{inst}$. Therefore we obtain that $\pi \models \varphi$ if and only if $\widehat{\pi}^2 \models \tau[\varphi]$, which corresponds to check if $\widehat{\pi} \models \neg inst\mathbf{U}(inst \wedge \tau[\varphi])$.

4 Domain-Dependent Properties

Domain-dependent properties stem from peculiar features of the specified institution and regard its functionality: for instance, we may want to check if it is possible that a participant is declared to be the winner of an auction. In specifying domain-dependent properties we must take into account two different aspects: (i) since we are considering open multiagent systems, agents may violate norms of institutions and (ii) agents may be permitted and not obliged to perform certain actions (see Section 2). For instance, in our specification of the English auction, participants are permitted to make bids and an agent can be declared to be the winner only it has offered the highest price. Therefore, certain executions end without a winner because none of the agents has made a bid, while if the auctioneer respects its obligations, it is always the case that if there is at least an offer, there will be a winner.

As a consequence, agents' violations and permissions led us to consider not only *validity* of LTL formulae, but also their *satisfiability*. In the sequel we will write $M \models_A \varphi$ to mean that φ is valid in M and $M \models_E \varphi$ to express that φ is satisfiable in M. The set of LTL formulae can be seen as a subset of CTL* formulae of the form $\mathbf{A}f$, where $\mathbf{A}$ is the universal quantifier over paths and f is a formula composed by atomic propositions, boolean operators, and temporal operators [2]. For the relation existing among the universal and the existential quantifiers, we can define satisfiability of formula φ as follows:

$$M \models_E \varphi \equiv M \not\models_A \neg\varphi$$

Therefore, since SPIN is able to check only validity of LTL formulae, to verify if $M \models_E \varphi$, we check whether $\neg\varphi$ is a valid formula, and if the model checker generates a counterexample we assume that φ is satisfiable. Despite our interest for the existence of certain paths, we still prefer LTL to CTL because it is simpler and it helps the designer to focus his or her attention on single runs of the system.

Domain-dependent properties can be specified in FIEVeL by combining temporal operators with expressions that refer to institutional states (expressed in terms of status functions) and events. Despite FIEVeL expressions correspond to plain LTL formulae, we think that it is worth specifying properties of institutions with FIEVeL for three main reasons: i) a FIEVeL formula represents an abbreviated form for a long and complex LTL formula, ii) FIEVeL guarantees syntactic type checking of formulae, and

iii) designers can reason in terms of institutional concepts ignoring their translation into Promela models. Moreover, institutions describe rules that typically are independent of the number of agents, objects, etc. involved in the interaction, which can be naturally expressed in FIEVeL by using quantification over sorts. Temporal operators and FIEVeL expressions can be combined because we assume that domains are fixed at all states of our system. For the same reason, we admit that domain-dependent properties can be externally quantified with respect to basic domains (see Section 2). For instance, we may want to verify that only an auctioneer can open an auction or that a participant may eventually become the winner. These properties are formalized in FIEVeL as follows:

$$\mathtt{|=A\ forall\ X\ in\ AID\ G(done}(open,X)\mathtt{->\ exists\ A\ in\ AUCTIONEER}$$
$$\mathtt{[A.subject=\ X]);} \qquad (1)$$

$$\mathtt{|=E\ exists\ X\ in\ AID\ (\ exists\ P\ in\ PARTICIPANT\ [P.subject=X]}$$
$$\mathtt{->\ F\ exists\ W\ in\ CURWINNER\ [W.subject=\ X]);} \qquad (2)$$

While properties that hold in paths where agents may violate norms are useful to evaluate *worst cases* and to check whether an institution is *robust*, the *functionality* of an institution can be better evaluated by assuming that all agents are compliant (i.e., behave according to the norms of the system). For this reason, domain-dependent properties are specified in two different sections, one where agents are assumed to be compliant and another where all possible paths are considered.

To express agents compliance, we introduce a new proposition, *violation*, which is set to *true* whenever an obligation is violated. Therefore, *illegal states* where at least an obligation has been violated evaluates *violation* to true: in doing so, our treatment of agents violations is somehow similar to the approach presented in [16] and [24]. Therefore, to check whether $\models_E \varphi$ under the hypothesis of agent compliance we verify whether:

$$\models_E \mathbf{G}\neg violation \wedge \varphi$$

while under the hypothesis of agent compliance $\models_A \varphi$ is checked as follows:

$$\models_A \mathbf{G}\neg violation \rightarrow \varphi \text{ and } \models_E \mathbf{G}\neg violation \wedge \varphi$$

For example, as mentioned above, assuming that the auctioneer is compliant with its obligations, we would expect that if a participant makes a bid, the auctioneer will declare the winner of that round, which can be expressed as follows:

$$\mathtt{|=A\ G(happens}(offer)\mathtt{->F\ happens}(currentWinner)); \qquad (3)$$

As we can see in Figure 3, property (3) holds only if we assume agents compliance. Verifying domain-dependent properties by assuming that agents will conform to the norms of the system not only allows us to check the functionality of an institution, but also considerably speeds up the verification process (see Table 1).

We think that the availability of a tool for the automatic verification of institutions is especially useful when a designer wants to change an existing institution by introducing new institutional actions or norms. By defining new possibilities of actions or limiting existing ones, certain properties may cease to hold, compromising the functionality of an institution. In an earlier version of our specification of the English auction, we

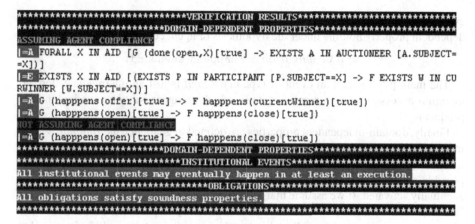

```
***************************VERIFICATION RESULTS***************************
***************************DOMAIN-DEPENDENT PROPERTIES***************************
ASSUMING AGENT COMPLIANCE
|=A FORALL X IN AID [G (done(open,X)[true] -> EXISTS A IN AUCTIONEER [A.SUBJECT=
=X])]
|=E EXISTS X IN AID [(EXISTS P IN PARTICIPANT [P.SUBJECT==X] -> F EXISTS W IN CU
RWINNER [W.SUBJECT==X])]
|=A G (happpens(offer)[true] -> F happpens(currentWinner)[true])
|=A G (happpens(open)[true] -> F happpens(close)[true])
NOT ASSUMING AGENT COMPLIANCE
|=A G (happpens(open)[true] -> F happpens(close)[true])
***************************DOMAIN-DEPENDENT PROPERTIES***************************
***************************INSTITUTIONAL EVENTS***************************
All institutional events may eventually happen in at least an execution.
***************************OBLIGATIONS***************************
All obligations satisfy soundness properties.
******************************************************************************
```

Fig. 3. The report generated by our tool during the verification of domain-dependent properties presented in Section 4

introduced the participant status function as an entry point for agents to participate to an auction. In that specification, among others, we checked, under the hypothesis of agents compliance, if every opened auction would be eventually closed, as stated by the following property:

$$|\text{=A } \mathbf{G}(\mathbf{happens}(open) \text{ -> } \mathbf{F} \ \mathbf{happens}(close)); \tag{4}$$

After that, we authorized participants to leave the auction during the time comprised among two consecutive rounds. In our first attempt, property (4) did not loger hold, since the auctioneer was authorized to declare a new round only if there were at least two agents (see Figure 1), while it was authorized to close the auction in such circumstances but was not obliged to do so. We solve this problem by introducing a new obligation for the auctioneer, and now property (4) is valid in our specification (see Figure 3).

5   Domain-Independent Properties

Domain-independent properties represent general desirable properties of institutions which stem from our metamodel (see [27]). For instance, a sound specification should be characterized by the fact that every institutional event must eventually happen in at least an execution where no violations occur. On the contrary, it would mean that either the preconditions of the institutional event are never met, that the designer has not defined the necessary authorizations, or that norms of the institution forbid agents from executing it whenever they are authorized. In any case, it is important that the designer becomes aware of this fact, and consider how to modify the institution, otherwise the definition of such institutional event would be useless.

A second important aspect that distinguishes domain-independent properties from domain dependent properties is that the former can be automatically generated by statically analyzing a specification of an institution, without considering the actual purposes of the designer when he or she has specified it. For instance, we can check whether an event of type *newRound* may occur by specifying the following property as a domain dependent property holding under the hypothesis of agent compliance:

$$\models_E \mathbf{G}\neg violation \wedge \mathbf{F}\text{happens}(\text{newRound})$$

The main point is that an event of type *newRound* is just an intermediate step, although a necessary one, to reach a state in which an agent wins the auction and the product is sold.

Finally, domain-independent properties are defined to guarantee the *rationality* of an institution with respect to the intended semantics of the concepts defined by our meta-model. For example, norms are introduced in open multiagent systems to constrain possible agents' behaviour, and therefore it must be the case that each norm can be eventually activated. If we assume that agents are autonomous, it should be possible for an agent both to violate and fulfill its obligations (and prohibitions), which means that norms regulate aspects of (social) reality which are contingent. It would be irrational to define an obligation characterized by an expression that makes it always fulfilled (or violated) independently of agent actions. Moreover, it should be the case that once a norm is activated, it ought to eventually reach a final state (fulfilled, violated, revoked), which guarantees that the whole life-cycle of a norm is limited and regulated only by the institution that defines it. Assuming that propositions $activated_i$, $violated_i$, and $fulfilled_i$ represent the fact that the i-th obligation associated to the j-th status function are respectively *activated, fulfilled,* or *violated,* and that $imposed\_sf_j$ and $revoked\_sf_j$ are true when the j-th status function is assigned or revoked, we can formalize the properties mentioned above as follows:

1. $\models_A \mathbf{G}((imposed\_sf_j \wedge (activated_i) \rightarrow \mathbf{F}(violated_i \vee fulfilled_i \vee revoked\_sf_j))$
2. $\models_E \mathbf{G}(imposed\_sf_j \rightarrow \mathbf{F}activated_i)$
3. $\models_E \mathbf{G}(imposed\_sf_j \rightarrow \mathbf{F}fulfilled_i)$
4. $\models_E \mathbf{G}(imposed\_sf_j \rightarrow \mathbf{F}violated_i)$

At the moment, these properties cannot be expressed in FIEVeL. Instead, they are generated by defining new constants in the Promela model which refer to the state of each obligation. We are considering how to extend FIEVeL such that a specification may refer to the current state of agents' obligations, which is a fundamental step to specify recovery policies and sanctions for the management of violations.

We think that the definition of a library of domain-independent properties, their automatic generation and verification is an important aspect of the development of sound institutions, since they regard the rationality of an institution and reflect certain aspects that may be critical in the development of an institution. Also, if we consider that a specification may be composed by many institutional events and norms, the support provided by a tool spares the designer the tedious task of hand coding them. Finally, their automatic definition allows the designer to focus his or her attention on the most relevant aspects of an institution to comply with his or her objectives.

6 The Verification Framework

To check with our tool whether an institution satisfies a set of domain-dependent properties, the designer must provide a *model definition* by describing which elements compose each basic domain (see Section 2) and the initial state of the system, defined in terms of which status functions are imposed on agents at the initial state. Moreover, the user can select which domain-independent properties must be generated to guarantee the soundness of the specification. At the moment, we have fully implemented only the verification of properties described in Section 5, although new domain-independent properties can be easily defined and incorporated into our tool thanks to its modular architecture.

Given an institution, a model description, a set of domain dependent properties specified by the designer, and a set of soundness aspects that should be checked, the tool automatically verifies the specification and creates a report of the verification activity as shown in Figure 3, which shows results obtained by checking most of the properties mentioned in this paper.

When a property does not hold, the model checker generates a counterexample [2,12], which is used to extract the sequence of base-level events that characterize that execution. To better interpret why a trace violates a property, we have started to implement a translation of FIEVeL into a set of Java classes, which should help the designer to reason in terms of the abstractions provided by FIEVeL and to hide the details related with Promela and its syntax. Also, such classes represent a fist step to develop a simulator of institutions, which can help the designer to test his or her own specifications and to understand how they will evolve by interactively determining events that will be processed by the institution.

To provide the reader with a feeling of the computational costs of our approach, we report results obtained during the verification of property (1) presented in Section 4 on a desktop PC with installed Windows and equipped with a pentium 3.0 GHz and 0.5 GB of RAM. Table 1 reports our experiments, where "*" represents the fact that the verification process requires more than 500 seconds and therefore it has been interrupted. Analyzing results showed in Table 1, we can observe that by increasing the size of domains representing agents and prices we obtain a very fast growth of time and memory required to verify such property. This is essentially due to the fact that the number of agents and prices determines the number of possible events that can be interleaved with time events. Also, in our formalization of the English auction we keep trace of the order in which agents make their bids, so that the auctioneer is able to declare a *current winner* even if two agents have offered the same price during a round (the first agent that has bid the highest price is declared to be the current winner). Clearly, this fact contributes to increasing the number of possible paths that the model checker has to consider, and hence the amount of required memory and time.

Despite that, we consider our results interesting, considered the complexity of the specification and compared with our experience in the verification of systems specified in Promela. Instead, we are not able to offer to the reader any comparison with results obtained by related works, because most of them do not report any experimental result [13,28,24] or they mention results related with very simple properties [4]. In every case, Table 1 clearly indicates that our approach is able to cope only with small domains. In fact, performances rapidly decay with the growth of the size of the model due to the number of variables that concur to represent the state of the system and due to embedded code used to compute events preconditions and propositions of LTL formulas. Several

Table 1. Time and memory required to verify Property (1) of Section 4. Results are reported showing the size of the considered models and if they have been obtained assuming agent compliance.

Agents	Prices	Memory (MB) agent compliance	Time (sec) agent compliance	Memory (MB)	Time (sec)
3	1	11.164	0.18	61.962	0.93
3	3	12.342	6.17	107.826	74.75
3	5	52.093	42.14	*	*
3	7	155.772	170.49	*	*
4	1	12.867	0.26	67.81	1.29
4	3	13.162	16.06	116.841	198.10
4	5	58.65	128.34	*	*
4	7	179.131	499.59	*	*

techniques have been proposed in the literature to solve these problems, and we think that the most promising for the verification of institutions are *predicate abstraction* [11] and *symbolic representation* [3] of institutional transitions.

7   Discussion and Conclusions

In this paper we have presented a framework for the definition and verification of institutions. The main advantage of our approach consists in the definition of a language that allows a designer to specify institutions and their desired properties in terms of a set of legal and philosophical concepts, and to automatically translate them into the input language of a model checker. Although in this paper we have exemplified our approach with a well known protocol, we expect that our framework is suitable for the specification and verification of systems where normative constraints and authorizations are generated by different sources and do not specify a precise sequence of messages and events. In presence of a collection of deontic positions that come from different sources, it is important to check that certain properties hold, to guarantee that agents and their designers can fulfill their objectives.

A few attempts have been previously carried out to apply model checking to verify institutions. [13] and [4] developed techniques to translate certain aspects of *electronic institutions* [8] into the input languages of SPIN or NuSMV [1]. Roughly speaking, the language presented in [8] describes institutions as composed by protocols, defined as finite automata, and a systems of norms, which may also regulate the execution of protocols by prohibiting agents from exchanging certain messages. [13] and [4] focus their attention only on properties of finite automata (e.g. "it is always possible to reach a final state"), while they do not take into account *normative rules*, that is, norms that model obligations agents get as a consequence of previous actions [8]. Instead, in our approach the attention is essentially focused on verifying properties of institutional states, described in terms of status functions, which are intrinsically related with the norms of the system. Moreover, in [13] each transition of the automata is interpreted an obligation, while according to [8] transitions represent agents' permissions. Therefore, it may occur that properties verified by the model checker actually do not hold in the original model and *vice versa*.

In [5,22] the authors distinguish among *institutional domain facts* and *normative facts* (obligations, institutionalized power, and permissions), while in our approach we proposed a unified view of institutional domain and normative facts. Indeed, we claim that institutional facts are such only because they imply new normative facts for the interacting agents, which also represents a significant difference with respect to our previous attempts to model institutional reality [9].

In the literature only agent actions have been considered relevant to describe institutions [5,9,22,24], and the attention has been focused on a single action type, namely the act of exchanging a message [8]. The importance of time events has been neglected [8,24], while not only time events are important for the management of obligations, but also they can count as institutional events (see Figure 1). For instance, in most cultures the 18th birthday imposes new status functions on a person.

As we have discussed in Section 6, we are considering how to improve the performance of the verification process by applying *predicate abstractions* [11]. In particular, we think that the approach presented in [3], where SAT solvers-techniques have been proposed to increase the efficiency of the abstraction process, could be applied both to reduce the size of the state space and to obtain institutional paths starting from computational paths by symbolically representing institutional transitions.

Acknowledgments. The author would like to thank his Ph.D. advisor, Marco Colombetti, for fruitful discussions and criticisms about the contents presented in this paper.

References

1. Cimatti, A., Clarke, E., Giunchiglia, E., Giunchiglia, F., Pistore, M., Roveri, M., Sebastiani, R., Tacchella, A.: NuSMV Version 2: An OpenSource Tool for Symbolic Model Checking. In: Brinksma, E., Larsen, K.G. (eds.) CAV 2002. LNCS, vol. 2404, Springer, Heidelberg (2002)

2. Clarke, E.M., Grumberg, O., Peled, D.: Model Checking. MIT Press, Cambrige, MA (1999)

3. Clarke, E.M., Kroening, D., Sharygina, N., Yorav, K.: Predicate Abstraction of ANSI-C Programs Using SAT. Formal Methods in System Design 25(2-3), 105–127 (2004)

4. Cliffe, O., Padget, J.: A Framework For Checking Interactions Within Agent Institutions. In: Proceedings of the ECAI Workshop on Model Checking and Artificial Intelligence (MoChart I) (2002)

5. Cliffe, O., Vos, M.D., Padget, J.: Specifying and Analysing Agent-based Social Institutions using Answer Set Programming. In: Boissier, O., Padget, J., Dignum, V., Lindemann, G., Matson, E., Ossowski, S., Sichman, J.S., Vázquez-Salceda, J. (eds.) Coordination, Organizations, Institutions, and Norms in Multi-Agent Systems. LNCS (LNAI), vol. 3913, pp. 99–113. Springer, Heidelberg (2006)

6. Dijkstra, E.W.: Guarded commands, nondeterminacy and formal derivation of programs. Communication of the ACM 18(8), 453–457 (1975)

7. Esteva, M., de la Cruz, D., Sierra, C.: ISLANDER: an electronic institutions editor. In: Castelfranchi, C., Johnson, W.L. (eds.) Proceedings of the first international joint conference on Autonomous Agents and Multiagent Systems (AAMAS '02), pp. 1045–1052. ACM Press, New York, NY, USA (2002)

8. Esteva, M., Rodríguez-Aguilar, J.A., Sierra, C., Garcia, P., Arcos, J.L.: On the Formal Specification of Electronic Institutions. In: Dignum, F., Sierra, C. (eds.) Agent Mediated Electronic
   Commerce. LNCS (LNAI), vol. 1991, pp. 126–147. Springer, Heidelberg (2001)
9. Fornara, N., Viganò, F., Colombetti, M.: Agent Communication and Institutional Reality. In:
   van Eijk, R.M., Huget, M.-P., Dignum, F.P.M. (eds.) AC 2004. LNCS (LNAI), vol. 3396, pp.
   1–17. Springer, Heidelberg (2005)
10. García-Camino, A., Rodríguez-Aguilar, J.A., Sierra, C., Vasconcelos, W.W.: A distributed architecture for norm-aware agent societies. In: Baldoni, M., Endriss, U., Omicini, A., Torroni,
   P. (eds.) DALT 2005. LNCS (LNAI), vol. 3904, pp. 89–105. Springer, Heidelberg (2007)
11. Graf, S., Saidi, H.: Construction of Abstract State Graphs with PVS. In: Proceedings of the
   9th International Conference on Computer Aided Verification, pp. 72–83. Springer, Heidelberg (1997)
12. Holzmann, G.: The SPIN Model Checker: Primer and Reference Manual. Addison-Wesley,
   London (2003)
13. Huget, M.-P., Esteva, M., Phelps, S., Sierra, C., Wooldridge, M.: Model Checking Electronic
   Institutions. In: Proceedings of the ECAI Workshop on Model Checking and Artificial Intelligence (MoChArt I) (2002)
14. Jones, A., Sergot, M.J.: A formal characterisation of institutionalised power. Journal of the
   IGPL 4(3), 429–445 (1996)
15. Kowalski, R.A., Sergot, M.J.: A Logic-based Calculus of Events. New Generation Computing 4, 67–95 (1986)
16. Lomuscio, A., Sergot, M.: A formulation of violation, error recovery, and enforcement in
   the bit transmission problem. Journal of Applied Logic (Selected articles from DEON02 -
   London) 1(2), 93–116 (2002)
17. Masolo, C., Vieu, L., Bottazzi, E., Catenacci, C., Ferrario, R., Gangemi, A., Guarino, N.: Social Roles and their Descriptions. In: Dubois, D., Welty, C., Williams, M.,(eds.) Proceedings
   of the Ninth International Conference on the Principles of Knowledge Representation and
   Reasoning (KR2004), pp. 267–277 (2004)
18. Meinke, K., Tucker, J.V. (eds.): Many-sorted logic and its applications. John Wiley & Sons,
   Inc, New York, NY, USA (1993)
19. Morzenti, A., Mandrioli, D., Ghezzi, C.: A Model Parametric Real-Time Logic. ACM Transactions on Programming Languages and Systems 14(4), 521–573 (1992)
20. Moses, Y., Tennenholtz, M.: Artificial Social Systems. Computers and AI 14(6), 533–562
   (1995)
21. Ostroff, J.S.: Deciding properties of timed transition models. IEEE Transactions on Parallel
   Distributed Systems 1(2), 170–183 (1990)
22. Pitt, J., Kamara, L., Sergot, M., Artikis, A.: Formalization of a voting protocol for virtual organizations. In: Proceedings of the 4th International Joint Conference on Autonomous agents
   and Multi-Agent Systems (AAMAS 2005), pp. 373–380. ACM Press, New York, NY, USA
   (2005)
23. Searle, J.R.: The construction of social reality. Free Press, New York, USA (1995)
24. Sergot, M.J.: Modelling unreliable and untrustworthy agent behaviour. In: Dunin-Keplicz,
   B., Jankowski, A., Skowron, A., Szczuka, M. (eds.) Monitoring, Security, and Rescue Techniques in Multiagent Systems, Advances in Soft Computing, pp. 161–178. Springer, Heidelberg (2005)
25. Vasconcelos, W.: Logic-based electronic institutions. In: Leite, J.A., Omicini, A., Sterling, L.,
   Torroni, P. (eds.) DALT 2003. LNCS (LNAI), vol. 2990, pp. 221–242. Springer, Heidelberg
   (2003)

26. Viganò, F.: FIEVeL, a Language for the Specification and Verification of Institutions. Technical Report 3, Institute for Communication Technologies, Università della Svizzera Italiana (2006)
27. Viganò, F., Colombetti, M.: Specification and Verification of Institutions through Status Functions. In: Proceedings of the AAMAS Workshop on Coordination, Organization, Institutions and Norms in agent systems (COIN06) (2006)
28. Walton, C.D.: Model Checking Agent Dialogues. In: Leite, J.A., Omicini, A., Torroni, P., Yolum, P. (eds.) DALT 2004. LNCS (LNAI), vol. 3476, pp. 132–147. Springer, Heidelberg (2004)

SAT-Based Verification of Security Protocols Via Translation to Networks of Automata [*]

Mirosław Kurkowski[1], Wojciech Penczek[2,3], and Andrzej Zbrzezny[1]

[1] Institute of Mathematics and Computer Science, Jan Długosz University,
Armii Krajowej 13/15, 42-200 Częstochowa
m.kurkowski@ajd.czest.pl, a.zbrzezny@ajd.czest.pl
[2] Institute of Computer Science, PAS, Ordona 21, 01-237 Warsaw, Poland
penczek@ipipan.waw.pl
[3] Institute of Informatics, Podlasie Academy, Sienkiewicza 51, 08-110 Siedlce, Poland

Abstract. In this paper we show a novel method for modelling behaviours of security protocols using networks of communicating automata in order to verify them with SAT-based bounded model checking. These automata correspond to executions of the participants as well as to their knowledge about letters. Given a bounded number of sessions, we can verify both correctness or incorrectness of a security protocol proving either reachability or unreachability of an undesired state. We exemplify all our notions on the Needham Schroeder Public Key Authentication Protocol (NSPK) and show experimental results for checking authentication using the verification tool VerICS.

Keywords: security protocols, model checking, authentication.

1 Introduction

Security protocols define the rules of exchanging messages between the parties in order to establish a secure communication channel between them. Similarly to communicating protocols there are several approaches to verification of security protocols. These protocols are usually verified using deductive methods (e.g., theorem proving) or algorithmic ones. Deductive methods have been exploited in many verification systems like: Isabelle [2], Murϕ [26], TAPS [9], PVS [13], and NRL [25]. Algorithmic approaches include mainly methods based on model checking, which have been an object of an intensive research for several years in both academic and commercial institutions.

Intuitively, model checking of a security protocol consists in checking whether a model of the protocol accepts an execution (or contains a reachable state) that is representing an attack on the protocol. Comparing to standard model checking methods for communicating protocols or for distributed systems, the main difficulty is caused by the need to model both the intruder who is responsible

---

[*] The authors acknowledge partial support from the Ministry of Science and Information Society Technologies under the grant number 3 T11C 01128.

S. Edelkamp and A. Lomuscio (Eds.): MoChart IV, LNAI 4428, pp. 146–165, 2007.

for generating attacks as well as changes of knowledge (about keys, nonces, etc.) of the participants. Typically, a model is constructed as a product of processes representing the participants and the intruder.

Properties expressing correctness of security protocols are usually formulated as reachability properties or in linear (branching) time temporal logic. Following early achievements in model checking of cryptographic protocols by the teams of E. Clarke [8], C. Meadows [25], G. Lowe [23], or D. Bolignano [4], over the last five years the state-of-the-art verification system AVISPA [1] has been designed and implemented as the result of the EU research project. AVISPA is composed of the following four self-complementing modules: *OFMC* applying symbolic verification on-the-fly via analysis of a transition system described in the specification language IF, *CL-AtSe* using 'constrain solving' and enables discovering of type flaws, *SATMC* being a bounded model checker exploiting a SAT-solver, and *TA4SP* applying a method based on regular tree languages and therm rewriting.

On the other hand, verification systems for distributed and real time systems like SMV [24], Spin [14], KRONOS [29], UppAal [3], or Verics [11] enjoy a much longer history and experience in use. It is clearly very interesting to investigate methods of applying the above tools to verification of security protocols [17,28,10,16,15]. In this paper we are interested in using tools that accept inputs represented by networks of (timed) automata as these can be then verified with most of the existing symbolic and non-symbolic model checkers. Verification can be performed either indirectly by specifying a protocol in a higher order language and then translating it to automata or directly by modelling a protocol by a network of automata. In this paper[1] we offer a new syntax and semantics of security protocols, and an entirely novel approach to their verification (to the best of our knowledge). Our main and original idea about consists in using networks of automata for modelling separately the participants and their knowledge about secrets. Thanks to that we get a very distributed representation of the protocol executions, which is important for an efficient symbolic encoding and model checking. To this aim we develop a novel semantics of security protocols, where the notion of a computational structure and an interpretation is based on the ideas that appeared in [18,5]. Next, we give a method for representing the executions of a security protocol (within a computational structure for a bounded number of sessions) by the runs of the product automaton of a network of the above mentioned automata and show how to look for attacks on authentication. To this aim we use Bounded Model Checking (BMC), which consists in translating the problem of reachability in the product automaton to satisfiability of some propositional formula. Moreover, in addition to prove reachability of an undesired state (in case there is an attack on the protocol), we can also prove unreachability of such a state if there is no attack in the computational structure. This seems to be as well a novel application of BMC to verification of security protocols.

---

[1] Some preliminary results [19] were presented at CS&P'06.

Our model allows for specification and verification of untimed cryptographic protocols which realise the well-known *challenge-response* idea. The Needham-Schroeder public key protocol [6] is the best known example here, but there are other more complicated protocols like NSPK-Lowe, Andrew, TMN, Otway-Rees, and Yahalom [6,7] that fall into that class as well. In this paper, for simplicity of a translation to automata, we assume that letters sent in the executions of the protocols cannot include nested ciphers. We focus on the public key cryptography, but it is easy to observe that this model is adequate in the case of symmetric cryptography too. Our model of the Intruder's behaviour follows the well known Dolev-Yao model [12] in which the Intruder can intercept and modify all the letters. However, in our experiments we are dealing with a limited model of the Intruder in which he can only receive letters sent to him when playing the role of himself or impersonating another participant. This limitation allows to look for attacks in a more efficient way as the size of a state space is then much limited.

The rest of the paper is organised as follows. In Section 2 we introduce syntax for dealing with untimed security protocols. A computational structure generating all the runs of the protocols considered is defined in Section 3. A method for finding attacks by analysing computations of the protocol is shown in Section 4. Section 5 defines network of automata for representing the participants of a protocol and their knowledge about secrets. Then, experimental results are given in Section 6 and some concluding remarks in Section 7.

2   Syntax of Security Protocols

In this section we introduce syntax for dealing with untimed security protocols. To this aim, we give some notations used in the rest of the paper. Next, we define the following basic syntactic notions of our model.

- $\mathcal{T}_P = \{\mathcal{P}_1, \mathcal{P}_2, \ldots, \mathcal{P}_{n_P}\}$ is a set of symbols representing the users of the computer network,
  $\mathcal{T}_I = \{\mathcal{I}_{\mathcal{P}_1}, \mathcal{I}_{\mathcal{P}_2}, \ldots, \mathcal{I}_{\mathcal{P}_{n_P}}\}$ is a set of symbols representing the identifiers of the users,
- $\mathcal{T}_K = \bigcup_{i=1}^{n_P} \{\mathcal{K}_{\mathcal{P}_i}, \mathcal{K}_{\mathcal{P}_i}^{-1}\}$ is a set of symbols representing the cryptographic keys of users (public and private respectively),
- $\mathcal{T}_N = \bigcup_{i=1}^{n_P} \{\mathcal{N}_{\mathcal{P}_i}^1, \ldots, \mathcal{N}_{\mathcal{P}_i}^{n_N}\}^2$ is a set of symbols representing the users' *nonces*,
- $\{"(", ")", "\{", "\}", ","\}$ is a set of the auxiliary symbols.

Definition 1 (Letter Terms). *By a set of letter terms $\mathcal{T}$ we mean the smallest set satisfying the following conditions:*

1. $\mathcal{T}_P \cup \mathcal{T}_I \cup \mathcal{T}_K \cup \mathcal{T}_N \subseteq \mathcal{T}$.
2. *If $X \in \mathcal{T}$ and $Y \in \mathcal{T}$, then the concatenation $X \cdot Y \in \mathcal{T}$,*

---

[2] We assume that n_P and n_N are some fixed natural numbers.

3. If $X \in T$ and $K \in T_K$, then $\langle X \rangle_K \in T^3$.

Next, we define some useful relations over the set T.

Definition 2. *Let $\prec_T \subseteq T \times T$ be the smallest relation (called (immediate) subterm relation), which satisfies the following conditions:*

1. If $X, Y \in T$, then $X \prec_T X \cdot Y$ and $Y \prec_T X \cdot Y$,
2. If $X \in T$ and $K \in T_K$, then $X \prec_T \langle X \rangle_K$ and $K \prec_T \langle X \rangle_K$.

By $\preceq_T$ we denote the transitive and reflexive closure of $\prec_T$. Next, for any $X \subseteq T$ we define a sequence of the sets $(X^n)_{n \in \mathbf{N}}$ that are subsets of T:

- $X^0 \overset{def}{=} X$,
- $X^{n+1} \overset{def}{=} X^n \cup \{Z \in T \mid (\exists X, Y \in X^n, K \in X \cap T_K)\, Z = X \cdot Y \vee Z = \langle X \rangle_K\}$.

Intuitively, the set X^{n+1} contains the, gradually built, letter terms from X^n using the operations of composition and encryption. In what follows, for any set Z by 2^Z_{fin} we denote a set of all the finite subsets of Z.

For $X \in 2^T_{fin}$ the set $Comp(X) \overset{def}{=} \bigcup_{n \in \mathbf{N}} X^n$ is composed of all the letters that can be constructed out of elements of X only[4].

Now, we are ready to define the syntax for a protocol step and then for a protocol itself. A notion of a step is clearly more complicated than in the common language as it provides the information not only about the sender P, the receiver Q, and the letter L sent from P to Q, but also about letters necessary to compose L as well as generated secrets necessary to compose L. The intended aim of this extra information is to point out to additional actions of the sender like generating new secrets or composing the letter L.

Definition 3. *By a (protocol) step α we mean a five-tuple $(P, X, G, Q, L) \in T_P \times 2^T_{fin} \times 2^{T_K \cup T_N}_{fin} \times T_P \times T$, with the following intuitive meaning:*
  P - the sender of the step,
  X - the set of letters necessary to compose L,
  G - the set of generated secrets necessary to compose L,
  Q - the receiver of L, and
  L - the letter sent from P to Q,
that satisfies the following conditions:

1. $P \neq Q$ (nobody can send letters to himself),
2. $L \in Comp(X) \wedge (\forall Y \subseteq X)(L \in Comp(Y) \Rightarrow Y = X)$,
   (X is a minimal set from which L can be constructed)
3. $G \subseteq X$ (the secrets of G are elements of X).

By a protocol Σ we mean a finite sequence $(\alpha_1, \ldots, \alpha_n)$ of steps.

---

[3] $\langle X \rangle_K$ is a term that is interpreted as a ciphertext containing the letter X encrypted with the key K.

[4] Description is not allowed here.

Example 1. We consider Needham Schroeder Public Key Authentication Protocol (NSPK) as a working example. Below, syntax of NSPK is defined. $T_P = \{\mathcal{A}, \mathcal{B}\}$, $T_I = \{\mathcal{I}_\mathcal{A}, \mathcal{I}_\mathcal{B}\}$, $T_K = \{\mathcal{K}_\mathcal{A}, \mathcal{K}_\mathcal{B}\}$, $T_N = \{\mathcal{N}_\mathcal{A}, \mathcal{N}_\mathcal{B}\}$. The protocol NSPK is given by the following sequence of steps: $(\alpha_1, \alpha_2, \alpha_3)$, where:

$$\alpha_1 = (\mathcal{A}, \{\mathcal{N}_\mathcal{A}, \mathcal{I}_\mathcal{A}, \mathcal{K}_\mathcal{B}\}, \{\mathcal{N}_\mathcal{A}\}, \mathcal{B}, \langle \mathcal{N}_\mathcal{A}, \mathcal{I}_\mathcal{A} \rangle_{\mathcal{K}_\mathcal{B}}),$$
$$\alpha_2 = (\mathcal{B}, \{\mathcal{N}_\mathcal{A}, \mathcal{N}_\mathcal{B}, \mathcal{K}_\mathcal{A}\}, \{\mathcal{N}_\mathcal{B}\}, \mathcal{A}, \langle \mathcal{N}_\mathcal{A}, \mathcal{N}_\mathcal{B} \rangle_{\mathcal{K}_\mathcal{A}}),$$
$$\alpha_3 = (\mathcal{A}, \{\mathcal{N}_\mathcal{B}, \mathcal{K}_\mathcal{B}\}, \emptyset, \mathcal{B}, \langle \mathcal{N}_\mathcal{B} \rangle_{\mathcal{K}_\mathcal{B}}). \qquad \square$$

3   Computational Structure

In this section we define a computational structure generating all the computations (under the interpretations considered) of an authentication protocol investigated. Later, we aim at representing these computations by runs of some network of automata. In general, we could deal with an infinite number of sessions in a computational structure, but because we aim at verifying our protocols in an automatic way, we restrict ourselves to a bounded number of sessions by limiting the number of nonces. We start with defining the following sets:

- $\mathbf{P} = \{p_1, p_2, \ldots, p_{n_p}\}$ - a set of the honest participants in the network,
- $\mathbf{P}_\iota = \{\iota, \iota(p_1), \iota(p_2), \ldots, \iota(p_{n_p})\}$ - a set of the dishonest participants containing the Intruder and the Intruder impersonating the participant p_i for $1 \leq i \leq n_p$,
- $\mathbf{I} = \{i_{p_1}, \ldots, i_{p_{n_p}}, i_\iota\}$ - a set of the identifiers of the participants in the network,
- $\mathbf{K} = \bigcup_{i=1}^{n_p} \{k_{p_i}, k_{p_i}^{-1}\} \cup \{k_\iota, k_\iota^{-1}\}$ - a set of the cryptographic keys of the participants,
- $\mathbf{N} = \bigcup_{i=1}^{n_p} \{n_{p_i}^1, \ldots, n_{p_i}^{k_N}\} \cup \{n_\iota^1, \ldots, n_\iota^{k_N}\}$ - a set of the *nonces*[5].

Definition 4. *By a set of letters* $\mathbf{L}$ *we mean the smallest set satisfying the following conditions:*

1. $\mathbf{P} \cup \mathbf{P}_\iota \cup \mathbf{I} \cup \mathbf{K} \cup \mathbf{S} \subseteq \mathbf{L}$,
2. *If* $x, y \in \mathbf{L}$, *then the concatenation* $x \cdot y \in \mathbf{L}$,
3. *If* $x \in \mathbf{L}$ *and* $k \in \mathbf{K}$, *then* $\langle x \rangle_k \in \mathbf{L}$,
   $\langle x \rangle_k$ *is a ciphertext consisting of the letter* x *encrypted with the key* k.

Next, we define some auxiliary relations over the set $\mathbf{L}$.

Definition 5. *Let* $\prec \subseteq \mathbf{L} \times \mathbf{L}$ *be the smallest relation (called* (immediate) *subletter relation) satisfying the following conditions:*

1. *If* $x, y \in \mathbf{L}$, *then* $x \prec x \cdot y$ *and* $y \prec x \cdot y$,
2. *If* $x \in \mathbf{L}$ *and* $k \in \mathbf{K}$, *then* $x \prec \langle x \rangle_k$ *and* $k \prec \langle x \rangle_k$.

---

[5] As before, we assume that n_p and k_N are some fixed natural numbers. For simplicity, we take the same number of nonces for each user.

By $\preceq$ we denote the transitive and reflexive closure of $\prec$. Next, for any $X \subseteq \mathbf{L}$ we define a sequence of the sets $(X^n)_{n \in \mathbf{N}}$ that are also subsets o $\mathbf{L}$, where

- $X^0 \overset{def}{=} X$,
- $X^{n+1} \overset{def}{=} X^n \cup \{z \in \mathbf{L} \mid (\exists x, y \in X^n, \ k \in X \cap \mathbf{K}) \ z = x \cdot y \ \lor \ z = \langle x \rangle_k\}$.

The intuition behind this definition is the same as for the corresponding one in Section 2, i.e., the set X^{n+1} contains the, gradually built, letters from X^n using the operations of composition and encryption. Next, define the set $Comp(X) \overset{def}{=} \bigcup_{n \in \mathbf{N}} X^n$ which consists of all the letters that can be composed out of elements of X only[6] and the set $Sublet(X) \overset{def}{=} \{l \in \mathbf{L} \mid (\exists x \in X) \ l \preceq x\}$ which contains all the subletters of X.

Definition 6. *Let $X \subseteq \mathbf{L}$ and $K \subseteq \mathbf{K}$. Define the set $\xi_K(X) \subseteq \mathbf{L}$ as the smallest set of letters satisfying the following conditions:*

1. $X \subseteq \xi_K(X)$,
2. *if $l \cdot m \in \xi_K(X)$, then $l \in \xi_K(X)$ and $m \in \xi_K(X)$,*
3. *if $\langle l \rangle_k \in \xi_K(X)$ and $k \in \xi_K(X) \cup K$, then $l \in \xi_K(X)$.*

The set $\xi_K(X)$ contains all the letters which can be retrieved from X by decomposing a concatenation or decrypting a letter using a key, which is either in $\xi_K(X)$ or in K. By $\xi(X)$ we mean the set $\xi_\emptyset(X)$.

Next, we define interpretations of the terms of $\mathcal{T}$. Each interpretation determines one execution of the protocol (defined as a syntactical object).

Definition 7. *By an interpretation of the set of the letter terms $\mathcal{T}$ we mean any injection $f : \mathcal{T} \to \mathbf{L}$ satisfying the following conditions:*

1. $f(\mathcal{T}_P) \subseteq \mathbf{P} \cup \mathbf{P}_\iota, \ f(\mathcal{T}_I) \subseteq \mathbf{I}, \ f(\mathcal{T}_K) \subseteq \mathbf{K}, \ f(\mathcal{T}_N) \subseteq \mathbf{N}$,
2. $(\forall X, Y \in \mathcal{T}) \ f(X \cdot Y) = f(X) \cdot f(Y)$ *(homomorphism),*
3. $(\forall X \in \mathcal{T})(\forall \mathcal{K} \in \mathcal{T}_K) \ f(\langle X \rangle_\mathcal{K}) = \langle f(X) \rangle_{f(\mathcal{K})}$ *(homomorphism),*
4. *If $f(\mathcal{P}) = p$ for $p \in \mathbf{P}$, then $f(\mathcal{I}_\mathcal{P}) = i_p, \ f(\mathcal{N}_\mathcal{P}) \in \{n_p^1, \ldots, n_p^{k_S}\}$, $f(\mathcal{K}_\mathcal{P}) = k_p$ and $f(\mathcal{K}_\mathcal{P}^{-1}) = k_p^{-1}$.*
5. *If $f(\mathcal{P}) = \iota$, then $f(\mathcal{I}_\mathcal{P}) = i_\iota, \ f(\mathcal{K}_\mathcal{P}) = k_\iota$ and $f(\mathcal{K}_\mathcal{P}^{-1}) = k_\iota^{-1}$.*
6. *If $f(\mathcal{P}) = \iota(p)$, then $f(\mathcal{I}_\mathcal{P}) = i_p, \ f(\mathcal{K}_\mathcal{P}) = k_p$ and $f(\mathcal{K}_\mathcal{P}^{-1}) = k_p^{-1}$,*
7. $f(\mathcal{T}_\mathcal{P}) \setminus \mathbf{P}_\iota \neq \emptyset$

The condition 1 states that the atomic terms are mapped into corresponding objects of the computational structure, i.e., symbols representing participants are mapped into participants, etc. The condition 2 and 3 guarantee the homomorphical separation between the mapped symbols. The condition 4 says that the symbols related to a given participant are mapped into corresponding objects (identifiers, keys, nonces) in the structure. The conditions 5-7 are related to our model of the Intruder. The condition 5 determines that if the Intruder

---

[6] Description is not allowed here.

wants to play in an execution of the protocol the role of himself, then he uses his own identifier and keys. There is no condition on the nonces used by the Intruder, as we assume that he can use any nonce. The condition 6 states that if the Intruder ι impersonates another participant p in some interpretation, then in any execution under this interpretation p's keys and p's identifier need to be used by ι. Then, due to the condition 1, no participant symbol is mapped to p in this interpretation. The last condition says that at least one honest participant takes part in each interpretation.

In order to define later an interpretation of a protocol step in which the Intruder is the sender, we need the notion of a set of generators for a letter.

Definition 8. *Let $l \in \mathbf{L}$ be a letter and $X \subseteq \mathbf{L}$. The set X is said to be a set of generators of l (denoted by $X \vdash l$) if the following conditions are met:*

1. $X \subseteq Sublet(\{l\})$,
2. $l \in Comp(X)$,
3. $(\forall m \in X)(m \notin Comp(X \setminus \{m\}))$,
4. $(\forall m \in X)(l \notin Comp(X \setminus \{m\}))$.

Intuitively, we have $X \vdash l$ if all the elements of X are subletters of l, l can be composed out of the elements of X, and X is a minimal such a set.

Example 2. Consider the letter $l = \langle i_a, n_a \rangle_{k_b}$. Observe that the sets $X_1 = \{i_a, n_a, k_b\}$ and $X_2 = \{\langle i_a, n_a \rangle_{k_b}\}$ are sets of independent generators of l, i.e., we have $X_1 \vdash l$ and $X_2 \vdash l$.

Having defined a set of letter generators and an interpretation of $\mathcal{T}$, we are now ready to apply it to a protocol step and then to the whole protocol.

Definition 9. *Consider a step $\alpha = (\mathcal{P}, \mathcal{X}, \mathcal{G}, \mathcal{Q}, \mathcal{L})$ of a given protocol Σ and an interpretation f of $\mathcal{T}$. By the f-interpretation of the step α (denoted by $f(\alpha)$) we mean the following five-tuple:*

- $(f(\mathcal{P}), f(\mathcal{X}), f(\mathcal{G}), f(\mathcal{Q}), f(\mathcal{L})^7)$, *if $f(\mathcal{P}) \in \mathbf{P}$,*
- $(f(\mathcal{P}), \{X \mid X \vdash f(\mathcal{L})\}, \emptyset, f(\mathcal{Q}), f(\mathcal{L}))$, *if $f(\mathcal{P}) \in \mathbf{P}_\iota$.*

In the case when the Intruder is the sender, we assume that he can compose a letter $f(\mathcal{L})$ from any set which generates $f(\mathcal{L})$. We also assume that the Intruder has got a set of nonces at his disposal and he does not need to generate them. The reason is that the Intruder can use the same nonce many times and in different sessions.

By *the execution of a protocol $\Sigma = (\alpha_1, \alpha_2, \ldots, \alpha_n)$ under an interpretation f* we mean the sequence $f(\Sigma) = (f(\alpha_1), f(\alpha_2), \ldots, f(\alpha_n))$.

Example 3. Again, we exemplify the above notions on NSPK. $\mathbf{P} = \{a, b\}$, $\mathbf{P}_\iota = \{\iota, \iota(a), \iota(b)\}$, $\mathbf{I} = \{i_a, i_b, i_\iota\}$, $\mathbf{K} = \{k_a, k_b, k_\iota\}$, $\mathbf{N} = \{n_a, n_b, n_\iota\}$. Consider the interpretation f_1 defined as follows: $f_1(\mathcal{A}) = a$, $f_1(\mathcal{B}) = b$, $f_1(\mathcal{I}_\mathcal{A}) = i_a$, $f_1(\mathcal{I}_\mathcal{B}) = i_b$, $f_1(\mathcal{N}_\mathcal{A}) = n_a$, $f_1(\mathcal{N}_\mathcal{B}) = n_b$, $f_1(\mathcal{K}_\mathcal{A}) = k_a$, $f_1(\mathcal{K}_\mathcal{B}) = k_b$. We have the following execution of NSPK: $(f_1(\alpha_1), f_1(\alpha_2), f_1(\alpha_3))$, where:

---

[7] We assume that any private key cannot be an element of the contents of $f(\mathcal{L})$.

- $f_1(\alpha_1) = (a, \{n_a, i_a, k_b\}, \{n_a\}, b, \langle n_a, i_a \rangle_{k_b})$,
- $f_1(\alpha_2) = (b, \{n_a, n_b, k_a\}, \{n_b\}, a, \langle n_a, n_b \rangle_{k_a})$,
- $f_1(\alpha_3) = (a, \{n_b, k_b\}, \emptyset, b, \langle n_b \rangle_{k_b})$.   □

In order to define knowledge of the participants and the Intruder we need to introduce the following auxiliary notions. If $f(\alpha_i) = (p, X, G, q, l)$, for some $p, q \in \mathbf{P} \cup \mathbf{P}_\iota$, $X \in 2^{\mathbf{L}}_{fin}$, $G \in 2^{\mathbf{K} \cup \mathbf{N}}_{fin}$, and $l \in \mathbf{L}$, then we use the following notations:

$Send^{f(\alpha_i)} = p$ (the sender of $f(\alpha_i)$),

$Lett^{f(\alpha_i)} = l$ (the letter of $f(\alpha_i)$),

$Gen^{f(\alpha_i)} = G$ (the set of generated new secrets in $f(\alpha_i)$),

$Resp^{f(\alpha_i)} = q$ (the responder of $f(\alpha_i)$), and

$Part^{f(\alpha_i)} = \{Send^{f(\alpha_i)}, Resp^{f(\alpha_i)}\}$.

Additionally if $Send^{f(\alpha_i)} \in \mathbf{P}$, then let $Comp^{f(\alpha_i)} = X$ (the set of letters that are sufficient to compose $Lett^{f(\alpha_i)}$) and if $Send^{f(\alpha_i)} \in \mathbf{P}_\iota$, then let $Comp^{f(\alpha_i)} = \bigcup_{X \vdash Lett^{f(\alpha_i)}} X$ (the union of sets which generate $Lett^{f(\alpha_i)}$).

For a set of interpretations $\mathcal{F}$, we define the set $Comp^p_{\mathcal{F}}$ ($Comp^\iota_{\mathcal{F}}$) of the letters, which the participant $p \in \bigcup_{f \in \mathcal{F}} f(\mathcal{T}_P) \setminus \mathbf{P}_\iota$ (the Intruder ι, resp.) needs to compose all the letters sent in an execution under any interpretation $f \in \mathcal{F}$.

Definition 10. *The set* $Comp^p_{\mathcal{F}} = \bigcup_{1 \leq i \leq n} \bigcup_{\{f \in \mathcal{F} | Send^{f(\alpha_i)} = p\}} Comp^{f(\alpha_i)}$ *for an honest user p is the union of all the sets $Comp^{f(\alpha_i)}$ for all $i \leq n$ and $f \in \mathcal{F}$, where $Send^{f(\alpha_i)} = p$.*

The set $Comp^\iota_{\mathcal{F}} = \bigcup_{1 \leq i \leq n} \bigcup_{\{f \in \mathcal{F} | Send^{f(\alpha_i)} \in \mathbf{P}_\iota\}} Comp^{f(\alpha_i)}$ *is the union of all the sets $Comp^{f(\alpha_i)}$ for all $i \leq n$ and $f \in \mathcal{F}$, where $Send^{f(\alpha_i)} \in \mathbf{P}_\iota$.*

Consider any finite sequence of interpretations of k protocol steps $\mathbf{r} = (f^1(\alpha_{i_1}), f^2(\alpha_{i_2}), \ldots, f^k(\alpha_{i_k}))$. For every $p \in \bigcup_{i=1}^{k} f^i(\mathcal{T}_P)$ we define a sequence of the participant's knowledge $(\kappa^j_p)_{j=1,\ldots,k}$ at the steps of the protocol.

Definition 11. *For an honest participant $p \in \bigcup_{f \in \mathcal{F}} f(\mathcal{T}_P) \setminus \mathbf{P}_\iota$ his knowledge at the step j is given inductively as follows:*
$$\kappa^0_p = \mathbf{I} \cup \{k_p^{-1}\} \cup \{k_q \mid q \in \mathbf{P}\} \cup \{k_\iota\},$$

$$\kappa^{j+1}_p = \begin{cases} \kappa^j_p & \text{if } p \notin Part^{f^{j+1}(\alpha_{i_{j+1}})}, \\[2mm] \kappa^j_p \cup Gen^{f^{j+1}(\alpha_{i_{j+1}})} & \text{if } p = Send^{f^{j+1}(\alpha_{i_{j+1}})}, \\[2mm] Comp^p_{\mathcal{F}} \cap \xi_{\{k_p^{-1}\}}(\kappa^j_p \cup \{Lett^{f^{j+1}(\alpha_{i_{j+1}})}\}) & \text{if } p = Resp^{f^{j+1}(\alpha_{i_{j+1}})}. \end{cases}$$

The intuition behind the above definition is as follows. The knowledge of a participant not participating in a protocol step is not changing. If a participant is the initiator of a step, then his knowledge is extended with the set of the generated nonces. If a participant is the responder of a step, then his knowledge is extended by all the letters, which can be retrieved from the former knowledge and the letter actually received. But, for efficiency reasons it is restricted to a subset of $Comp^p_\mathcal{F}$, i.e., to the letters which the participant needs in order to compose any letter in any execution determined by $\mathcal{F}$.

We define two models of the Intruder's knowledge. The first one is the full Dolev-Yao model the Intruder's knowledge, whereas the second model restricts the Intruder such that if he is not the responder of a letter, then his knowledge does not change.

Definition 12. *The Intruder's knowledge at each step j of the protocol is common for all $p \in \bigcup_{f \in \mathcal{F}} f(T_P) \cap \mathbf{P}_\iota$ and it is given inductively as follows:*

$\kappa^0_\iota = \mathbf{I} \cup \{k_\iota^{-1}, k_\iota\} \cup \{k_q \mid q \in \mathbf{P}\} \cup \{n_\iota^1, \ldots, n_\iota^{k_N}\},$
For the D-Y model of the Intruder:
$\kappa^{j+1}_\iota = Comp^\iota_\mathcal{F} \cap \xi_{\{k_\iota^{-1}\}}(\kappa^j_\iota \cup \{Lett^{f^{j+1}(\alpha_{i_{j+1}})}\}).$
For the restricted model of the Intruder:

$$\kappa^{j+1}_\iota = \begin{cases} \kappa^j_\iota & \text{if } Resp^{f^{j+1}(\alpha_{i_{j+1}})} \notin P_\iota, \\ Comp^\iota_\mathcal{F} \cap \xi_{\{k_\iota^{-1}\}}(\kappa^j_\iota \cup \{Lett^{f^{j+1}(\alpha_{i_{j+1}})}\}) & \text{if } Resp^{f^{j+1}(\alpha_{i_{j+1}})} \in P_\iota. \end{cases}$$

Notice the Intruder is retrieving all the possible letters from his knowledge and the letter he has interecepted (received), which is restricted to a subset of $Comp^\iota_\mathcal{F}$ for efficiency reasons. For simplicity, we assume that the Intruder does not generate his nonces as he can use them several times in many executions. This does not introduce any limitations.

In the following definition we formulate the conditions which guarantee that a sequence of protocol step interpretations is a computation of the protocol.

Definition 13. *By a computation of the protocol Σ we mean any injective finite sequence of protocol step interpretations: $\mathfrak{r} = (f^1(\alpha_{i_1}), f^2(\alpha_{i_2}), \ldots, f^k(\alpha_{i_k}))$ which meets the following conditions:*

1. $(\forall k \in \mathbf{N}_+)[i_k > 1 \Rightarrow (\exists j < k)(f^j = f^k \wedge i_j = i_k - 1)],$
2. $(\forall k, j \in \mathbf{N}_+)[k \neq j \Rightarrow Gen^{f^k(\alpha_{i_k})} \cap Gen^{f^j(\alpha_{i_j})} = \emptyset],$
3. $(\forall j \in \mathbf{N}_+)[Lett^{f^j(\alpha_{i_j})} \in Comp(\kappa^{j-1}_{Send^{f^j(\alpha_{i_j})}} \cup Gen^{f^j(\alpha_{i_j})})].$

The first condition states that for each protocol step (except for the first one) in interpretation f, there is a preceding step in the same interpretation. The second one says that the sets of generated nonces are disjoint, whereas the third one guarantees that the letter $Lett^{f^j(\alpha_{i_j})}$ can be sent by $Send^{f^j(\alpha_{i_j})}$ only if it can be composed from the set of currently generated nonces and the knowledge of the participant $Send^{f^j(\alpha_{i_j})}$ at the step $j-1$.

4   Attacks Upon Protocols

Security protocols are used in order to establish a secure communication channel between two parties involved in the communication. This is obtained by ensuring that each party is confident about several security properties: e.g., that the other party is who they say they are (*authentication*), a confidential information is not visible to non-authorised parties (*secrecy*), the information exchanged by two parties cannot be altered by an intruder (*integrity*), and finally the parties taking part in the transaction cannot deny it later (*non-repudiation*).

Below, we focus on checking authentication only. We say that a given protocol is *correct* if the protocol cannot be executed in such a way that identifiers or keys of one participant are used by someone else. Having this in mind, we give the following definition.

Definition 14 (Attacking execution). *By* an attacking execution *we mean any execution under an interpretation f, where $f(\mathcal{P}) = \iota(p)$, for some $\mathcal{P} \in \mathcal{T}_P$ and $p \in \mathbf{P}$.*

Example 4. Consider the interpretation f_2 defined as follows: $f_2(\mathcal{A}) = \iota(a)$, $f_2(\mathcal{B}) = b$, $f_2(\mathcal{I}_A) = i_a$, $f_2(\mathcal{I}_B) = i_b$, $f_2(\mathcal{N}_A) = n_a$, $f_2(\mathcal{N}_B) = n_b$, $f_2(\mathcal{K}_A) = k_a$, $f_2(\mathcal{K}_B) = k_b$. We have the following execution of the NSPK protocol: $(f_1(\alpha_1), f_1(\alpha_2), f_1(\alpha_3))$, where:

$\quad f_2(\alpha_1) = (\iota(a), \{X_1, X_2\}, \emptyset, b, \langle n_a, i_a \rangle_{k_b})$,
$\quad f_2(\alpha_2) = (b, \{n_a, n_b, k_a\}, \{n_b\}, \iota(a), \langle n_a, n_b \rangle_{k_a})$,
$\quad f_2(\alpha_3) = (\iota(a), \{X_3, X_4\}, \emptyset, b, \langle n_b \rangle_{k_b})$,
$\quad X_1 = \{n_a, i_a, k_b\}, X_2 = \{\langle n_a, i_a \rangle_{k_b}\}, X_3 = \{n_b, k_b\}, X_4 = \{\langle n_b \rangle_{k_b}\}.$ □

Definition 15 (Attack). *By* an attack *upon a protocol we mean any of its computations such that an attacking execution is its subsequence.*

The following example shows an attack on NSPK.

Example 5. Consider the interpretation f_2 of Example 4 and the interpretation f_3 defined below: $f_3(\mathcal{A}) = a$, $f_3(\mathcal{B}) = \iota$, $f_3(\mathcal{I}_A) = i_a$, $f_3(\mathcal{I}_B) = i_\iota$, $f_3(\mathcal{N}_A) = n_a$, $f_3(\mathcal{N}_B) = n_b$, $f_3(\mathcal{K}_A) = k_a$, $f_3(\mathcal{K}_B) = k_\iota$.
For f_3 we have the following execution of NSPK: $(f_3(\alpha_1), f_3(\alpha_2), f_3(\alpha_3))$, where:

$\quad f_3(\alpha_1) = (a, \{n_a, i_a, k_\iota\}, \{n_a\}, \iota, \langle n_a, i_a \rangle_{k_\iota}).$
$\quad f_3(\alpha_2) = (\iota, \{X_5, X_6\}, \emptyset, a, \langle n_a, n_b \rangle_{k_a}),$
$\quad f_3(\alpha_3) = (a, \{n_b, k_\iota\}, \emptyset, \iota, \langle n_b \rangle_{k_\iota})$

with $X_5 = \{n_a, n_b, k_a\}$ and $X_6 = \{\langle n_a, n_b \rangle_{k_a}\}$.
Observe that the sequence $\mathfrak{r} = (f_3(\alpha_1), f_2(\alpha_1), f_2(\alpha_2), f_3(\alpha_2), f_3(\alpha_3), f_2(\alpha_3))$ is a computation [8] which contains an attacking execution. Thus, $\mathfrak{r}$ is an attack.

---

[8] A simplified notation of this computation is the following:

$$
\begin{array}{rcll}
a & \to & \iota & : \quad \langle n_a, i_a \rangle_{k_\iota}, \\
\iota(a) & \to & b & : \quad \langle n_a, i_a \rangle_{k_b}, \\
b & \to & \iota(a) & : \quad \langle n_a, n_b \rangle_{k_a}, \\
\iota & \to & a & : \quad \langle n_a, n_b \rangle_{k_a}, \\
a & \to & \iota & : \quad \langle n_b \rangle_{k_\iota}, \\
\iota(a) & \to & b & : \quad \langle n_b \rangle_{k_b}.
\end{array}
$$

5 Networks of Communicating Automata

In this section we represent the computations of a protocol by runs of a *network of communicating automata*, where each automaton represents one component of the protocol.

Definition 16 (Automaton). *An automaton A_i is a 4-tuple $(\Sigma_i, L_i, s_i^0, T_i)$, where*

- Σ_i *is a finite set of actions,*
- L_i *is a finite set of locations,*
- $s_i^0 \in L_i$ *is the initial location,*
- $T_i \subseteq L_i \times \Sigma_i \times L_i$ *is a transition relation.*

A set of communicating automata can be composed into the global (*product*) automaton by the standard multi-synchronisation approach: the transitions that do not correspond to a shared action are interleaved, whereas the transitions labelled with a shared action are synchronised. Assume a set of n communicating automata $\{A_1, \ldots, A_n\}$ and let $\Sigma(a) = \{1 \leq i \leq n \mid a \in \Sigma_i\}$.

Definition 17 (Product Automaton). *The product automaton of the automata A_i is defined by $\mathcal{A} = (\Sigma, G, s^0, T)$, where:*

- $\Sigma = \bigcup_{i=1}^{n} \Sigma_i$ *is a finite set of actions,*
- $G = L_1 \times \ldots \times L_n$ *is a finite set of global states,*
- $s^0 = (s_1^0, \ldots, s_n^0)$ *is the initial state,*
- T *is a transition relation, where $((l_1, \ldots, l_n), a, (l_1', \ldots, l_n')) \in T$ iff*
  $\forall_{i \in \Sigma(a)}\ (l_i, a, l_i') \in T_i$ *and* $\forall_{i \in \{1,\ldots,n\}\setminus\Sigma(a)}\ l_i = l_i'$.

By a *run* of $\mathcal{A}$ on a word $a_1 \cdots a_n$ we mean a sequence of states $(s_0, \ldots, s_n)$ such that $s_0, \ldots, s_n \in G$, $s_0 = s^0$, and $(s_i, a_i, s_{i+1}) \in T$ for all $1 \leq i \leq n-1$. A state $s \in G$ is *reachable* if there is a run of $\mathcal{A}$ s.t. its final state is equal to s.

Now, we are going to use networks of automata for modelling executions of the protocol as well as for modelling the knowledge of the participants.

5.1 Automata for Modelling Executions of the Participants

Assume we are dealing with a protocol $\Sigma = (\alpha_1, \ldots, \alpha_n)$.

Definition 18 (Automaton for execution). *Consider the execution of the protocol Σ under an interpretation f, i.e., $(f(\alpha_1), f(\alpha_2), \ldots, f(\alpha_n))$. This execution is modelled by the automaton $A_f = (\Sigma_f, Q_f, f(\alpha_0), \delta_f)$, where:*

- $Q_f = \{s_0^f, s_1^f, s_2^f, \ldots, s_n^f\}$ *is the set of states, where s_0^f is the initial state,*
- $\Sigma_f = \{k_{f(\alpha_i)} \mid 1 \leq i \leq n \wedge Send^{f(\alpha_i)} \in \mathbf{P}\} \cup$
  $\bigcup_{i=1}^{n} \bigcup_{X \subseteq L} \{k_{f(\alpha_i)}^X \mid Send^{f(\alpha_i)} \in \mathbf{P}_\iota \wedge X \vdash Lett^{f(\alpha_i)} \wedge X \neq \{Lett^{f(\alpha_i)}\}\}$,
- $\delta_f = \{(s_{i-1}^f, k_{f(\alpha_i)}, s_i^f) \mid 1 \leq i \leq n \wedge k_{f(\alpha_i)} \in \Sigma_f\} \cup$
  $\{(s_{i-1}^f, k_{f(\alpha_i)}^X, s_i^f) \mid 1 \leq i \leq n \wedge k_{f(\alpha_i)}^X \in \Sigma_f\}$.

The intuition behind the above definition is as follows. Each state s_i^f of the automaton is reached after executing the step α_i of the execution (under f) of the protocol. If the sender of this step is honest, then there is only one possibility to execute this step as the sender needs to have the required knowledge for composing the letter sent in this step. However, if the sender of this step is the Intruder, then there are many possibilities to execute this step determined by the sets of generators of the letter to be sent. Each of these possibilities is labelled with a different label $k_{f(\alpha_i)}^X$.

5.2   Automata for Modelling the Knowledge of the Participants

Consider a finite set of protocol interpretations $\mathcal{F}$.

Definition 19 (Automaton for the knowledge of a honest participant)
For each honest participant $p \in (\bigcup_{f \in \mathcal{F}} f(\mathcal{T}_P) \setminus \mathbf{P}_\iota)$ and each element $l \in Comp_{\mathcal{F}}^p \setminus \kappa_p^0$, we define the following (knowledge) automaton $A_l^p = (\Sigma_l^p, Q_l^p, q_l^p, \delta_l^p)$, where

- $\Sigma_l^p \stackrel{def}{=} \{k \in \bigcup_{f \in \mathcal{F}} \Sigma_f \mid Cond_1(k) \vee Cond_2(k)\}$ with
  $Cond_1(k) := (\exists f \in \mathcal{F})(\exists i \leq n)(s_{i-1}^f, k, s_i^f) \in \delta_f \wedge$
  (i) $(p = Send^{f(\alpha_i)} \wedge l \in Gen^{f(\alpha_i)}) \vee$
  (ii) $(p = Resp^{f(\alpha_i)} \wedge l \in \xi_{\{k_p^{-1}\}}(\{Lett^{f(\alpha_i)}\}) \wedge$
    $\wedge (\forall j \in \{1, \ldots, i-1\})((p = Resp^{f(\alpha_j)} \Rightarrow l \notin \xi_{\{k_p^{-1}\}}(Lett^{f(\alpha_j)})) \wedge$
    $\wedge (p = Send^{f(\alpha_j)} \Rightarrow l \notin Gen^{f(\alpha_j)}))$
  $Cond_2(k) := (\exists f \in \mathcal{F})(\exists i \leq n)(s_{i-1}^f, k, s_i^f) \in \delta_f \wedge$
  (iii) $(p = Send^{f(\alpha_i)} \wedge l \in Comp^{f(\alpha_i)} \setminus Gen^{f(\alpha_i)}) \vee$
  (iv) $(p = Resp^{f(\alpha_i)} \wedge l \in \xi_{\{k_p^{-1}\}}(\{Lett^{f(\alpha_i)}\}) \wedge$
    $\wedge (\forall j \in \{1, \ldots, i-1\})((p = Resp^{f(\alpha_j)} \Rightarrow l \notin \xi_{\{k_p^{-1}\}}(Lett^{f(\alpha_j)})) \wedge$
    $\wedge (p = Send^{f(\alpha_j)} \Rightarrow l \notin Gen^{f(\alpha_j)}))$
- $Q_l^p = \{q_l^p, s_l^p\}$ is the set of states,
- q_l^p is the initial state,
- δ_l^p is the transition relation given as follows
  $(q_l^p, k, s_l^p) \in \delta_l^p$ iff $Cond_1(k)$, $(s_l^p, k, s_l^p) \in \delta_l^p$ iff $Cond_2(k)$.

If the automaton A_l^p is in the state q_l^p, then this means that the participant p does not know l. If the automaton A_l^p moves to the state s_l^p, then this corresponds to the fact that p learns about l and can use it. The condition (i) specifies that l is generated by p at the step $f(\alpha_i)$. The condition (ii) says that p learns about l at the step $f(\alpha_i)$. This is modelled only once in order to reduce the number of the transitions. The condition (iii), which defines the loop, enables p to use l while composing new letters. The condition (iv) enables to receive l in a different execution that the one, which was used to define the condition (ii).

Example 6. The network of automata that model the execution and the knowledge of the participants of Example 3 is shown in the figure below.

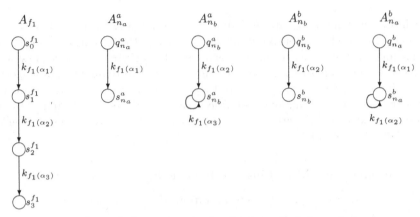

We give two versions of the automata for the Intruder's knowledge.

Definition 20 (Automaton for the knowledge of the Intruder). *First, we give the automaton corresponding to the full D-Y Intruder's knowledge and then we discuss the modifications for the restricted model.*

The D-Y model of the Intruder: *for each letter*

- $l \in Comp_{\mathcal{F}}^{\iota} \cap \xi_{\{k_{\iota}^{-1}\}}(\bigcup_{f \in \mathcal{F}} \bigcup_{i \leq n} \{Lett^{f(\alpha_i)}\}) \setminus \kappa_{\iota}^0$,

we define the knowledge automaton $A_l^{\iota} = (\Sigma_l^{\iota}, Q_l^{\iota}, q_l^{\iota}, \delta_l^{\iota})$, *where*

- $\Sigma_l^{\iota} \overset{def}{=} \{k \in \bigcup_{f \in \mathcal{F}} \Sigma_f \mid Cond_1^{\iota}(k) \vee Cond_2^{\iota}(k)\}$ *with*

  $Cond_1^{\iota}(k) := (\exists f \in \mathcal{F})(\exists i \leq n)(s_{i-1}^f, k, s_i^f) \in \delta_f \wedge$

  (i) $[(l \in \xi_{\{k_{\iota}^{-1}\}}(\{Lett^{f(\alpha_i)}\}) \wedge (\forall j \in \{1, \ldots, i-1\})(l \notin \xi_{\{k_{\iota}^{-1}\}}(Lett^{f(\alpha_j)}))$

  $Cond_2^{\iota}(k) := (\exists f \in \mathcal{F})(\exists i \leq n)(s_{i-1}^f, k, s_i^f) \in \delta_f \wedge$

  (ii) $(Send^{f(\alpha_i)} \in \mathbf{P}_{\iota} \wedge (\exists X \subseteq \mathbf{L})(X \vdash Lett^{f(\alpha_i)} \wedge l \in X \wedge k = k_{f(\alpha_i)}^X)) \vee$

  (iii) $(l \in \xi_{\{k_{\iota}^{-1}\}}(\{Lett^{f(\alpha_i)}\}) \wedge (\forall j \in \{1, \ldots, i-1\})(l \notin \xi_{\{k_{\iota}^{-1}\}}(Lett^{f(\alpha_j)})))$.

- $Q_l^{\iota} = \{q_l^{\iota}, s_l^{\iota}\}$ *is the set of states,*
- q_l^{ι} *is the initial state,*
- δ_l^{ι} *is the transition relation given as follows:*
  $(q_l^{\iota}, k, s_l^{\iota}) \in \delta_l^{\iota}$ *iff* $Cond_1^{\iota}(k)$, $(s_l^{\iota}, k, s_l^{\iota}) \in \delta_l^{\iota}$ *iff* $Cond_2^{\iota}(k)$.

The following changes to the above definition are made for the restricted model of the Intruder's knowledge:

- $l \in Comp_{\mathcal{F}}^{\iota} \setminus \kappa_{\iota}^0$,

(i) $[(Resp^{f(\alpha_i)} \in \mathbf{P}_{\iota} \wedge l \in \xi_{\{k_{\iota}^{-1}\}}(\{Lett^{f(\alpha_i)}\}) \wedge$

  $\wedge (\forall j \in \{1, \ldots, i-1\})((Resp^{f(\alpha_j)} \in \mathbf{P}_{\iota} \Rightarrow l \notin \xi_{\{k_{\iota}^{-1}\}}(Lett^{f(\alpha_j)}))),$

(iii) $(Resp^{f(\alpha_i)} \in \mathbf{P}_{\iota} \wedge l \in \xi_{\{k_{\iota}^{-1}\}}(\{Lett^{f(\alpha_i)}\}) \wedge$

  $\wedge (\forall j \in \{1, \ldots, i-1\})(Resp^{f(\alpha_j)} \in \mathbf{P}_{\iota} \Rightarrow l \notin \xi_{\{k_{\iota}^{-1}\}}(Lett^{f(\alpha_j)}))).$

If the automaton A_l^{ι} is in the state q_l^{ι}, then this means that the Intruder does not know l. If the automaton A_l^{ι} moves to the state s_l^{ι}, then this corresponds to the fact that ι learns about l and can use it. The condition (i) says that ι learns about l at the step $f(\alpha_i)$. This is modelled only once in order to reduce the number of the transitions. The condition (ii) enables ι to use l while composing new letters. The condition (iii) enables to receive l in a different execution that the one, which was used to define the condition (i).

Recall that we are dealing with the protocol Σ and a set $\mathcal{F}$ of its interpretations. Let $\mathcal{A} = (N, Q, s^0, \delta)$ be the product automaton of the following set of the automata $\{A_f \mid f \in \mathcal{F}\} \cup \{A_l^p \mid p \in \bigcup_{f \in \mathcal{F}} f(\mathcal{T}_P) \cap (\mathcal{P} \cup \{\iota\}) \wedge l \in Comp_{\mathcal{F}}^p\}$.

The following theorem says that for each computation in the computation structure there is the corresponding run in the product automaton $\mathcal{A}$ built for this structure and moreover each run of $\mathcal{A}$ corresponds to some computation.

Theorem 1. *Let $f^i \in \mathcal{F}$ for $1 \leq i \leq k$. A sequence of protocol steps $\mathfrak{r} = (\ f^1(\alpha_{i_1}), f^2(\alpha_{i_2}), \ldots, f^k(\alpha_{i_k})\ )$ is a computation iff there is a run in the product automaton $\mathcal{A}$ on a word $(\overline{k_{f^1(\alpha_{i_1})}}, \overline{k_{f^2(\alpha_{i_2})}}, \ldots, \overline{k_{f^k(\alpha_{i_k})}})$, where:*

$$
\overline{k_{f^j(\alpha_{i_j})}} \in
\begin{cases}
\{k_{f^j(\alpha_{i_j})}\} & \text{if } Send^{f^j(\alpha_{i_j})} \in \mathbf{P}, \\[2mm]
\{k_{f^j(\alpha_{i_j})}^X \mid X \vdash Lett^{f^j(\alpha_{i_j})}\} & \text{if } Send^{f^j(\alpha_{i_j})} \in \mathbf{P}_\iota.
\end{cases}
$$

Proof. By induction on the length of a computation (run). Omitted because of the lack of space (see [20] for a proof).

Thanks to the above theorem, we can reduce an analysis of a security protocol for interpretations assumed to verification of the corresponding product automaton. Specifically, there is an attack on the protocol iff there is a run in the product automaton corresponding to some attacking execution.

6 Experimental Results

We start by describing a SAT-based method of testing reachability for a network of automata, i.e., checking whether a state satisfying certain (usually undesired) property is reachable in the product automaton. For this, assume that φ is a property to be verified. Let $\alpha_k(\varphi)$, for $k \in \mathbb{N}$, be a propositional formula that is satisfiable if and only if there exists a run π of length k such that the property φ holds at some state of π. Moreover, let β_k, for $k \in \mathbb{N}$, be a propositional formula that is satisfiable if and only if there exists a run of length k.

Algorithm 1 searches for the greatest natural number k_0 such that every run is of length less or equal to k_0. Such a number k_0 exists if the set of the reachable states is finite and there are no loops in the set of the reachable states, and this is the case for all the networks of automata considered in this paper. Notice that that if there exists a run π on which φ is reachable, then the length of π has to be less or equal to k_0. Therefore, we can conclude that if the property φ is not reachable on any run of length less or equal to k_0, then it is unreachable.

In Algorithm 1 we use the procedure $checkSat(\gamma)$ that for any given propositional formula γ returns one of the following three possible values: $SAT, UNSAT,$

or $UNKNOWN$. The meanings of the values SAT and $UNSAT$ are self-evident. The value $UNKNOWN$ is returned in two cases: either the procedure $checkSat$ is not able to decide satisfiability of its argument within some timeout period[9] or it has to terminate due to exhaustion of the available memory.

The above method can be applied to all the networks of automata considered in this paper in view of the fact that there are no loops, at least in the set of the reachable states. We would like to stress that for such networks of automata the method is complete. Another SAT-based method of testing reachability can be found in [30].

Algorithm 1. Algorithm for deciding reachability problem

```
 1: k ← 0
 2: loop
 3:     result ← checkSat(α_k(φ))
 4:     if result = SAT then
 5:         return REACHABLE
 6:     else if result = UNKNOWN then
 7:         return UNKNOWN
 8:     end if
        /* α_k(φ) is not satisfiable */
 9:     k ← k + 1
10:     result ← checkSat(β_k)
11:     if result = UNSAT then
12:         return UNREACHABLE
13:     else if result = UNKNOWN then
14:         return UNKNOWN
15:     end if
        /* β_k is satisfiable */
16: end loop
```

We have tested the correctness (Definition 15) of the NSPK protocol defined in Example 1. The computational structure (defined in Example 3) is given by 18 automata modelling executions of the principals and 20 knowledge automata (for the restricted model of the Intruder's knowledge). Some of them are shown in Examples 7 and 8. According to Definition 14 there are 4 attacking executions. The experiments consisted in checking reachability (in the product automaton) of the final states of the automata representing these four executions. We have verified that one of these states is reachable at a run of the length 6. This run corresponds to the attack discovered by Lowe [21] (see Example 5).

We have also verified two other protocols:

- an improved version of NSPK, known as the protocol NSPK-Lowe [21],
- an untimed version of the Wide-Mouth Frog Protocol ([6]).

The NSPK-Lowe protocol is defined as: $\Sigma_{NSPK-Lowe} = (\alpha_1, \alpha_2, \alpha_3)$, where:

---
[9] This is preset in advance.

$$\alpha_1 = (\mathcal{A}, \{\mathcal{N_A}, \mathcal{I_A}, \mathcal{K_B}\}, \{\mathcal{N_A}\}, \mathcal{B}, \langle \mathcal{N_A}, \mathcal{I_A} \rangle_{\mathcal{K_B}}),$$
$$\alpha_2 = (\mathcal{B}, \{\mathcal{N_A}, \mathcal{N_B}, \mathcal{I_B}, \mathcal{K_A}\}, \{\mathcal{N_B}\}, \mathcal{A}, \langle \mathcal{N_A}, \mathcal{N_B}, \mathcal{I_B} \rangle_{\mathcal{K_A}}),$$
$$\alpha_3 = (\mathcal{A}, \{\mathcal{N_B}, \mathcal{K_B}\}, \emptyset, \mathcal{B}, \langle \mathcal{N_B} \rangle_{\mathcal{K_B}}).$$

For the same computational structure we have obtained 18 automata for the executions of the participants and 24 knowledge automata. It turned out that the length of the longest possible run is equal to 13. Additionally, it has been verified that no final state of the automata corresponding to the attacking executions is reachable at runs of length up to 13. According to Theorem 1 this proves that in the computational structure considered there is no attack upon the protocol NSPK-Lowe.

We have also investigated the untimed Wide-Mouth Frog Protocol[10]. For the same computational structure we have obtained 15 automata for all the executions and 12 knowledge automata. It turned out that the length of the longest possible run in the network for untimed WMF is equal to 6. Additionally, it has been verified that no final state of the automata corresponding to the attacking executions is reachable at runs of length up to 6. Thus, we conclude that there is no attack in the computational structure considered.

The experimental results are shown in the tables below. The computer used to perform experiments was equipped with the processor Intel Pentium D (3000 MHz), 2 GB main memory, the operating system Linux and the SAT-solver MiniSat.

Table 1. Experimental results for NSPK Protocol

Trace length	Variables	Literals	Clauses	Time (s.)	Result
4	3514	24044	10136	0.040	UNSAT
6	5226	35880	15124	0.036	SAT

Table 2. Experimental results for Lowe's NSPK Protocol

Trace length	Variables	Literals	Clauses	Time (s.)	Result
4	3299	22539	9491	0,052	UNSAT
7	5708	39180	16496	0.300	UNSAT
10	8117	55821	23501	2,140	UNSAT
13	10526	72462	30506	54,85	UNSAT

Table 3. Experimental results for Untimed WMF Protocol

Trace length	Variables	Literals	Clauses	Time (s.)	Result
3	3513	5479	15639	0,43	UNSAT
5	6417	7771	22715	0,86	UNSAT

---

[10] This protocol is defined as follows:
$$\alpha_1 = (\mathcal{A}, \{\mathcal{I_A}, \mathcal{N_A}, \mathcal{I_B}, \mathcal{K}, \mathcal{K_{AS}}\}, \{\mathcal{N_A}, \mathcal{K}\}, \mathcal{S}, < \mathcal{N_A}, \mathcal{I_B}, \mathcal{K} >_{\mathcal{K_{AS}}}),$$
$$\alpha_2 = (\mathcal{S}, \{\mathcal{I_A}, \mathcal{N_S}, \mathcal{K}, \mathcal{K_{BS}}\}, \{\mathcal{N_S}\}, \mathcal{B}, < \mathcal{N_S}, \mathcal{I_A}, \mathcal{K} >_{\mathcal{K_{BS}}}).$$

Table 4. Experimental results from VerICS and SATMC

Tool	Protocol	Time (s)
VerICS	NSPK	0,09
SATMC	NSPK	0,20
VerICS	NSPK-Lowe	0,31
SATMC	NSPK-Lowe	0,27

We have compared[11] our results to these obtained from SATMC[12] of AVISPA ([1]). The results are quite comparable (see the table below), but in our case in addition to finding or not finding attacks, we can also automatically verify with BMC that an attack does not exist at all in the computational structure considered.

In case of verification of NSPK we have got a shorter time whereas for NSPK-Lowe our result is slightly worse (for runs of length 7 as used by SATMC). Clearly, much more experiments need to be made to fully compare our method with AVISPA or other tools. But, these experiments should be conducted only after our implementation has been optimised in order to get an honest comparison.

7   Conclusions and Perspectives

In this paper we have considered attacks on authentication only, but we can easily extend them to attacks on secrecy. In order to prove that an information at is insecure, we have to prove that the state s_i^t of A_i^t is reachable.

Our next step is to see what the limits of our method are in terms of the number of sessions as well as in the number of participants for all the protocols which satisfy our restrictions. Then, we are going to relax the assumption on non-nesting ciphers and again conduct experiments with multi-session and multi-user security protocols.

Acknowledgements

The authors wish to thank to Kamil Grondys, Anna Sowik, and Izabela Szczypior for their help and the discussions.

References

1. Armando, A., Basin, D., Boichut, Y., Chevalier, Y., Compagna, L., Cuellar, J., Drielsma, P.H., Heám, P.C., Kouchnarenko, O., Mantovani, J., Mödersheim, S., von Oheimb, D., Rusinowitch, M., Santiago, J., Turuani, M., Viganò, L., Vigneron, L.: The AVISPA tool for the automated validation of internet security protocols and applications. In: Etessami, K., Rajamani, S.K. (eds.) CAV 2005. LNCS, vol. 3576, pp. 281–285. Springer, Heidelberg (2005)

---

[11] In this experiment we have used the same SAT-solver as SATMC uses, i.e., zChaff.
[12] SATMC is a SAT-based bounded model checker.

2. Bella, G., Paulson, L.C.: Using Isabelle to prove properties of the Kerberos authentication system. In: Orman, H., Meadows, C., (eds). Proceedings of the DIMACS Workshop on Design and Formal Verification of Security Protocols (CD-ROM) (DIMACS'97) (1997)

3. Bengtsson, J., Larsen, K.G., Larsson, F., Pettersson, P., Yi, W., Weise, C.: New generation of Uppaal. In: Proc. of the Int. Workshop on Software Tools for Technology Transfer (STTT'98), BRICS Notes Series, pp. 43–52 (1998)

4. Bolignano, D.: An approach to the formal verification of cryptographic protocols. In: Proceedings of the 3rd ACM Conference on Computer and Communication Security, pp. 106–118 (1996)

5. Bozga, L., Ene, C., Lakhnech, Y.: A Symbolic Decision Procedure for Cryptographic Protocols with Time Stamps. Journal of Logic and Algebraic Programming 65(1), 1–35 (2005)

6. Burrows, M., Abadi, M., Needham, R.: A Logic of Authentication. In: Proceedings of the Royal Society of London A, vol. 426, pp. 233–271 (1989)

7. Clark, J.A., Jacob, J.L.: A survey of authentication protocol literature. Technical Report 1.0, http://www.cs.york.ac.ukjac/papers/drareview.ps.gz (1997)

8. Clarke, E.M., Jha, S., Marrero, W.: Verifying security protocols with Brutus. ACM Transactions on Software Engineering and Methodology 9(4), 443–487 (2000)

9. Cohen, E.: Taps: A first-order verifier for cryptographic protocols. In: CSFW '00: Proceedings of the 13th IEEE Computer Security Foundations Workshop (CSFW'00), pp. 144–158. IEEE Computer Society, Los Alamitos (2000)

10. Corin, R., Etalle, S., Hartel, P.H., Mader, A.: Timed model checking of security protocols. In: Atluri, V., Backes, M., Basin, D., Waidner, M. (eds.) 2nd ACM Workshop on Formal Methods in Security Engineering: From Specifications to Code (FMSE), pp. 23–32. ACM Press, New York (2004)

11. Dembiński, P., Janowska, A., Janowski, P., Penczek, W., Półrola, A., Szreter, M., Woźna, B., Zbrzezny, A.: VerICS: A tool for verifying timed automata and Estelle specifications. In: Garavel, H., Hatcliff, J. (eds.) ETAPS 2003 and TACAS 2003. LNCS, vol. 2619, pp. 278–283. Springer, Heidelberg (2003)

12. Dolev, D., Yao, A.: On the security of public key protocols. IEEE Transactions on Information Theory 29(2), 198–208 (1983)

13. Evans, N., Schneider, S.: Analysing time dependent security properties in csp using pvs. In: Cuppens, F., Deswarte, Y., Gollmann, D., Waidner, M. (eds.) ESORICS 2000. LNCS, vol. 1895, pp. 222–237. Springer, Heidelberg (2000)

14. Holzmann, G.J.: The model checker SPIN. IEEE Trans. on Software Eng. 23(5), 279–295 (1997)

15. Jakubowska, G., Penczek, W.: Is Your Security Protocol on Time? In: Proc. of International Symposium on Fundamentals of Software Engineering (FSEN'07) (to appear) (2007)

16. Jakubowska, G., Penczek, W., Srebrny, M.: Verifying security protocols with timestamps via translation to timed automata. In: Czaja, L., (ed). In: Proc. of the Int. Workshop on Concurrency, Specification and Programming (CS&P'05), Warsaw University Press, pp. 100–115 (2005)

17. Jha, S., Clarke, E.M., Marrero, W.: Using state space exploration and a natural deduction style message derivation engine to verify security protocols. In: Gries, D., De Roever, W.P. (eds.) Proceedings of the IFIP Working Conference on Programming Concepts and Methods (PROCOMET'98), pp. 87–106. Chapmann and Hall, Sydney (1998)

18. Kurkowski, M.: Deductive methods for verification of correctness of the authentication protocols (in polish). PhD thesis, Institute of Computer Science, Polish Academy of Sciences (2003)
19. Kurkowski, M., Penczek, W.: Verifying Cryptographic Protocols modeled by networks of automata. In: Proc. of CS&P'06, Humboldt University Press, pp. 292–303 (2006)
20. Kurkowski, M., Penczek, W.: SAT-based Verification of Security Protocols via Translation to Networks of Automata. Report 998 of ICS PAS, Warsaw, http://www.imi.ajd.czest.pl/pub/report_kp_07.zip (2007)
21. Lowe, G.: Breaking and Fixing the Needham-Schroeder Public-Key Protocol Using FDR. In: Margaria, T., Steffen, B. (eds.) TACAS 1996. LNCS, vol. 1055, pp. 147–166. Springer, Heidelberg (1996)
22. Lowe, G., Roscoe, B.: Using CSP to Detect Errors in The TMN Protocol. IEEE Transaction on Software Engineering 23(10), 659–669 (1997)
23. Lowe, G.: Casper: A compiler for the analysis of security protocols. Journal of Computer Security 6(1-2), 53–84 (1998)
24. McMillan, K.L.: Symbolic Model Checking. Kluwer Academic Publishers, Dordrecht (1993)
25. Meadows, C.: The NRL protocol analyzer: An overview. Journal of Logic Programming 26(2), 13–131 (1996)
26. Mitchell, M., Mitchell, J.C., Stern, U.: Automated analysis of cryptographic protocols using murϕ. In: Proc. of the 1997 IEEE Symposium on Security and Privacy, pp. 141–151. IEEE Computer Society Press, Los Alamitos (1997)
27. Needham, R., Schroeder, M.: Using Encryption for Authentication in large networks of computers. Communications of the ACM 21(12), 993–999 (1978)
28. Panti, M., Spalazzi, L., Tacconi, S.: Using the NUSMV model checker to verify the Kerberos Protocol. In: Proc. of the Third Collaborative Technologies Symposium (CTS-02), pp. 27–31 (2002)
29. Yovine, S.: KRONOS: A verification tool for real-time systems. International Journal of Software Tools for Technology Transfer 1(1/2), 123–133 (1997)
30. Zbrzezny, A.: SAT-based reachability checking for timed automata with diagonal constraints. Fundamenta Informaticae 67(1-3), 303–322 (2005)

Appendix

Example 7. A part of the network of automata that model the execution and the knowledge of the participants of Example 4 is shown in the figure below.

Example 8. The full network of automata that model both the executions f_2 and f_3 is shown in the figure below.

$\square$

Distributed Extended Beam Search for Quantitative Model Checking

A.J. Wijs and B. Lisser

CWI, P.O. Box 94079, 1090 GB Amsterdam, The Netherlands
{wijs,bert.lisser}@cwi.nl

Abstract. In this paper, we mainly focus on solving scheduling problems with model checking, where a finite number of entities needs to be processed as efficiently as possible, for instance by a machine. To solve these problems, we model them in untimed process algebra, where time is modelled using a special *tick* action. We propose a set of distributed state space explorations to find schedules for the modelled problems, building on the traditional notion of *beam search*. The basic approach is called distributed (detailed) beam search, which prunes parts of the state space while searching using an evaluation function in order to find near-optimal schedules in very large state spaces. Variations on this approach are presented, such as distributed *flexible*, distributed *g-synchronised*, and distributed *priority* beam search, which can also practically be used in combinations.

Keywords: directed model checking, distributed model checking, scheduling, beam search.

1 Introduction

Traditionally, model checking concerns modelling systems and checking properties, which either hold or not, in other words, the checks can be answered with either "yes" or "no". In more recent years, however, the awareness has grown that often other kinds of checks, which cannot be answered in such a manner, are as important. For these checks, one is usually interested in some measurements, such as the throughput or efficiency of a particular system. Markov Chains, for instance, have shown to be useful when one needs to do performance analysis of a system [9]. Although not common yet, sometimes scheduling problems are also addressed using model checking techniques [2,28,37,41], since the tools are usually equipped with highly expressive languages, making it possible to specify complex industrial scheduling questions. Comparing the two kinds of property checks, one could label traditional model checking as *qualitative* model checking and the latter one as *quantitative* model checking [22].

Furthermore, as state explosion is a big problem in model checking, research is being done to efficiently explore state spaces to find deadlocks fast, particularly using Artificial Intelligence (AI) heuristic techniques, such as A^* [15] and genetic algorithms [19]. This approach is referred to as *directed* model checking [15]. Although mostly used for qualitative model checking, techniques like beam search [5] can be applied for quantitative model checking, in particular to solve scheduling problems.

In an earlier paper [41], we made a first attempt at solving scheduling problems, where a finite number of products needs to be processed as efficiently as possible by a

S. Edelkamp and A. Lomuscio (Eds.): MoChart IV, LNAI 4428, pp. 166–184, 2007.

machine, by modelling them using untimed process algebra and generating state spaces from the models using a specialised toolset. Within such a state space a *minimal-time trace* represents an optimal schedule for the problem at hand.

We experienced the limits of our first attempt quite soon; state spaces tend to be very big, sometimes in the order of hundreds of gigabytes. Although we developed an on-the-fly search algorithm, which enables us to find optimal solutions while generating, we were still confronted with technological limits. Because of this we moved to a distributed setting with our minimal-time search algorithm. In [41], results of applying this distributed algorithm on finding schedules for a clinical chemical analyser can be found. The algorithm enabled us to deal with bigger problems, but still we had the impression that the technique could be improved if we were able to avoid the (many) non-promising traces and guide the search through the state space towards near-optimal schedules using a heuristic method. When looking at available pruning techniques in the literature, we found beam search [5]. Beam search is a heuristic method for combinatorial optimisation problems, which has extensively been studied in AI and operations research [27,35]. Later this technique has been applied to scheduling problems, for example in systems designed for complex job shop[1] environments [12,17,31,38,41]. Since then new variants of beam search have been introduced, such as filtered beam search [30] and recovery beam search [12].

Using beam search proved to be very fruitful, as we were able to find near-optimal schedules for all the considered batches of tests of the clinical chemical analyser [41]. It sometimes took a lot of time, though, mostly due to the extra computation needed to evaluate states. This could be improved if we moved the beam search techniques to a distributed setting. In this paper we propose several distributed beam search variants, focussing on detailed beam search, since due to its global view when pruning, it is not obvious how a distributed algorithm should function.

Contributions. We show how a technique for solving scheduling problems can be adapted to a distributed setting. The technique, beam search, is a heuristic which prunes parts of a state space while searching, in order to find near-optimal solutions. We extend the distributed technique to deal with arbitrary state spaces and make it more effective.

Structure of the paper. First we will present some preliminaries. Next we describe the kind of scheduling problems we are dealing with. After that we explain the most common forms of beam search, followed by descriptions of the distributed versions we propose. We show how some of these versions perform in practice, looking at, as we call it, the Zebra Finch problem, which is a combination of several river crossing problems [14]. Finally, we discuss related work and conclude the paper.

2   Preliminaries

We use the following formalism to represent state spaces.

---

[1] The job shop problem is the most classic scheduling problem in the literature. In its most basic form, we have a finite set M of resources, and a number of jobs $J_1,\ldots,J_n$ which compete in using the resources in a specific order and for a finite number of time units. The problem is to allocate the resources such that the jobs are finished in minimal time.

Definition 1 (Labelled transition system). *A Labelled Transition System (LTS) is a tuple* (Σ, s_0, Act, Tr), *where* Σ *is a finite set of states, which is usually not known a priori, but generated on-the-fly,* $s_0 \in \Sigma$ *is the initial state, Act is a given finite set of action labels and* $Tr \subseteq \Sigma \times Act \times \Sigma$ *is the transition relation. A transition* $(s, a, s') \in Tr$, *denoted* $s \xrightarrow{a} s'$, *indicates that the system can move from state s to s' by performing action a.*

For $T \subseteq Tr$, we define $nx(s, T) = \{s' \in \Sigma \mid \exists a \in Act.\ s \xrightarrow{a} s' \in T\}$. We define a state s to be an *endstate* iff $nx(s, Tr) = \emptyset$.

Breadth-first State Space Generation. State space generation algorithms are provided with a specification as input and produce the state space which is described by that specification. A breadth-first state space generation (BFS) algorithm, as presented in Algorithm 1, starts from the initial state of the specification and names it s_0. State s_0 is placed in the set S_0. Sets $S_1, S_2, \dots$ are generated iteratively.

In Algorithm 1, *expand* : $\Sigma \to \mathscr{P}(Tr)$ is the function that provides the interface between the state space generation algorithm and the underlying specification. For a state s, *expand*(s) is the set of transitions which root in s. Set S_i with $i \in \mathbb{N}$ denotes the set of states in the $i + 1$th level of the state space. The set *Closed* is used to perform *delayed* duplicate detection [34] when expanding states; if a state has already been expanded before, we do not need to expand it again. This is checked at the end of generating a new set, hence it is *delayed*.

Algorithm 1. Breadth-first state space generation

---

procedure bfs(s_0)
   $i := 0$
   $S_i := \{s_0\}$
   Closed $:= \emptyset$
   while $S_i \setminus$ *Closed* $\neq \emptyset$ **do**
      $S_{i+1} := \emptyset$
      for all s in $S_i \setminus$ *Closed* **do**
         $S_{i+1} := S_{i+1} \cup nx(s, expand(s))$
      Closed $:=$ *Closed* $\cup S_i$
      $i := i + 1$
   return Finished

Distributed State Space Generation. Moving to a distributed setting, we no longer deal with one machine, but one manager and n clients $C_1, \dots, C_n$, where $n \in \mathbb{N}$. For this paper, it suffices to say, that in distributed BFS state space generation, every client performs a BFS on the states it gets. After generating the set S_{i+1}, given a set S_i, how the states in S_{i+1} should be distributed over the n clients is determined by a hash function *Checksum* : $\Sigma \to \mathbb{N}$. For more information on distributed state space generation, the reader is referred to, for instance, [11].

The language μCRL. The process algebra μCRL [21], an extension of ACP [4] with abstract data types, is a language for specifying distributed systems and protocols in an algebraic style. A μCRL specification describes an LTS, in which states represent process terms and edges are labelled with actions. This process algebra is used as input to a state space generation toolset [7], which is accompanied by symbolic reduction techniques. The toolset has also been extended for a distributed setting [6].

Based on the work from [8,40], we use a special *tick* action, which models time progression. This is comparable to relative discrete time [1]: A *tick* action indicates that the system moves to the next time slice.

Definition 2 (minimal-time trace [41]). *Given an LTS and a transition label* a, *we say that there is a trace with execution time t ($t \in \mathbb{N}$) to a transition with label* a *iff there is a trace in the LTS starting from the starting state s_0 and reaching a transition with label* a, *such that the number of* tick *transitions occurring in this trace equals t. We define a trace from s_0 to a transition with label* a *to be* minimal-time *iff there is no other trace in the LTS from s_0 to* a *with less* tick *transitions.*

Using this definition, we can formulate a scheduling problem as a reachability problem: finding an optimal schedule to perform a batch of tasks successfully can also be seen as finding a minimal-time trace to a transition indicating successful termination in a state space containing all possible schedules as traces. That we can also in this manner deal with scheduling problems involving parallel execution of tasks, will be explained in the following section.

3   Modelling Scheduling Problems Using μCRL

Scheduling problems, in this paper, are typically about processing a certain number of entities (for instance, products or jobs, in the case of jobshop scheduling). The processing is usually done by a machine, or combination of machines, which can perform tasks $t_1,\ldots,t_m \in Ta$, where Ta is a set of task labels[2], provided, that the accompanying sets of constraints $C_1,\ldots,C_m$ are met[3]. Furthermore, each task t_i has an execution time $d(t_i)$ associated with it, given by the function[4] $d : Ta \to \mathbb{N}$. In these problems, a certain goal should be reached, usually having completely processed a finite batch of entities. The question asked in scheduling is not mainly *if* this goal can be reached, but *how efficiently* this can be done.

As we perform scheduling using model checking tools, we are able to deal with complex industrial systems, the models of which tend to lead to very big, arbitrarily structured state spaces. We model tasks as transitions, meaning that performing task t_i in an execution appears as $s_j \xrightarrow{t_i} s_{j+1}$ in the LTS, where s_j and s_{j+1} are two states in the trace corresponding to the execution. In state spaces, where the traces represent schedules, we can observe the following.

A function *progress*: $\Sigma \to \mathbb{N}$ can be constructed, which can access the state variables of a state s, using the underlying μCRL specification of the LTS (similar to *expand(s)*

---

[2] Later on, in our approach, action labels from *Act* represent task labels from *Ta*.

[3] To keep things general, we do not fix these constraints to a specific notation here. Suffice it so say that they can deal with time and data.

[4] Since execution times are here represented using natural numbers, we use discrete time.

in section 2) and quantifies the progress made to reaching some predetermined goal, for instance having completely processed a given batch of entities. In general, say we have $c_0, c_{end} \in \mathbb{N}, \forall s \in \Sigma . c_0 \leq progress(s) \leq c_{end}$ and $progress(s_0) = c_0$, in other words, c_0 is the initial (no) progress and c_{end} represents having reached the goal. We do not claim any monotonicity of this function, as in general one can imagine tasks which provide negative progress, which, for instance, is the case in our example in section 7.

Building on Definition 1, we can now distinguish two kinds of endstates.

Definition 3 (termination and deadlock). *A state s is a* termination *state iff it is an endstate and* $progress(s) = c_{end}$. *A state s is a* deadlock *state iff it is an endstate and* $progress(s) \neq c_{end}$.

The intuition behind this, is that we can distinguish two kinds of endstates: one where the predetermined goal is reached, and one where it is not.

The general structure of a μCRL model of a scheduling problem can be described as consisting of a process (or processes), which is an alternative composition of all tasks t_i, each followed by a sequence of *tick* actions, to indicate the execution time. The tasks t_i can only be executed if the accompanying conditions C_i are met, written in the model as conditions for the actions representing the tasks, and, once executed, a task has an effect on the progress of the processing (as expressed by function *prog*). So this model can execute all available tasks as long as the constraints are satisfied. Which tasks to execute and when is decided non-deterministically; there are no built-in priorities.

Besides that, we introduce a special action called *finished*. We use this action in such a way that it can be executed iff it leads to a termination state.

Sometimes, a system consists of several processes running in parallel, and the scheduling problem involves the parallel execution of tasks. In μCRL, it is possible to model multiple processes in parallel and have them work with time correctly. For this it must be enforced that all *tick* actions are synchronised; only if all processes can do a *tick* action, a *tick* action occurs. Explaining in detail how this can be achieved is outside the scope of this paper, since it involves a detailed explanation of μCRL. The interested reader is referred to [8,40]. We can note here, that having several processes in the structure mentioned earlier, means that we can still relate a schedule to a path in the state space. For this, we need to interpret a sequence of tasks, not containing any *tick* actions, as a set of tasks happening at the same time. Consider, for example, the sequence $a \cdot b \cdot tick$ in a trace, where '·' is the sequential composition operator of μCRL. Due to the structure of the processes, we know that a and b originate from different processes; if not, they would be seperated by at least one *tick* action (assuming that the execution of each task takes at least one time unit). Furthermore, we can interpret $a \cdot b \cdot tick$ as a and b happening at the same time, which makes sense, considering that they happen in the same time unit (i.e. between the same two *tick* actions). If we do this, then we do not differentiate $a \cdot b \cdot tick$ from $b \cdot a \cdot tick$. Note, that this relates to the notion of independent actions for partial order reduction [32]. Using this terminology in our case, given a solution path, we abstract away the particular action arrangement of independent actions.

Having created a μCRL model, it is possible, using the μCRL toolset, to generate a state space from it. This state space incorporates all possible behaviour of the system described by the model. Somewhere in this state space there is at least one minimal-time trace to a finish. Given Definition 2, we use the *finished* action as transition a, in order to formulate a minimal-time trace to a termination. In [41], this modelling approach is applied on a clinical chemical analyser, and a specific minimal-cost search is explained (the search is mentioned again later in this paper in section 6).

4 Beam Search

Beam search [5] is similar to breadth-first search as it progresses level by level. At each level, it uses a heuristic evaluation function to estimate the promise of encountered states. The β most promising states are selected for further examination. Because of this aggressive pruning, the generation time is a linear function of β and is thus heavily decreased. When $\beta \rightarrow \infty$, beam search behaves as breadth-first search [39].

The beam search approach is a branch-and-bound technique where only the β most promising states at each level of the search tree are selected for further branching. This β is the so-called *beam width*, which is fixed to a value before searching. Other states are discarded, so searching can be done relatively quickly. Because of this, using the beam search technique does not guarantee finding an optimal solution, since wrong decisions can be made while pruning. To limit the possibility of wrong decisions one can increase the beam width, at the cost of an increase in computational effort.

Clearly the evaluation function used to select states is very important. In the past, two types of evaluation functions have been used: *priority* and *total cost evaluation functions*. A priority evaluation function calculates a priority for each task, while a total cost evaluation function calculates an estimate of the total cost of the best schedule that can be found continuing from the partial schedule represented by the state. Priority evaluation functions have a local view of the problem, since they only consider the next task to be scheduled, while total cost evaluation functions have a global view, taking the complete schedule into account. These types of functions lead to two classic beam searches, namely priority and detailed beam search, using a priority and a total cost evaluation function, respectively.

In a detailed beam search, at each level up to β nodes are selected to continue, regardless of what their parent states are, therefore it could be the case, that some nodes have multiple selected children, while others have none. A total cost evaluation function allows comparison of states from different executions as it shows the progress each execution is making (i.e. it has a global view). This in contrast to priority evaluation functions, which only allow comparison of alternatives, which are part of the same trace up to that point.

In [39], detailed and priority beam search were extended for usage on arbitrary state spaces, as opposed to highly structured trees. In the following section we present extended detailed beam search, as implemented in the μCRL state space generator. For a detailed comparison between the basic notion of this beam search and the extension and eventual adaptation to the μCRL toolset setting, the reader is referred to [39].

5 Extended Detailed Beam Search

In this section we first present the extended detailed beam search in its sequential form. After that we adapt it to a distributed setting. From now on, whenever detailed beam search is mentioned, we refer to the search extended for arbitrarily structured state spaces.

5.1 Sequential Detailed Beam Search

A user of the μCRL toolset can perform a detailed beam search, i.e. a beam search using a total cost evaluation function. The user can provide a function using constants and variables from the model, combining them using mathematical operators.

Algorithm 2 shows in pseudo-code the detailed beam search algorithm as used in the μCRL toolset. The evaluation function is called $f : \Sigma \rightarrow \mathbb{N}$. This function is decomposed to $f(s) = g(s) + h(s)$, where $g(s)$ represents the cost taken to reach s from the root of the tree, which is defined as $g(s) = g(s') + cost(a)$ if $s' \xrightarrow{a} s$. The function $cost : Act \rightarrow \mathbb{N}$ assigns weights to actions that can, for instance, denote the time needed to perform different jobs in a scheduling problem. These are usually fixed to certain values before searching starts. Since the range of $cost$ is non-negative numbers, if $s \xrightarrow{a} s'$, then $g(s') \geq g(s)$, for any action a. The $h(s)$ function is an estimation of the cost it would take to efficiently complete the schedule continuing from s. Here, we consider *admissible* heuristics, i.e. for all states s, $h(s)$ is an underestimation of the real minimal cost needed to complete the schedule. The function $get f_{max} : \mathscr{P}(\Sigma) \rightarrow \Sigma$, given a set of states, returns one of the states that has the highest f value. It thus computes $f(s) = g(s) + h(s)$ for each member of the set. Contrary to Algorithm 1, here, all S_i and *Closed* contain pairs of states and corresponding g-values. Finally, the functions $unify(X)$ and $update(X,Y)$ are defined as follows: $unify(X) = \{\langle s, g \rangle \in X \mid \forall \langle s', g' \rangle \in X . s = s' \implies g \leq g'\}$ and $update(X,Y) = \{\langle s, g \rangle \in X \mid \neg \exists g' \leq g . \langle s, g' \rangle \in Y\}$. These functions are used to perform a delayed duplicate detection, where revisiting of a state is allowed if it is reached via a path with a lower cost than the g-cost assigned to it so far.

Note, that no additional stopping condition appears in Algorithm 2, i.e. it appears as though we exclude searching for something in particular, for instance the violation of a property. This, however, can in practice be done on top of any search. Relating back to section 3, we can perform a detailed beam search and at the same time check, whether a transition $s \xrightarrow{a} s'$ is found, such that $a = finished$. Once this is the case, the search can be stopped and a trace from s_0 to s' can be returned, which corresponds to a schedule. This approach is used in our experiments (see section 7).

5.2 Distributed Detailed Beam Search

Because of the global view of total cost evaluation functions, designing a distributed version of detailed beam search is non-trivial. Clients should not select states for further exploration in isolation of each other, but have to communicate.

Say we have a manager and n clients to do a distributed detailed beam search. As described in 2, we have a hash function $Checksum:\Sigma \rightarrow \mathbb{N}$, which is used to distribute generated states over the clients for future exploration. Say the LTS consists of levels S_0, S_1, etc. As detailed beam search is done in a breadth-first manner, each level of states S_i gets distributed over the n clients before exploration, leading to the subsets $S_i^1, \ldots, S_i^n$,

---

Algorithm 2. Detailed beam search for state space generation

---

procedure detbs (s_0, β)
   $s_0.g := 0$
   $i := 0$
   $S_i := \{\langle s_0, s_0.g\rangle\}$
   $Closed := \emptyset$
   while $S_i \neq \emptyset$ **do**
      $S_{i+1} := \emptyset$
      while $|S_i| > \beta$ **do**
         $S_i := S_i \setminus \{(s,g) \in S_i \mid s = get f_{max}(S_i)\}$
      for all $s \in S_i$ **do**
         for all $s \xrightarrow{a} s' \in expand(s)$ **do**
            $s'.g := s.g + cost(a)$
            $S_{i+1} := S_{i+1} \cup \{\langle s', s'.g\rangle\}$
      $Closed := unify(Closed \cup S_i)$
      $S_{i+1} := update(unify(S_{i+1}), Closed)$
      $i := i + 1$
   return Finished

---

such that $S_i^1 \cup \ldots \cup S_i^n = S_i$ for all levels i, where S_i^j is the subset of S_i designated to client j by the hash function.

Now, we define function $p_f : \mathscr{P}(\Sigma) \to \mathscr{P}(\mathscr{P}(\Sigma))$, which is used at each level i by each client j. For practical reasons, we say that k is an upper limit of f. Now, p_f distributes the states from a set S_i^j over k equivalence classes $[\sigma_0^j], \ldots, [\sigma_{k-1}^j]$, such that $\forall u \in \{0, 1, \ldots, k-1\}. \forall s \in [\sigma_u^j].f(s) = u$.

We refer to a selection of γ states from a set S_i^j using evaluation function f as $sel_\gamma^f(S_i^j) = [\sigma_0^j] \cup \ldots \cup [\sigma_r^j] \cup [\sigma']$, with $r \in \mathbb{N}$ and $r < k-1$, such that $|[\sigma_0^j] \cup \ldots \cup [\sigma_r^j]| < \gamma$, $[\sigma'] \subseteq [\sigma_{r+1}^j]$ and $|[\sigma_0^j] \cup \ldots \cup [\sigma_r^j] \cup [\sigma']| = \gamma$. In practice, $[\sigma'] \subseteq [\sigma_{r+1}^j]$ is composed according to a so-called tie-breaking rule. In the remainder of this paper, we denote sel_γ^f as sel_γ.

The goal to achieve now for the algorithm is the following:

$$\forall i. sel_{\gamma_{i,1}}(S_i^1) \cup \ldots \cup sel_{\gamma_{i,n}}(S_i^n) = sel_\beta(S_i) \quad (1)$$

Here, β is the beam width and $\gamma_{i,1}, \ldots, \gamma_{i,n} \in \mathbb{N}$, such that $\gamma_{i,1} + \ldots + \gamma_{i,n} = \beta$. If we could assume that $\gamma_{i,1} = \ldots = \gamma_{i,n}$, then there would be no problem moving the sequential beam search algorithm to a distributed setting. Then, however, besides assuming that the states of each level are evenly distributed over the clients, we also have to assume that the β most promising states of a level are evenly distributed. This we cannot assume in general. Instead,

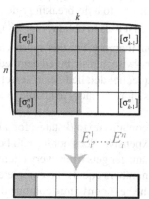

Fig. 1. Distributing, partitioning and selecting

we can move to a more general situation where the $\gamma_{i,j}$s are unequal to each other. In order to achieve this, extra communication is necessary.

Being in level i, let every client j first determine $sel_\beta(S_i^j)$, this to be prepared for the worst case scenario where all β most promising states end up at a single client. This is illustrated in the top part of Figure 1, where each row in the diagram represents a client, and each column represents an equivalence class. Having constructed the equivalence classes, $sel_\beta(S_i^j)$ is determined, which, in Figure 1, is highlighted in grey for each client. Once this is done, the clients send a set of tuples, each consisting of an evaluation value and the number of states in $sel_\beta(S_i^j)$ that have this evaluation value to the manager. To put it more formal, the following is sent by each client j, being in level i of the LTS:

$$E_i^j = \{(r, |[\sigma_r^j] \cap sel_\beta(S_i^j)|) | 0 \le r \le k - 1 \wedge |[\sigma_r^j] \cap sel_\beta(S_i^j)| \ne 0\} \qquad (2)$$

All the sets E_i^j sent by the clients are used by the manager to determine a final selection of β states. This is illustrated in the bottom part of Figure 1. First E_i is created as $E_i = \{(j,e,t)|(e,t) \in E_i^j\}$, where e and t correspond to the first and second element in the tuples calculated in (2). Similar to p_f, we define a function $p_e : \mathscr{P}(\mathbb{N}^3) \to \mathscr{P}(\mathscr{P}(\mathbb{N}^3))$, which allows us to distribute the elements of the set E_i over k equivalence classes $[e_0], \ldots, [e_{k-1}]$, such that $\forall u \in \{0,1,\ldots,k-1\}. \forall (j,e,t) \in [e_u].e = u$.

For selecting the β best states, we define a function $T_j : \mathscr{P}(\mathbb{N}^3) \to \mathbb{N}$, which returns the number of states from client j represented in the given evaluation set E; more specific, $T_j(E) = 0 + \sum_{(j,e,t) \in E'} t$, with $E' = \{(j',e',t') \in E \mid j' = j\}$. We define $T : \mathscr{P}(\mathbb{N}^3) \to \mathbb{N}$ as the total number of states represented in the given evaluation set E, so $T(E) = \sum_{j=1}^n T_j(E)$. We refer to a selection of β triples from E_i as $evsel_\beta(E_i) = [e_0] \cup \ldots \cup [e_r] \cup [e']$, with $r \in \mathbb{N}$ and $r < k - 1$, such that $T([e_0]) + \ldots + T([e_r]) < \beta$, $[e'] = evsubsel_{\beta - (T([e_0]) + \ldots + T([e_r]))}([e_{r+1}])$. Here, $evsubsel_{\beta'}([e_u]) = \{(j_0,e_0,t_0)\} \cup \ldots \cup \{(j_{w-1},e_{w-1},t_{w-1})\} \cup \{(j_w,e_w,t'_w)\}$, where $(j_0,e_0,t_0),\ldots,(j_w,e_w,t_w) \in [e_u], t'_w \le t_w$ and $t_0 + \ldots + t_{w-1} + t'_w = \beta'$. In practice, $[e']$ is composed according to a tie-breaking rule.

Each client j receives a width $\gamma_{i,j} = T_j(evsel_\beta(E_i))$, which it uses to obtain $sel_{\gamma_{i,j}}(S_i^j)$. Since $sel_{\gamma_{i,j}}(S_i^j) \subseteq sel_\beta(S_i^j)$, this set can be constructed from memory. For this approach only one extra communication round is necessary. Memory-wise, a distributed detailed beam search with beam width β is comparable with a sequential detailed beam search with beam width $n.\beta$, but, of course, on the whole, there is more memory available in a distributed setting than in a sequential one.

One advantage of detailed beam search is that if a level contains up to β states, for all states s in the level, $h(s)$, which can be computationally expensive, does not have to be calculated. To achieve this in the distributed version, the manager gets from every client the number of newly generated states. The sum of these numbers equals the complete size of the next level. If it sends this number together with the next continue command, the clients know whether or not to prune (see Algorithms 3 and 4).

In general, distributed state space generation algorithms benefit from symmetry. If all clients have to do a similar amount of work, than little to no idle time occurs in any of the clients and therefore no processing power is wasted. However, if we allow unequal $\gamma_{i,j}$s, then the workload of the clients can be very unequal at times. It makes no sense to have clients idle, while they could very well expand states. Exploring more states than originally asked for can in practice, where the accuracy of the evaluation function[5] and the minimally necessary beam width are in general not known, only be seen as an improvement in accuracy[6]. For this reason we decided to create a variant where the manager does not provide every client j with $\gamma_{i,j}$, but a single $\gamma_i = max(\gamma_{i,1}, \gamma_{i,2}, \ldots, \gamma_{i,n})$ is provided to all clients. In this way every client expands the same amount of states[7], and we know that the β most promising states are selected[8].

Algorithms 3 and 4 show what the clients and the manager do in a distributed detailed beam search, respectively. The selection procedure of the manager in order to obtain γ_i is done in *calculateLimit()*. Matching send and receive functions can be identified by their names. Note, that duplicate detection is now performed by each client after having received the new set of states to be expanded. This works thanks to the *Checksum* function, which ensures that a state s is always assigned to the same client j. During the generation, a client can receive the following commands from the manager:

- `continue`: In the next step, receive new states in S_i and expand them.
- `finish`: Stop the search algorithm.

6 Other Beam Search Variants

In general, minimal-time traces to a transition a are not necessarily shortest traces to this transition. This fact means that when first encountering a in a BFS, we cannot claim having found a minimal-time trace. This can, however, be achieved by searching a state space using minimal-cost, or minimal-time, search [41], which can be seen as uniform-cost search [24], where the costs are modelled using additional actions. There, compared to BFS, the sets S_i do not comprise of states which are i transitions removed from s_0, but, using a total cost function g, in each iteration, S_i is transformed into $\hat{S}_i = \{\langle s, g \rangle \in S_i \mid \forall \langle s', g' \rangle \in S_i . g \le g'\}$, $\hat{S}_i$ is expanded, leading to $\hat{S}_{i+1}$, and finally, $S_{i+1} = \hat{S}_{i+1} \cup (S_i \setminus \hat{S}_i)$. This technique can be combined with beam search, resulting in *g-synchronised* beam search, which is presented in [39] as an instance of *G-synchronised* beam search, where G can be any reasonable function. Compared to regular beam search, now only states with equal g-values are considered at the same time and states are selected purely on their h-value. It can be seen as *greedy search*, as described in [36], on top of minimal-cost, or uniform-cost, search. In each iteration, first, the current S_i is transformed to $\hat{S}_i$ like in minimal-cost search, as described earlier. Then, h is applied on $\hat{S}_i$, in order to keep up to β states, as is done

---

[5] Of course, an important problem is to find a very good evaluation function. This is however beyond the scope of this paper, where we assume a given function, its accuracy unknown.

[6] There are results where a bigger beam width does not correspond to a higher accuracy, such as in [29,41] and in section 7.2. However, this phenomenon mainly occurs when using relatively small beam widths (compared to the size of the state space), and can therefore be ignored for bigger cases.

[7] The exception to this is when a client has less states available than it is told to expand.

[8] One could argue that another approach is to redistribute the β selected states over the clients, in order to balance the workload. However, then we go against the distribution of the hash function, which means that clients will no longer be able to perform duplicate detection, leading possibly to redundant work.

Algorithm 3. Distributed detailed beam search - Client Instantiator

procedure ddbsclient(CLIENTNUMBER, {clientnumbers}, s_0, β)
  $s_0.g := 0$
  $i := 0$
  if $Checksum(s_0) =$ CLIENTNUMBER **then**
    $S_i := \{\langle s_0, s_0.g \rangle\}$
  else
    $S_i := \emptyset$
  $Closed := \emptyset$
  $SendToClientsNextLevel(S_i)$
  $(command, levelsize) := RecvFromMgr()$
  if $command \neq$ **finish then**
    repeat
      $S_i := update(unify(RecvFromClientsNextLevel()), Closed)$
      $S_{i+1} := \emptyset$
      if $levelsize > \beta$ **then**
        while $|S_i| > \beta$ **do**
          $S_i := S_i \setminus \{(s,g) \in S_i \mid s = get f_{max}(S_i)\}$
        $SendToMgrEvalInfo(I)$, with I as (2), $sel_\beta(S_i^j) = S_i$
        $\gamma_i := RecvFromMgrLimit()$
        while $|S_i| > \gamma_i$ **do**
          $S_i := S_i \setminus \{(s,g) \in S_i \mid s = get f_{max}(S_i)\}$
      for all $s \in S_i$ **do**
        for all $s \xrightarrow{a} s' \in expand(s)$ **do**
          $s'.g := s.g + cost(a)$
          $S_{i+1} := S_{i+1} \cup \{\langle s', s'.g \rangle\}$
      $Closed := unify(Closed \cup S_i)$
      $SendToClientsNextLevel(unify(S_{i+1}))$
      $SendToMgrSizeNextLevel(|unify(S_{i+1})|)$
      $i := i + 1$
      $(command, levelsize) := RecvFromMgr()$
    until $command =$ **finish**
  return Finished

Algorithm 4. Distributed detailed beam search - Manager Instantiator

procedure ddbsmanager({clientnumbers}, s_0, β)
  $levelsize := 1$
  $SendToClients($**continue**, $levelsize)$
  repeat
    if $levelsize > \beta$ **then**
      $SendToClientsLimit(calculateLimit(RecvFromClientsEvalInfo()))$
    $levelsize := RecvFromClientsSizeNextLevel()$
    if $levelsize = 0$ **then**
      $SendToClients($**finish**, $0)$
    else
      $SendToClients($**continue**, $levelsize)$
  until $levelsize = 0$
  return Finished

in greedy search. Greedy search from [36] corresponds to beam search with a constant g[9]. This variant not only allows finding minimal-time solutions within the beam before any other solutions. If one uses additional actions to model costs, it also removes the necessity to store the g-value of every state, since revisiting a state necessarily means having found a less efficient trace compared with a previous trace to the state.

Priority beam search is performed using a priority evaluation function $f : Tr \to \mathbb{Z}$, which assigns priorities to transitions. Therefore, priority beam search works on transitions, not states. A fixed number of outgoing transitions is selected *per state*, which makes the adaptation to a distributed setting straightforward. Since each selection does not consider the outgoing transitions of other states, communication with other clients is not needed. We can take the standard distributed state space generation algorithm, and insert an evaluation and selection step at the point where a state is expanded. Priority beam search for state spaces is described in more detail in [39].

Two other (related) variants are *flexible* priority beam search and *flexible* detailed beam search, introduced in [39,41]. Flexible priority beam search behaves as regular priority beam search, but at each state it also selects any transition which has the same priority as the least competent member of the usually selected set. In other words, tie-breaking is avoided, by making the beam dynamic in size. The benefit of this approach is that there are no selection criteria other than the evaluation function used. This not only leads to more insight in the effectiveness of the function, but in practice it may also mean that smaller beam widths can be used, compared to non-flexible beam search (see, for instance, the results in section 7). The drawback is that the memory requirement is no longer linear in the maximum search depth, since β is only a guideline for the beam width. This search can be implemented in a distributed setting, since the local view characteristic is not lost. Similarly, in flexible detailed beam search we achieve at each level closure on the worst evaluation value still selected. The algorithm described in section 5.2 can be made flexible by redefining some functions. First we say that function $sel_\gamma(S_i^j)$ selects at least γ states, where $sel_\gamma(S_i^j) = [\sigma_0^j] \cup \ldots \cup [\sigma_r^j] \cup [\sigma_{r+1}^j]$, with $r \in \mathbb{N}$ and $r < k - 1$, such that $|[\sigma_0^j] \cup \ldots \cup [\sigma_r^j]| < \gamma$ and $|[\sigma_0^j] \cup \ldots \cup [\sigma_r^j] \cup [\sigma_{r+1}^j]| \geq \gamma$. Likewise, we redefine $evsel_\beta(E_i) = [e_0] \cup \ldots \cup [e_r] \cup [e_{r+1}]$, with $r \in \mathbb{N}$ and $r < k - 1$, such that $T([e_0]) + \ldots + T([e_r]) < \beta$ and $T([e_0]) + \ldots + T([e_{r+1}]) \geq \beta$.

7 Experimental Results

In this section we will show some experimental results of trying to solve instances of what we call the *Zebra Finch problem*. We based this problem on a combination of several *river crossing problems* [14], such as *five jealous husbands* and *soldiers and children*. First we describe the problem and then we provide the results obtained using the techniques described in this paper.

---

[9] It should be noted, that in the literature greedy search is sometimes given a different meaning. At least one other greedy search exists, which corresponds to detailed beam search with $\beta = 1$ (e.g. [43]).

7.1 The Zebra Finch Problem

Zebra Finches (*Taeniopygia guttata*) are small birds living in Central Australia [42]. They are found in large colonies of pairs inhabiting open steppes with scattered bushes and trees. These birds can react aggressively towards each other, for instance when a jealous male bird tries to keep other male birds away from his mate. When young birds reach an age where they can live outside the nest they are quickly adopted by the group.

We consider a group consisting of *n* pairs and *m* young, sitting in a tree on an open steppe. They want to migrate to some bushes up ahead, but they have to travel in smaller groups, since there are some hawks flying in the distance, which can spot a group of more than *k* adult finches. Once a group has reached the bushes, at least one of the Zebra Finches needs to fly back, in order to signal that a new group can travel. On top of this there are two other conditions:

1. Considering the jealous nature of the male Zebra Finches, no female finch may ever be either in the tree, the travelling group or the bushes in the presence of other male birds, unless her partner is also present.

Fig. 2. A pair of Zebra Finches

2. The young in the colony have to be guided by at least one adult finch, so the travelling group cannot consist of only young finches. In limiting the group size, two young are equivalent to one adult.

Finally some costs are related to the travelling from tree to bushes and back:

- A group consisting of only adults needs 1 time unit to travel the distance, independent of the size of the group;
- If the number of young in the group does not exceed the number of adults, the time needed to travel is 2 time units (each adult needs to take care of at most one young);
- When, in the group, the number of young exceeds the number of adults, the travel takes 3 time units, since at least one adult takes care of more than one young.

We model the problem allowing all possible actions at all times. It demonstrates the techniques' ability to deal with arbitrary state spaces; problem instances lead to state spaces containing both cycles (while forming the group and when birds fly away and back again), and deadlocks (violations of the 'jealous male' condition).

7.2 Results

In Table 1 we present some results we found for instances of the Zebra Finch problem. We used minimal-cost search, *g*-synchronised detailed beam search and its flexible variant, where for the last two cases we defined the *h* for each state as the number of finches still in the tree, thereby encouraging fast removal and discouraging the returning of finches. Problem instances are described by providing *n*, *m* and *k*. For each search, the total execution time of the result found is given. Furthermore, the number of states searched to find the solution and the time needed to find it is provided. Searches not performed are marked with hyphens, and where the results could not be obtained due to technical reasons, dots are written. When a search is done in a distributed setting, an asterisk is placed after the number of states. Sequential searches were performed using a machine with a 64bit Athlon 2.2Ghz processor, 1 GB of memory and running Suse 9.3, while 16 of these machines together performed the distributed searches.

The minimal-cost search tells us that as the problem instances get bigger, the state spaces grow very rapidly. The beam searches on the other hand show a much nicer increase in states from instance to instance. Looking at the (50,50,10) instance though, we see an unwanted effect in the regular g-synchronised beam search, already briefly referred to in section 5.2, namely that increasing β not necessarily means getting a better result. This might be due to pruning sometimes not being done only based on f, but also on other criteria, simply because more than β states turn out to be promising enough. Although this mainly has a noticeable effect in smaller instances, it is undesired and does not occur in its flexible variant. The fact, by the way, that a much bigger beam width was also needed for the flexible search in comparison with previous instances may indicate that the evaluation function can still be improved.

Furthermore, it is interesting to note that for smaller instances, the distributed algorithm performs worse than the sequential version, which can be seen in the (50,50,20) case, where we performed both a sequential and a distributed search. The S_i sets in the state space are all relatively small, making the communication overhead of the distributed algorithm noticeable. This seems to be directly related to the argument found in the literature against distributed beam search in a more traditional setting [5], mentioned in more detail in section 8. Besides that, note that the result obtained with the distributed search is better than the one of the sequential search, even though the beam widths are equal. This is due to tie-breaking, which, in a distributed environment, can

Table 1. Zebra Finch problem results

Instance			minimal-cost search			g-synch. detailed BS				Flex. g-synch. det. BS			
n	m	k	result	# states	time	β	result	# states	time	β	result	# states	time
10	5	5	19	228,737	00:00:29	400	19	58,272	00:00:14	400	19	67,804	00:00:18
10	10	5	21	513,123	00:01:07	400	21	65,605	00:00:18	400	21	85,633	00:00:24
10	10	8	10	2,020,061	00:04:28	450	10	48,669	00:00:19	400	10	69,550	00:00:21
50	50	5	121	18,157,429	00:48:13	1,000	121	641,315	00:04:49	400	121	298,065	00:02:31
50	50	10	41	475,744,120 *	05:13:26	1,000	43	637,285	00:07:28	-	-	-	-
50	50	10	-	-	-	1,500	44	946,660	00:13:37	-	-	-	-
50	50	10	-	-	-	4,000	43	2,139,347	...	4,000	42	2,365,102	...
50	50	20	-	-	-	5,000	24	3,478,600	01:14:00	1,500	22	1,649,203	...
50	50	20	-	-	-	5,000	20	3,095,782 *	02:01:05	4,000	20	2,579,479 *	01:48:16
100	100	10	-	-	-	5,000	87	6,009,134 *	01:39:52	4,000	87	5,318,589 *	06:22:54
100	100	20	-	-	-	5,000	41	5,884,895 *	00:42:48	4,000	42	5,433,733 *	04:02:26
100	100	50	-	-	-	20,000	17	27,366,213 *	02:57:21	4,000	18	41,611,293 *	06:16:29
100	100	80	-	-	-	20,000	10	19,107,091 *	ca. 24h	...	...	...	...
200	200	50	-	-	-	50,000	35	135,964,662 *	ca. 36h	...	...	...	...

happen at multiple places in a single level, instead of only at one point. In the flexible search, where tie-breaking is avoided altogether, this behaviour does not appear.

The $(100,100,50)$ and the $(100,100,80)$ case have a big difference in execution time, while the number of states in the latter case is even lower. However, although the number of expanded states is lower in the $(100,100,80)$ case, the number of encountered and evaluated states is much higher. This is directly related to the maximum size of the travelling group k.

The last two cases could not be solved using flexible beam search. The main reason for this is that in many levels all states had to be expanded, since no states could be pruned based on f. This shows that the flexible variant can point to the necessity to design a better evaluation function, in this case for instance one, that also takes the number of finches in the group into account. Finally, as stated earlier in section 6, for the flexible search, overall β is more stable compared to the non-flexible search. This means in general, that, given some search results, it is easier to determine β for a new flexible search, than for a new non-flexible one.

8 Related Work

Concerning scheduling, quite some research has been done in the field of timed automata. In a paper by Niebert, et al. [28], the problem of minimum-time reachability for timed automata is considered. In several papers by Behrmann, et al. (e.g. [2]), linearly priced timed automata are introduced as an extension of timed automata with prices on both transitions and locations. They consider the minimum-cost reachability problem and an algorithmic solution is offered. In [37], an approach specific for SPIN is presented using a depth-first search algorithm.

There are many papers on solving job-shop scheduling problems, for instance [10]. Most approaches, however, are specifically designed for job-shop problems, while the techniques described in this paper are also meant for other, industrial systems.

Distributed state space generation has appeared in various forms and in various settings, we will just mention a few here. An early approach not limited to any specific input language was proposed in [11]. In [13], a distributed generation algorithm is presented for the MURϕ verifier. Based on this technique a distributed UPPAAL has been developed [3]. An implementation of a distributed state space exploration algorithm based on the SPIN model checker [26] exists. In [18], a method is described to generate LTSs in a distributed way by means of the CADP model checker. All these approaches, however, focus on exhaustive state space generation and not on heuristically pruning parts of the state space on-the-fly in order to solve a particular kind of problem. In [23], a distributed, external version of A^* is developed, combining the fields of distributed, directed and external model checking.

Attempts to create a distributed beam search can be found outside of model checking [5]. In those settings one usually works with search trees which have a much lower average branching factor (the number of outgoing transitions per state) compared to an average state space. Because of this, small beam widths, usually not bigger than 10, can be used, making a distributed beam search counter-productive due to the communication overhead (a similar result can be found in section 7.2). In model checking, however, we wish to deal with arbitrary state spaces, where the average branching factor can be much higher, thereby, for bigger instances, making a distributed beam search effective.

Relating our extensions of beam search to other work, in [16], best-first search is extended to k-best-first search, allowing to compensate for inaccuracies in the evaluation function by selecting in each iteration more than only the best state. Essentially, the difference between k-best-first search and beam search is the decision to keep states not selected in one iteration for the next iteration. This makes k-best first search a complete search, but it also means its memory requirement is higher, since there is no pruning done. A trade-off can, however, be achieved, by using inadmissible heuristics, such that fewer states are expanded, but the solution will be near-optimal. This trade-off is also used for weighted A^* [33] and linear-space best-first search [25], where the h-function is multiplied by some factor. Moreover, in the latter, the memory requirement is linear in the size of the search depth. Our extension of g-synchronised beam search can probably best be compared with filtered beam search [30], in the sense that in each iteration, the current set of states undergoes two phases; in filtered beam search, first a priority beam search is applied, and on the outcome of that, detailed beam search is used, this to lessen the computational complexity. In g-synchronised beam search, we first postpone some states, and then prune states from the remaining set.

In [20], the development of heuristics is the main focus, making it nicely connecting to this paper, in the sense that we start with the assumption of having a heuristic function. Their objective is to model check Java programs with heuristics constructed using the properties to check, the structure of the programs and additional input of the user. They use a number of search algorithms, one of which is beam search. Their beam search, however, seems to deviate from the traditional notion, in that $f(s) = h(s)$, making it practically a linear space greedy search. Furthermore, they include duplicate detection, but do not consider other extensions in order to deal more efficiently with arbitrary state spaces, such as a flexible search.

Finally, in [43], beam search is extended to a complete search, by using a new data structure, called a beam stack. With this it is possible to achieve a range of searches, from depth-first search ($\beta = 1$) to BFS ($\beta \rightarrow \infty$). Considering our extensions for arbitrary state spaces, it would be interesting to try to combined these two approaches.

9   Conclusions

We presented a distributed version of detailed beam search, used in a model checking setting. Due to the global view of detailed beam search, creating this version was non-trivial. In practice it shows that for bigger problem instances, the distributed algorithm pays off. We developed a variant called g-synchronised beam search, which considers the states sorted by increasing g. It does not need the storage of g-values of all states when using additional cost actions, since reopening is never necessary. Furthermore, we observed that sometimes increasing β does not lead to finding better results, due to the sometimes cutting away of states which are promising enough. To avoid this unwanted behaviour, we created a (distributed) flexible variant of beam search.

Future work. Usage in practice indicated that modelling time using a sequence of *tick* actions leads to state space explosions very quickly. The searches could be adapted to deal with $tick(t)$ actions, where $t \in \mathbb{N}$ denotes a number of time units delayed at once. Furthermore, as the construction of a suitable f is a big problem when using heuristics, it might be interesting to try to quantify the effectiveness of a given function.

Acknowledgements. We thank the anonymous reviewers of MoChArtIV for their constructive comments, and Mohammad Torabi Dashti for the help in designing the distributed detailed beam search algorithm.

References

1. Baeten, J.C.M., Middelburg, C.A.: Process Algebra with Timing. In: EATCS Monograph, Springer, Heidelberg (2002)
2. Behrmann, G., Fehnker, A., Hune, T., Larsen, K.G., Pettersson, P., Romijn, J.M.T.: Efficient Guiding Towards Cost-Optimality in UPPAAL. In: Margaria, T., Yi, W. (eds.) ETAPS 2001 and TACAS 2001. LNCS, vol. 2031, pp. 174–188. Springer, Heidelberg (2001)
3. Behrmann, G., Hune, T., Vaandrager, F.: Distributing Timed Model Checking - How the Search Order Matters. In: Emerson, E.A., Sistla, A.P. (eds.) CAV 2000. LNCS, vol. 1855, pp. 216–231. Springer, Heidelberg (2000)
4. Bergstra, J., Klop, J.: Algebra of Communicating Processes with Abstraction. Theor. Comput. Sci. 37, 77–121 (1985)
5. Bisiani, R.: Beam Search. In: Encyclopedia of Artificial Intelligence, pp. 1467–1568. Wiley Interscience Publication, Chichester (1992)
6. Blom, S., Orzan, S.: A Distributed Algorithm for Strong Bisimulation Reduction of State Spaces. In: Proc. of PDMC 2002, ENTCS, vol. 68 (4), Elsevier, Amsterdam (2002)
7. Blom, S.C.C., Fokkink, W.J., Groote, J.F., van Langevelde, I., Lisser, B., van de Pol, J.C.: μCRL: A Toolset for Analysing Algebraic Specifications. In: Berry, G., Comon, H., Finkel, A. (eds.) CAV 2001. LNCS, vol. 2102, pp. 250–254. Springer, Heidelberg (2001)
8. Blom, S.C.C., Ioustinova, N., Sidorova, N.: Timed verification with μCRL. In: Broy, M., Zamulin, A.V. (eds.) PSI 2003. LNCS, vol. 2890, pp. 178–192. Springer, Heidelberg (2003)
9. Bolch, G., Greiner, S., de Meer, H., Trivedi, K.S.: Queueing Networks and Markov Chains: Modeling and Performance Evaluation with Computer Science Applications, 2nd edn. Wiley, Chichester (2006)
10. Brucker, P., Jurisch, B., Sievers, B.: A branch and bound algorithm for the job-shop scheduling problem. Discrete Applied Mathematics 49(6), 107–127 (1994)
11. Ciardo, G., Gluckman, J., Nicol, D.: Distributed State Space Generation of Discrete-State Stochastic Models. INFORMS Journal on Computing 10(1), 82–93 (1998)
12. Della Croce, F., T'kindt, V.: A recovering beam search algorithm for the one-machine dynamic total completion time scheduling problem. Journal of the Operational Research Society 53, 1275–1280 (2002)
13. Dill, D.: The Murϕ Verification System. In: Alur, R., Henzinger, T.A. (eds.) CAV 1996. LNCS, vol. 1102, pp. 390–393. Springer, Heidelberg (1996)
14. Dudeney, H.E.: Amusements in Mathematics, chapter 9, Dover Publications, Inc, pp. 112–114(1958)
15. Edelkamp, S., Leue, S., Lluch-Lafuente, A.: Directed Explicit-state Model Checking in the Validation of Communication Protocols. STTT 5, 247–267 (2003)
16. Felner, A., Kraus, S., Korf, R.E.: KBFS: K-Best-First Search. AMAI 39(1-2), 19–39 (2003)

17. Fox, M.S.: Constraint-Directed Search: A Case Study of Job-Shop Scheduling. PhD thesis, CMU (1983)
18. Garavel, H., Mateescu, R., Smarandache, I.: Parallel State Space Construction for Model-Checking. In: Dwyer, M.B. (ed.) Model Checking Software. LNCS, vol. 2057, pp. 217–234. Springer, Heidelberg (2001)
19. Godefroid, P., Khurshid, S.: Exploring Very Large State Spaces Using Genetic Algorithms. In: Katoen, J.-P., Stevens, P. (eds.) ETAPS 2002 and TACAS 2002. LNCS, vol. 2280, pp. 266–280. Springer, Heidelberg (2002)
20. Groce, A., Visser, W.: Heuristics for Model Checking Java Programs. STTT 6(4), 260–276 (2004)
21. Groote, J.F., Reniers, M.A.: Handbook of Process Algebra, 17, pp. 1151–1208. Elsevier, Amsterdam (2001)
22. Huth, M., Kwiatkowska, M.: Quantitative Analysis and Model Checking. In: Proc. LICS'97, pp. 111–127. IEEE Computer Society Press, Los Alamitos (1997)
23. Jabbar, S., Edelkamp, S.: Parallel External Directed Model Checking With Linear I/O. In: Emerson, E.A., Namjoshi, K.S. (eds.) VMCAI 2006. LNCS, vol. 3855, pp. 237–251. Springer, Heidelberg (2006)
24. Korf, R.E.: Uniform-cost Search. In: Shapiro, S.C. (ed.) Encyclopedia of Artificial Intelligence, pp. 1461–1462. Wiley-Interscience, New York, NY (1992)
25. Korf, R.E.: Linear-space best-first search. Artificial Intelligence 62, 41–78 (1993)
26. Lerda, F., Sista, R.: Distributed-Memory model checking with SPIN. In: Dams, D.R., Gerth, R., Leue, S., Massink, M. (eds.) Theoretical and Practical Aspects of SPIN Model Checking. LNCS, vol. 1680, pp. 22–39. Springer, Heidelberg (1999)
27. Lowerre, B.T.: The HARPY speech recognition system. PhD thesis, CMU (1976)
28. Niebert, P., Tripakis, S., Yovine, S.: Minimum-time reachability for timed automata. In: Proc. MED 2000, IEEE Press, Los Alamitos (2000)
29. Oechsner, S., Rose, O.: Scheduling Cluster Tools Using Filtered Beam Search and Recipe Comparison. In: Proc. 2005 Winter Simulation Conference, pp. 2203–2210. IEEE Computer Society Press, Los Alamitos (2005)
30. Ow, P.S., Morton, E.T.: Filtered beam search in scheduling. International Journal of Production Research 26, 35–62 (1988)
31. Ow, P.S., Smith, S.F.: Viewing scheduling as an opportunistic problem-solving process. Annals of Operations Research 12, 85–108 (1988)
32. Peled, D., Pratt, V., Holzmann, G. (eds.): Partial Order Methods in Verification, vol. 29 of DIMACS series in discrete mathematics and theoretical computer science. AMS (1996)
33. Pohl, I.: Heuristic Search Viewed as Path Finding in a Graph. Artificial Intelligence 1, 193–204 (1970)
34. Roscoe, A.W.: Model-checking CSP. In: A Classical Mind: Essays in Honour of C.A.R. Hoare, pp. 353–378. Prentice-Hall, Englewood Cliffs (1994)
35. Rubin, S.: The ARGOS Image Understanding System. PhD thesis, CMU (1978)
36. Russell, S., Norvig, P.: Artificial Intelligence: A Modern Approach. Prentice-Hall, Englewood Cliffs (1995)
37. Ruys, T.C.: Optimal scheduling using Branch-and-Bound with SPIN 4.0. In: Ball, T., Rajamani, S.K. (eds.) Model Checking Software. LNCS, vol. 2648, pp. 1–17. Springer, Heidelberg (2003)
38. Sabuncuoglu, I., Bayiz, M.: Job shop scheduling with beam search. European Journal of Operational Research 118, 390–412 (1999)
39. Dashti, T. M., Wijs, A.J.: Pruning State Spaces Using Extended Beam Search. To be published, http://www.cwi.nl/~wijs/beamsearch.pdf (2006)

40. Wijs, A.J., Fokkink, W.J.: From χ_t to μCRL: Combining Performance and Functional Analysis. In: Proc. ICECCS'05, pp. 184–193. IEEE Computer Society Press, Los Alamitos (2005)
41. Wijs, A.J., van de Pol, J.C., Bortnik, E.: Solving Scheduling Problems by Untimed Model Checking. In: Proc. FMICS'05, pp. 54–61. ACM Press, 2005. Extended version as CWI technical report SEN-R0608, http://db.cwi.nl/rapporten/abstract.php?abstractnr=2034
42. Zann, R.A.: The Zebra Finch - A Synthesis of Field and Laboratory Studies. Oxford University Press Inc, Oxford (1996)
43. Zhou, R., Hansen, E.A.: Beam-Stack Search: Integrating Backtracking with Beam Search. In: Proc. ICAPS'05, pp. 90–98. AAAI (2005)

Author Index

Lecture Notes in Artificial Intelligence (LNAI)

Vol. 4399: T. Kovacs, X. Llorà, K. Takadama, P.L. Lanzi, W. Stolzmann, S.W. Wilson (Eds.), Learning Classifier Systems. XII, 345 pages. 2007.

Vol. 4390: S.O. Kuznetsov, S. Schmidt (Eds.), Formal Concept Analysis. X, 329 pages. 2007.

Vol. 4389: D. Weyns, H.V.D. Parunak, F. Michel (Eds.), Environments for Multi-Agent Systems III. X, 273 pages. 2007.

Vol. 4384: T. Washio, K. Satoh, H. Takeda, A. Inokuchi (Eds.), New Frontiers in Artificial Intelligence. IX, 401 pages. 2007.

Vol. 4371: K. Inoue, K. Satoh, F. Toni (Eds.), Computational Logic in Multi-Agent Systems. X, 315 pages. 2007.

Vol. 4369: M. Umeda, A. Wolf, O. Bartenstein, U. Geske, D. Seipel, O. Takata (Eds.), Declarative Programming for Knowledge Management. X, 229 pages. 2006.

Vol. 4342: H. de Swart, E. Orłowska, G. Schmidt, M. Roubens (Eds.), Theory and Applications of Relational Structures as Knowledge Instruments II. X, 373 pages. 2006.

Vol. 4335: S.A. Brueckner, S. Hassas, M. Jelasity, D. Yamins (Eds.), Engineering Self-Organising Systems. XII, 212 pages. 2007.

Vol. 4334: B. Beckert, R. Hähnle, P.H. Schmitt (Eds.), Verification of Object-Oriented Software. XXIX, 658 pages. 2007.

Vol. 4333: U. Reimer, D. Karagiannis (Eds.), Practical Aspects of Knowledge Management. XII, 338 pages. 2006.

Vol. 4327: M. Baldoni, U. Endriss (Eds.), Declarative Agent Languages and Technologies IV. VIII, 257 pages. 2006.

Vol. 4314: C. Freksa, M. Kohlhase, K. Schill (Eds.), KI 2006: Advances in Artificial Intelligence. XII, 458 pages. 2007.

Vol. 4304: A. Sattar, B.-h. Kang (Eds.), AI 2006: Advances in Artificial Intelligence. XXVII, 1303 pages. 2006.

Vol. 4303: A. Hoffmann, B.-h. Kang, D. Richards, S. Tsumoto (Eds.), Advances in Knowledge Acquisition and Management. XI, 259 pages. 2006.

Vol. 4293: A. Gelbukh, C.A. Reyes-Garcia (Eds.), MICAI 2006: Advances in Artificial Intelligence. XXVIII, 1232 pages. 2006.

Vol. 4289: M. Ackermann, B. Berendt, M. Grobelnik, A. Hotho, D. Mladenič, G. Semeraro, M. Spiliopoulou, G. Stumme, V. Svátek, M. van Someren (Eds.), Semantics, Web and Mining. X, 197 pages. 2006.

Vol. 4285: Y. Matsumoto, R.W. Sproat, K.-F. Wong, M. Zhang (Eds.), Computer Processing of Oriental Languages. XVII, 544 pages. 2006.

Vol. 4274: Q. Huo, B. Ma, E.-S. Chng, H. Li (Eds.), Chinese Spoken Language Processing. XXIV, 805 pages. 2006.

Vol. 4265: L. Todorovski, N. Lavrač, K.P. Jantke (Eds.), Discovery Science. XIV, 384 pages. 2006.

Vol. 4264: J.L. Balcázar, P.M. Long, F. Stephan (Eds.), Algorithmic Learning Theory. XIII, 393 pages. 2006.

Vol. 4259: S. Greco, Y. Hata, S. Hirano, M. Inuiguchi, S. Miyamoto, H.S. Nguyen, R. Słowiński (Eds.), Rough Sets and Current Trends in Computing. XXII, 951 pages. 2006.

Vol. 4253: B. Gabrys, R.J. Howlett, L.C. Jain (Eds.), Knowledge-Based Intelligent Information and Engineering Systems, Part III. XXXII, 1301 pages. 2006.

Vol. 4252: B. Gabrys, R.J. Howlett, L.C. Jain (Eds.), Knowledge-Based Intelligent Information and Engineering Systems, Part II. XXXIII, 1335 pages. 2006.

Vol. 4251: B. Gabrys, R.J. Howlett, L.C. Jain (Eds.), Knowledge-Based Intelligent Information and Engineering Systems, Part I. LXVI, 1297 pages. 2006.

Vol. 4248: S. Staab, V. Svátek (Eds.), Managing Knowledge in a World of Networks. XIV, 400 pages. 2006.

Vol. 4246: M. Hermann, A. Voronkov (Eds.), Logic for Programming, Artificial Intelligence, and Reasoning. XIII, 588 pages. 2006.

Vol. 4223: L. Wang, L. Jiao, G. Shi, X. Li, J. Liu (Eds.), Fuzzy Systems and Knowledge Discovery. XXVIII, 1335 pages. 2006.

Vol. 4213: J. Fürnkranz, T. Scheffer, M. Spiliopoulou (Eds.), Knowledge Discovery in Databases: PKDD 2006. XXII, 660 pages. 2006.

Vol. 4212: J. Fürnkranz, T. Scheffer, M. Spiliopoulou (Eds.), Machine Learning: ECML 2006. XXIII, 851 pages. 2006.

Vol. 4211: P. Vogt, Y. Sugita, E. Tuci, C.L. Nehaniv (Eds.), Symbol Grounding and Beyond. VIII, 237 pages. 2006.

Vol. 4203: F. Esposito, Z.W. Raś, D. Malerba, G. Semeraro (Eds.), Foundations of Intelligent Systems. XVIII, 767 pages. 2006.

Vol. 4201: Y. Sakakibara, S. Kobayashi, K. Sato, T. Nishino, E. Tomita (Eds.), Grammatical Inference: Algorithms and Applications. XII, 359 pages. 2006.

Vol. 4200: I.F.C. Smith (Ed.), Intelligent Computing in Engineering and Architecture. XIII, 692 pages. 2006.

Vol. 4198: O. Nasraoui, O. Zaïane, M. Spiliopoulou, B. Mobasher, B. Masand, P.S. Yu (Eds.), Advances in Web Mining and Web Usage Analysis. IX, 177 pages. 2006.

Vol. 4196: K. Fischer, I.J. Timm, E. André, N. Zhong (Eds.), Multiagent System Technologies. X, 185 pages. 2006.

Vol. 4188: P. Sojka, I. Kopeček, K. Pala (Eds.), Text, Speech and Dialogue. XV, 721 pages. 2006.

Vol. 4183: J. Euzenat, J. Domingue (Eds.), Artificial Intelligence: Methodology, Systems, and Applications. XIII, 291 pages. 2006.

Vol. 4180: M. Kohlhase, OMDoc – An Open Markup Format for Mathematical Documents [version 1.2]. XIX, 428 pages. 2006.

Vol. 4177: R. Marín, E. Onaindía, A. Bugarín, J. Santos (Eds.), Current Topics in Artificial Intelligence. XV, 482 pages. 2006.

Vol. 4160: M. Fisher, W. van der Hoek, B. Konev, A. Lisitsa (Eds.), Logics in Artificial Intelligence. XII, 516 pages. 2006.